Willard W. Glazier

Heroes of Three Wars

Comprising a Series of Biographical Sketches of the Most Distinguished...

Willard W. Glazier

Heroes of Three Wars

Comprising a Series of Biographical Sketches of the Most Distinguished...

ISBN/EAN: 9783337015183

Printed in Europe, USA, Canada, Australia, Japan

Cover: Foto ©ninafisch / pixelio.de

More available books at **www.hansebooks.com**

Heroes of Three Wars:

COMPRISING

A Series of Biographical Sketches of the most Distinguished
Soldiers of the War of the Revolution, the War with
Mexico, and the War for the Union, who have
contributed by their valor to establish
and perpetuate the Republic of
the United States.

BY

CAPTAIN WILLARD GLAZIER,

AUTHOR OF "SOLDIERS OF THE SADDLE," "CAPTURE, PRISON-PEN AND ESCAPE," "BATTLES
FOR THE UNION," "PECULIARITIES OF AMERICAN CITIES," ETC., ETC.

Illustrated.

PHILADELPHIA:
HUBBARD BROTHERS, PUBLISHERS,
1883.

TO
GENERAL WILLIAM TECUMSEH SHERMAN,
HERO OF THREE WARS,

WHOSE GRANDEST CAMPAIGN, HIS MARCH THROUGH GEORGIA, AND THE CAROLINAS OPENED AN AVENUE OF ESCAPE FOR THOUSANDS OF CAPTIVES IN REBEL STOCKADES, AND AMONG THEM THE AUTHOR, WHO IN ADMIRATION OF A VALIANT SOLDIER, AND IN GRATITUDE TO THE STRONG ARM THAT LED THE BOYS IN BLUE FROM ATLANTA TO THE SEA, DEDICATES

This Volume
As a Tribute to his Genius and Patriotism.

WILLARD GLAZIER.

ILLUSTRATIONS.

	PAGE
PORTRAIT OF THE AUTHOR (Steel)............Frontispiece.	
HEROES OF THE REVOLUTION	20
WASHINGTON CROSSING THE DELAWARE	37
BATTLE OF BUNKER HILL	52
PUTNAM RESCUED BY MOLANG	77
ETHAN ALLEN AT TICONDEROGA	94
FIGHT—SERAPIS AND BON HOMME RICHARD	129
HEROES OF THE MEXICAN WAR	171
HOUSTON CATCHING THE SOUND OF BATTLE	221
MAY'S CHARGE AT RESACA DE LA PALMA	233
HEROES OF THE REBELLION	243
SCENE AT THE SIEGE OF VICKSBURG	255
SHERMAN'S MARCH THROUGH GEORGIA	271
SHERIDAN BACK FROM WINCHESTER	282
GENERAL THOMAS AT CHICKAMAUGA	309
DEATH OF GENERAL McPHERSON	343
FARRAGUT LASHED TO THE MAST AT MOBILE	365
KILPATRICK AT BRANDY STATION	382
CUSTER'S LAST BATTLE	415

(6)

PREFACE.

IF the genius and valor of Washington and his compatriots gave us a Republic, the hero of Chippewa not less nobly accomplished the second conquest of Mexico. General Scott and his invincible army, the heroes of Monterey, Cerro Gordo, Palo Alto and Buena Vista, displayed all the best qualities of commanders and soldiers. Sieges were conducted and cities captured which were considered impregnable, with a force apparently inadequate for a forlorn hope. They fought pitched battles and won them, opposing fresh recruits to veteran troops. They accomplished marches over routes before considered utterly impassable; captured fortresses bristling with cannon by means of the rifle and bayonet, and planted the Star Spangled Banner upon the proud "Halls of Montezuma."

In the great war for the preservation of the Union, Grant, Sherman, Sheridan, Thomas, Meade, and the grand galaxy of brave hearts that rallied around their standards, gloriously vindicated the cause of freedom on the battle-fields of the Rebellion.

Washington, Scott and Grant are names that will live forever in our history; not because they were the subjects of a blind adulation, but because their worth was properly estimated, and their deeds truthfully recorded. The time for deifying men has long since passed; we prefer to see them as they are—though great, still human, and surrounded with human infirmities; worthy of immortal renown, not because they are unlike us, but because they excel us and have performed a work which entitles them to the lasting gratitude of their countrymen.

Another object of this book is to group around these three generals those officers and men who climbed to immortality by their side, shared their fortunes, helped to win their victories, and remained with them to the end.

Many brave and worthy officers and soldiers might be added to the list I have selected, but the introduction of every meritorious soldier would make the work too cumbersome for my purpose, unless the biographies were reduced to mere encyclopædia articles.

Much pains has been taken to have these sketches complete without being heavy, to give the leading qualities, peculiar traits and distinguishing characteristics of the subjects presented.

Biographies possess but little value unless they give living portraits, so that each man stands out clear and distinct in his true character and proportions. A careful study of the wars herein discussed leads me to feel that I can place my effort before the public without the fear of being charged with egotism. Whatever the verdict may be, the gallant heroes embraced in these pages "deserve well of their country," and richly merit all the honor they have so nobly won.

WILLARD GLAZIER.

PHILADELPHIA, JUNE 24th, 1878.

CONTENTS.

CHAPTER I.

GEORGE WASHINGTON.

Ancestral Lines.—Saxon Origin of Name.—Family Coat of Arms.—Emigration to Virginia.—Birth and Childhood.—School Life.—The Young Surveyor.—Commissioned Major.—A Six-Hundred-Mile Journey.—Battle at Fort Necessity.—Braddock's Defeat and Death.—Falling in Love.—Marriage with the Widow Custis.—Opening Scenes in the Revolution.—Appointed Commander-in-Chief.—Meeting the Army at Cambridge.—The Declaration.—The Long, Long War.—Retreat Through the Jerseys.—Crossing the Delaware.—Battle of Princeton.—Monmouth.—Close of the Revolution.—Farewell to Companions-in-Arms.—As President of the United States. 21

CHAPTER II.

JOSEPH WARREN.

Birthplace of Warren.—School Days.—Graduation at Harvard.—Studying Medicine.—Warren as a Physician.—The "Sons of Liberty."—Warren's Activity in Politics.—Boston Massacre.—Oration at the Old South Church.—Liberty's Advocate.—The Tea Party.—Faneuil Hall Meeting.—Fourth Anniversary of Boston Massacre.—Second Oration.—Fears of Assassination.—The Crisis Met.—Paul Revere's Ride.—Warren's Presentiment.—Battle of Bunker Hill.—Death of Warren.—"'Tis Sweet for One's Country to Die."—Honors to his Memory.—Bunker Hill Monument. 43

CHAPTER III.

NATHANIEL GREENE.

Birthplace and Ancestry.—Work at the Plough and the Anvil.—Studying Euclid over the Forge.—Education under Disadvantages.—Lindley Murray and Dr. Styles.—Love of the Dance.—Ingenious Shingle Device.—Marriage.—On the Road to Lexington.—Made a

(ix)

Major-General.—Expelled from the Quakers.—Sick in Camp.—At Trenton.—The Brandywine.—Greene's Bravery.—Germantown. —The Fight through the Fog.—Valley Forge and Monmouth.— The Army of the South.—The Long Chase of Cornwallis.—Siege of Ninety-six.—Retirement. 54

CHAPTER IV.

LAFAYETTE.

Noble Lineage of the Marquis.—Early Surroundings.—A Member of the King's Regiment.—Commissioned at Fifteen.—Marriage.— The Dinner at Metz.—Noble Resolve.—Preparations to Sail for America.—Obstacles Everywhere.—Voyage of the "Victory."— Arrival.—Home of Benjamin Huger.—Journey to Philadelphia. —Fighting for Liberty.—Battle of Brandywine.—Services in the Revolution.—Arnold and Lafayette.—Return to France.—Visit to the United States.—Terrors of the French Revolution.—Flight and Imprisonment.—The Magdeburg Dungeon.—Liberated by Napoleon.—Visit to the United States in 1824.—Joyful Welcome. —The Citizen King of the French.—Last Days of Lafayette. 61

CHAPTER V.

ISRAEL PUTNAM.

Ancestry of Putnam.—Boyhood Days.—Marriage.—Removal to Pomfret.—Adventure with the Wolf.—Seven Years' War.—Putnam in Command of a Company.—Adventures along the Hudson. —Surprised by Indians.—Down the Rapids.—Indian Superstition. —Putnam at the Stake.—The Rescue.—The Guns of Lexington. —The Plow Exchanged for the Sword.—Murray Hill and the Quakeress.—Putnam's Rapid Rise in the Army.—*Ruse* at Princeton.—Escape at Horseneck.—Paralysis.—The Last of Earth.— Eulogiums. 74

CHAPTER VI.

ETHAN ALLEN.

Birthplace of Allen.—The New Hampshire Grants.—The Green Mountain Boys.—Ethan Allen a Leader.—Price on his Head.— Allen's Fearlessness.—The Revolution.—Capture of Ticonderoga. —Benedict Arnold's Part in the Affair.—Allen in Canada.—The Army of Invasion.—Plans for the Capture of Montreal.—The Fatal Snare.—Allen a Prisoner.—Brutal Treatment by British Officers.—In Falmouth, England.—The Gentlemen of Cork.— Exchanged.—Liberty and the Green Mountains Once More.— Joyful Welcome.—Allen Again Fighting the Battles of Young Vermont.—Review of his Character. 87

CONTENTS. xi

CHAPTER VII.

FRANCIS MARION.

The Huguenot Blood of Marion.—Boyhood Days.—Early Adventures.—The Shipwreck.—Battle with Cherokee Indians.—Marion Leads the Forlorn Hope.—The Bloody Pass.—He Leaves Congress for the Army.—Fame of Marion's Men.—Battle around Savannah.—The Williamsburg Band.—Marion's Brigade.—The Camp in the Swamp.—Successful Surprises.—The Dinner in the Woods.—Tarleton and the *Swamp-Fox.*—Song of Marion's Men. —Fighting for Liberty without Clothes or Food.—Marriage.— Closing Scenes. 106

CHAPTER VIII.

JOHN PAUL JONES.

The Sailor-Boy of Solway Frith.—Ancestry.—Boyish Pursuits.—His First Voyage.—Rapid Rise in the Marine Service.—In Virginia. —America his Adopted Country.—Created an Officer of the United States.—Adventures on the Sea.—The Terror of the English.—Action of the "Bon Homme Richard" and "Serapis." —Glorious Generalship.—Surrender of the English Ship.—Fame of the Chevalier Paul Jones.—The Gold Sword and the Cross of Merit.—American Prisoners Liberated.—At the Courts of Denmark and Russia.—Last Days of the Hero. 118

CHAPTER IX.

THADDEUS KOSCIUSZKO.

Early History of Kosciuszko.—Education in the Art of War.—An Affair of the Heart.—Exile.—Position on Washington's Staff.— Siege of Ninety-Six.—Service in Poland.—Dictator and Generalissimo.—Battle of Raczlawice.—Victory Followed by Defeat.— Decisive Battle of Maciejowice.—Overwhelmed by Superior Numbers.—"Finis Poloniæ!"—Imprisonment.—Freedom Regained.—Retirement at Fontainebleau.—The Fall from the Precipice.—Closing Scenes. 140

CHAPTER X.

HUGH MERCER.

The Moors of Culloden.—The Assistant-Surgeon of the Highland Army.—Emigration to Pennsylvania.—Indian Wars.—Wounded and Alone.—Outbreak of the Revolution.—The Fredericksburg Home.—Farewells.—Days of '76.—First Campaign.—A Gloomy Time.—Influence of Washington.—Across the Delaware.—Affairs in Philadelphia.—Putnam's Order.—Hasty Adjournment of Congress.—Change of Policy.—Attack on Trenton.—Victory.—The Night March on Princeton.—Desperate Fighting.—Ten to One.— Mercer Mortally Wounded.—The Farm-House Scene.—Last Moments.—Victory and Death. 145

CHAPTER XI.
ANTHONY WAYNE.

Birth and Ancestry.—Youthful Bent Towards Military Studies.—Marriage.—Beginning of Public Life.—In the Legislature.—Commissioned as Colonel.—Expedition to Canada.—At Brandywine.—Engagement of Germantown.—Service at Valley Forge.—Monmouth.—Storming of Stony Point.—Splendid Victory.—Revolt of the Pennsylvania Line.—Investment of Yorktown.—War with the Indians.—Peace Commissioner.—Death at Presque Isle.—Monument of the Cincinnati. 153

CHAPTER XII.
JOHN STARK.

Chivalrous Character of Stark.—Incident of Bunker Hill.—Birthplace and Early Life.—The Young Hunter.—On a Trapping Excursion.—Captured by the Indians.—On the Way to St. Francis.—Running the Gauntlet.—Admiration of the Tribe for the White Hunter.—He is made a Chief.—Seven Years' War.—New Hampshire Rangers.—Battle in the Snow.—Brilliant Fighting of Stark.—Promoted.—The Guns of Lexington.—The Muster at Medford.—Advance on Trenton.—Princeton.—Re-enlistment.—Popularity of Stark.—Under a Cloud.—Defence of Vermont.—Battle of Bennington.—Close of the War.—1812.—The Warrior's Last Sleep. 160

CHAPTER XIII.
WINFIELD SCOTT.

Lineage and Early Life.—A Captain of Artillery.—Court-Martialled.—Queenstown Heights.—Tomahawks.—Fort George.—Battle of Chippewa.—Lundy's Lane.—Wounded.—Public Enthusiasm.—Through a Score of Years.—War in Mexico.—Vera Cruz.—"Don't Expose Yourselves, Men!"—Cerro Gordo.—At Puebla.—Churubusco.—Contreras.—Chapultepec.—Molino del Rey.—City of Mexico Taken.—Grand Plaza Scene.—Results.—"Hail to the Chief!" 173

CHAPTER XIV.
ZACHARY TAYLOR.

His Characteristics.—Duty, his Constant Watchword.—Lineage.—Early Plantation Life.—Indian Foes.—Lieutenant in the United States Army.—At Fort Harrison.—Battle with Tecumseh.—Brevet Major.—The Florida War.—Okeechobee.—Ordered to Corpus Christi.—Palo Alto.—Resaca de la Palma.—Promoted to Major-General.—At Monterey.—Bloody Buena Vista.—Colonel Marshall's Opinion.—General Taylor's Dislike for a Uniform.—Ovations on his Return.—Elected President.—Stern Death.—Last Scenes.—Universal Sorrow. 188

CONTENTS. xiii

CHAPTER XV.

WILLIAM JENKINS WORTH.

Early Life.—The War of 1812.—At West Point.—The Seminole War.—With Taylor in Mexico.—At Monterey.—Given an Independent Command.—Description of the Assault.—His Generalship.—Storming of Federacion Hill.—Conducting the Capitulation.—At Vera Cruz.—Perote and Puebla.—Capture of El Molino del Rey.—Storming of Chapultepec.—Brevetted Major-General.—Monument in Madison Square. 203

CHAPTER XVI.

JOHN E. WOOL.

War of 1812.—Wool's Volunteer Corps.—Captaincy in the Thirteenth.—Bravery at Queenstown.—Death of General Brock.—Battle of Plattsburg.—Promoted for Gallantry.—Letter from President Madison.—Another Promotion.—Mexican War.—The March to Monclova.—Capture of Parras.—The Mission of Mercy.—Buena Vista.—Wool Entrusted with the Details.—Birthplace.—Where he Died.—Fortress Monroe.—*Hic Jacet.*—The Chief's War Horse.—Military Funeral. 209

CHAPTER XVII.

SAM HOUSTON.

Early History.—Scotch Ancestry.—Birthplace.—School Days in the Forest.—Hard Work on the Farm.—Homer's Iliad.—Off to the Woods.—Among the Cherokees.—Military Service.—The Soldier under Jackson.—Battle of the Horse-Shoe.—Desperate Bravery.—Wounded.—Promotion.—Role as a Lawyer.—Rises Rapidly to Distinction.—The Domestic Cloud.—Return to the Forest.—Emigration to Texas.—Houston as General.—Massacre of the Alamo.—Battle of San Jacinto.—The Young Republic and her President.—Annexation.—In the United States Senate.—Houston as Governor.—Last Days. 212

CHAPTER XVIII.

JAMES SHIELDS.

The Land of his Nativity.—First Army Experience.—The Mexican War-cloud.—Promotion.—The March through Mexico.—At Cerro Gordo.—Brilliant Achievement.—Wounded unto Death.—The Storming of Contreras.—Aid to Smith.—A Generous Piece of Conduct.—Chapultepec.—Under a Galling Fire.—Refuses to Leave the Field though Wounded.—His Return to the United States.—The War of Rebellion.—The Spring of '62.—Defeat of "Stonewall" Jackson.—Leaving the Army. 227

CHAPTER XIX.

CHARLES MAY.

Colonel May a Native of Washington.—Commissioned a Lieutenant by President Jackson.—Ordered to Florida.—Participates in the Capture of the Indian Chief Philip.—Opening of the Mexican War.—Joins General Taylor.—Co-operates with Captain Walker. —Famous Charge at Resaca de la Palma.—Gallant Conduct at Buena Vista.—Returns to the United States. 230

CHAPTER XX.

ULYSSES SIMPSON GRANT.

The Grants of the Early Scotch Monarchy.—Family Crests.— Direct Ancestry.—Boyhood.—Feats of Horsemanship.—Loading Wood.—Old "Dave" and Young Ulysses.—At West Point.— Experience in Mexican War.—Marriage.—Resigns His Commission.—In the Leather Business.—Beginning of Last War.— Recruiting a Company.—Battle of Belmont.—Cairo Expedition. —Fort Donelson.—Shiloh.—Vicksburg.—Chattanooga.—Missionary Ridge and Lookout Mountain.—Opinions of a Sachem. —The Last Campaign.—Lee's Surrender.—Elected and Reelected President. 245

CHAPTER XXI.

WILLIAM TECUMSEH SHERMAN.

Distinguishing Characteristic of Political Revolutions.—Birth of General Sherman.—Suddenly Left an Orphan.—Adopted by Hon. Thomas Ewing.—Sent to West Point.—Ordered to California.—Becomes a Banker.—Is Made President of the Louisiana Military Academy.—Opposed to Secession.—Tenders his Resignation.—Assists in Organizing Troops for the Suppression of the Rebellion.—At Bull Run.—At Shiloh, Pittsburgh Landing, Chattanooga and Missionary Ridge.—Defeats Hood.—From Atlanta to the Sea.—Campaign of the Carolinas.—Receives the Surrender of Johnston.—Enthusiastic Reception at Washington. . . 263

CHAPTER XXII.

PHILIP HENRY SHERIDAN.

Impetuosity of Character.—A Poor Irish Boy.—At West Point.— Wild Conduct.—Graduation.—Service in Western Territories.— Captain of the Thirteenth Infantry.—Quarter-master under Halleck.—As a Cavalry Officer.—Battle of Booneville.—Promotion to Brigadier-General.—Murfreesboro'.—At Chickamauga and Missionary Ridge.—In Pursuit of Early.—Cedar Creek.—Sheridan's Ride.—The Victory.—At Five Forks and Appomattox.— After the War. 278

CONTENTS. xv

CHAPTER XXIII.

GEORGE BRINTON MCCLELLAN.

Birth and Education.—In the Mexican War.—Services in Survey of Railroad Routes.—A Model Report.—Sent to the Crimea.— Superintendent of the Illinois Central.—Response to Governor Dennison.—Over the Department of the Ohio.—Virginia Campaigns.—In Command of the Army of the Potomac.—Movement to the Peninsula.—Siege of Yorktown.—Army Withdrawn.— McClellan's Letter.—Again in Command of the Potomac Army. —South Mountain and Antietam.—Relieved of his Command at Warrenton.—Nominated for the Presidency.—In Europe.—Governor of New Jersey. 287

CHAPTER XXIV.

AMBROSE EVERETT BURNSIDE.

His Scotch Blood.—Graduates at West Point.—In New Mexico.— As an Inventor.—Marching to the Front.—At Bull Run.—Promotion.—In Command of the North Carolina Expedition.— Capture of Newbern, Fort Macon and Beaufort.—At Antietam. —Slaughter at Fredericksburg.—Tenders his Resignation.— Brilliant Capture of East Tennessee.—Before Petersburg.— Elected Governor of Rhode Island.—In Congress. . . . 298

CHAPTER XXV.

GEORGE HENRY THOMAS.

A Second Washington.—Birth and Education.—Promotion for Bravery.—In Mexico.—Prompt Response at the Outbreak of Civil War.—The Battle of Mill Spring.—Declines to Supersede Buell.—At Murfreesboro'.—Chickamauga.—Position of Troops Under Thomas.—Their Firm Stand.—"The Rock of Chickamauga."—At Chattanooga.—The Atlanta Campaign.—Grant's Telegram.—Battle of Nashville.—Thanks of Congress and Gold Medal.—End of the War.—Goes to the Pacific Coast. . . 304

CHAPTER XXVI.

JOSEPH HOOKER.

Lookout Mountain.—The Battle Above the Clouds.—The Splendor of Victory.—The Strange Thanksgiving Day.—Taylor's Description.—The Old Flag at the Top.—General Howard in Lookout Valley.—Hooker at Chattanooga.—The Peninsular Campaign.— "Fighting Joe."—Wounded.—Chief in Command.—Chancellorsville.—The Atlanta Campaign.—Promotion of Howard.—Hooker Resigns in Consequence.—Mustered out of Service. . . . 314

CHAPTER XXVII.

GEORGE GORDON MEADE.

Ancestry.—A Fragment of Eventful History.—Birth in Spain.—At West Point.—In the Florida War.—In the Mexican War.—His Part in the Peninsular Campaign.—At Antietam.—In Command of the Army of the Potomac.—A Remarkable Order.—At Gettysburg.—The Desperate Last Effort.—His Report.—Congratulatory Address.—Thanks of Congress.—Advance to the Rappahannock.—Close Friendship between Meade and Grant.—Over the Atlantic Department.—Death in Philadelphia. . . . 326

CHAPTER XXVIII.

HENRY WARNER SLOCUM.

Birth and Education.—A Lawyer in Syracuse.—On the War-Path. —In the Chickahominy.—At Antietam, South Mountain and Chancellorsville.—The Field of Gettysburg.—The Repulse of Ewell's Troops.—In Tennessee.—Commanding the Vicksburg District. — The Georgia Campaign. — Marching through the Enemy's Country.—Battle of Bentonville.—A Splendid Fight.— Genius of Slocum. 332

CHAPTER XXIX.

JAMES BIRDSEYE M^cPHERSON.

His Ability.—Ancestry and Early Life.—Superior Scholarship at West Point.—In New York Harbor.—On the Pacific Coast.— Sent to Boston Harbor.—Slow Promotion.—On Halleck's Staff.— Services at Forts Henry and Donelson.—Engineering Work at Corinth. — His First Independent Command. — Vicksburg.— Grant's Endorsement.—With Sherman.—In Command of the Army of the Tennessee.—Postponement of Marriage.—March to the Sea.—Battle with Hood.—His Death.—Grant's Letter. 337

CHAPTER XXX.

WINFIELD SCOTT HANCOCK.

The Brilliant Charge at Williamsburg.—Popular Favor.—Birth and Early Training.—In the Mexican War.—The Florida Campaign.—Ordered to Washington.—At Antietam.—Fredericksburg and Chancellorsville. — His Stand at Gettysburg. — Cemetery Hill.—Wounded.—In the Last Grant Campaign.—Battle at Ely's Ford.—Assault of May Twelfth.—Capture of Stuart.—" I Decline to Take Your Hand."—In Charge of the Veteran First Corps In the Shenandoah Valley.—Characteristics. 347

CHAPTER XXXI.

JOHN CHARLES FREMONT.

The Hundred Days in Missouri.—Birth and Early Life.—On Board the "Natchez."—Beginning to be an Explorer.—Marriage with Jessie Benton.—Westward Ho!—Discoveries.—Conquest of California.—Across the Continent.—Senator from California.—In Command of the Western Department.—Causes of Removal.—Presidential Candidate.—An Extraordinary Ride.—What He Achieved. 352

CHAPTER XXXII.

OLIVER OTIS HOWARD.

The Christian Soldier.—Early Life.—Off to the Wars.—Bravery in Battle.—Loss of an Arm.—Antietam.—Fredericksburg.—Chancellorsville.—Gettysburg.—The Atlanta Campaign,—Chief of the Army of the Tennessee.—Convalescence.—His Religious Convictions.—Story of a Wagon-Master.—In Charge of the Freedman's Bureau.—Sherman's Letter. 357

CHAPTER XXXIII.

DAVID GLASCOE FARRAGUT.

The Power of the Navy.—Early Years of Farragut.—Remarkable Instance of Boyish Bravery.—Forty-eight Years of Quiet Life.—Union Sentiments.— Extract from Private Letter.—Castilian Ancestry.—Naval Combats on the Mississippi.—Capture of New Orleans.—The Bay Fight at Mobile.—Lashed to the Mast in the "Hartford."—Official Tour of European Ports.—Personal Habits of Farragut. 361

CHAPTER XXXIV.

FRANZ SIGEL.

Early Military Education and Career.—Espousal of the Cause of the Revolutionists.—Exiled.—Arrival in the United States.—Life Previous to the War.—A Volunteer in the Union Army.—His Military Ability.—At Wilson's Creek.—The Battle of Pea Ridge.—Fighting Against Enormous Odds.—Splendid Skill Exhibited by Sigel.—Difficulties with Halleck.—New York Indignation Meeting.—In Command at Harper's Ferry.—Battle of Newmarket.—Close of Military Career. 368

CHAPTER XXXV.

HUGH JUDSON KILPATRICK.

Born for the Cavalry.—Romance of Early Life.—Married on the Eve of Going to the Front.—Her Name on his Banner.—Big Bethel.—Wounded.—To the Front again.—Falmouth Heights.—

Kilpatrick's First Famous Raid.—Brandy Station.—" Men of Maine, Follow Me!"—Aldie.—Gettysburg.—Night Battle at Monterey.—New Baltimore.—Attempt to Rescue Prisoners.—Atlanta Campaign.—Resaca.—Wounded.—Georgia Campaign.—Waynesboro'.—At Savannah.—Sherman's Letter.—Promotion.—In the Carolinas.—Close of the War. 375

CHAPTER XXXVI.

PHILIP KEARNY.

Birthplace.—Where Educated.—In Europe.—Fighting Abroad.—Honors.—Participates in the Mexican War.—Loss of an Arm.—In Europe Again.—At Magenta and Solferino.—At the Front in our Last War.—Bravery at Williamsburg.—Promotion.—Kearny's Power over his Men.—The Battle of Chantilly.—Death's Sad Eclipse.—" Lay Him Low." 387

CHAPTER XXXVII.

NATHANIEL LYON.

Of Soldier Ancestry.—Early Childhood.—Graduates at West Point. —In the Mexican War.—On the Frontier.—Rescue of the St. Louis Arsenal.—Given the Chief Command in Missouri.—At Wilson's Creek.—Fighting Against Terrible Odds.—Twice Wounded.—The Last Charge.—Lyon's Fall.—His Civilian's Dress.—Funeral Honors.—The Sorrowful Multitudes.—Funeral Oration at Eastford.—Resolutions of Respect. 391

CHAPTER XXXVIII.

ELMER EPHRAIM ELLSWORTH.

" How Knightly looked he as he rode to Hounds!"—Character.—An Enthusiast in Military Science.—The French Zouave Tactics.—A Noble Ambition.—Early Struggles.—The Chicago Zouaves.—Their Perfection of Drill and Character.—A Tour of Triumph.—In New York.—A Favorite of Lincoln.—The War Clarion.—New York Fire Zouaves.—Sword Presentations.—In the South.—Last Night at Alexandria.—Letter Home.—The Dread Tragedy.—Universal Grief.—Lincoln's Sorrow.—The Genius of Ellsworth. 396

CHAPTER XXXIX

EDWARD DICKINSON BAKER.

The English Boy on American Shores.—Early Struggles.—Off for the West.—Efforts as a Young Lawyer in Springfield.—Congressional Honors.—Leadership on the Forum.—In the Mexican War.—Removal to the Pacific Coast.—Popularity as an Advocate.—Oration over Broderick.—Sent to the United States Senate from

Oregon.—Union Square Speech.—Organization of the California Regiment.—To the Front.—Ball's Bluff.—Last Scenes. . 407

CHAPTER XL.

GEORGE ARMSTRONG CUSTER.

Early Life of General Custer.—School Experience.—First Love.—Sent to West Point.—Trials of a Plebe.—The Attack on Fort Sumter.—Graduates and Goes to Washington.—Ordered to join his Regiment.—Incidents of the Battle of Bull Run.—Describes his First Emotions.—On Staff Duty.—The Peninsula Campaign.—Custer's First Charge.—Winning the Bars.—General McClellan Relieved.—Custer at Monroe.—The Course of True Love.—Battle of Aldie.—Made a General.—Battle of Gettysburg.—The Last Raid.—Appomattox Court House.—The Seventh Cavalry.—Life on the Plains.—Battle of the Washita.—Rain-in-the-face. Sitting Bull and Crazy Horse.—The Last Battle. 415

PART FIRST.

The War of the Revolution.

SUBJECTS:

Chapter		Page
I.	GEORGE WASHINGTON	21
II.	JOSEPH WARREN	43
III.	NATHANIEL GREENE	54
IV.	GILBERT MOTTIER LAFAYETTE	61
V.	ISRAEL PUTNAM	74
VI.	ETHAN ALLEN	87
VII.	FRANCIS MARION	106
VIII.	JOHN PAUL JONES	118
IX.	THADDEUS KOSCIUSZKO	140
X.	HUGH MERCER	145
XI.	ANTHONY WAYNE	153
XII.	JOHN STARK	160

HEROES OF THREE WARS.

CHAPTER I.

GEORGE WASHINGTON.

Ancestral Lines.—Saxon Origin of Name.—Family Coat of Arms.—Emigration to Virginia.—Birth and Childhood.—School Life.—The Young Surveyor.—Commissioned Major.—A Six-Hundred-Mile Journey.—Battle at Fort Necessity.—Braddock's Defeat and Death.—Falling in Love.—Marriage with the Widow Custis.—Opening Scenes in the Revolution.—Appointed Commander-in-Chief.—Meeting the Army at Cambridge.—The Declaration.—The Long, Long War.—Retreat Through the Jerseys.—Crossing the Delaware.—Battle of Princeton.—Monmouth.—Close of the Revolution.—Farewell to Companions-in-Arms.—As President of the United States.

THIS wonderful *Life* is enveloped in the pure rays of a fame which can find no equal: in which Justice became embodied as a noble passion united to a nobler fortitude: the channel of whose genius was world-wide—like the ocean, touching all shores: everywhere the liberator and firm champion of duty, which, to him, was the only gateway to glory: standing fearlessly in the breach, in defence of young Liberty, when the despotism of decay and king-craft attempted its destruction: the wise architect of a nation's destiny, laying deep its foundations in universal law as the expression of universal .right: whom Honor crowned with her most blazing star, and who remained unspoiled, though on him "affluent Fortune emptied all her horn:" the adulation of millions could not divest him of his gentle humility. He was the incarnate spirit of the New-World Thermopylæ, hurling back to their Upas soil the swarming desecrators of freedom. America yet feels his breath upon her, nor could she, without him, have risen to her present state. The rays of such a glorious sun must still continue to illumine her future—as they have gilded the past and enriched the present—with an ever-accumulating wealth of light!

There is a singular unanimity of opinion in ascribing to George Washington an exceptional character. It was certainly one of peculiar symmetry, in which a happy combination of qualities, moral, social and intellectual, were guided to appropriate action by a remarkable power of clear judgment. It was just the combination calculated to lead a spirited and brave people through such a trying crisis as the American Revolution. His star was not dark and bright by turns—did not reveal itself in uncertain and fitful glimmerings—but shone with a full and steady luminosity across the troubled night of a nation's beginning. Under these broad and beneficent rays the Ship of State was guided, through a sea of chaos, to safe anchorage. The voyage across those seven, eventful years was one that tried men's souls. Often, appalling dangers threatened. Wreck on the rocks of disunion, engulfment in the mountain waves of opposition, starvation and doubt and mutiny on shipboard—these were a few of the perils which beset their course. But a royal-souled Commander stood at the helm, and discerned, afar off, the green shores of Liberty. On this land the sunshine fell with fruitful power. The air was sweet with the songs of birds. Contentment, peace, prosperity, reigned. Great possibilities were shadowed forth within its boundaries, and a young nation, growing rapidly towards a splendid era of enlightenment, was foreseen as a product of the near future. It took a man with deep faith in the ultimate rule of right and in humanity to occupy that position; a man with large heart, with unselfish aims, with prophetic instincts, with clear and equalized brain. George Washington possessed all of these qualities—and more.

It is difficult to estimate what might have been the destiny of America with this man's influence left out. No one can well calculate how much he had to do with the formative stages of American Independence.

The masses may become agitated with germinal ideas, may seethe with internal fires; but it takes the mind of the *leader* to crystallize those ideas into form—to convert floating material into *use*. This was the mission of Washington, and nobly did he fulfil the sacred trust. His life naturally divides itself into three parts: First, that of the youthful *soldier;* Second, the *commander;* Third, the nation's beloved *champion* and *ruler*.

There is ever a questioning gaze, a kind of loving curiosity, turned towards the streams of birth and ancestry of the world's great leaders of men who have won imperishable renown in the service of their country, and a quiet satisfaction fills us if we discover that such lineage flows back to a beginning of noble men and women.

The origin of the name of Washington, the faraway springs of blood which coursed through the veins of those who bore the manorial title, cannot fail to be of interest to the reader. We learn of them first in the "Bolden Book," a record of all lands contained in a certain diocese in the county of Durham, England, in 1183. One William De Hertburn, during this time of the Conquest, held the village of De Hertburn in knight's fee; probably the same now called Hartburn, on the banks of the Tees. It is stated in the "Bolden Book" that this gentleman exchanged his village of Hertburn for the manor and village of Wessyngton, in the same diocese—engaging to pay the bishop a quit-rent of four pounds and to attend him with two greyhounds in grand hunts, and furnish a man-at-arms whenever military aid should be required of the palatinate.

With a change of estate came a change of surname, and from that time the family took the title of De Wyssington. The name is supposed to be of Saxon origin, and existed in England prior to the Conquest. The village of Wassengtone is mentioned in a Saxon charter granted by King Edgar, in 973, to Thorney Abbey. From the ancient De Wyssington we have the modern Washington.

Laurence Washington, of "Gray's Inn," was for some time Mayor of Northampton, and on the dissolution of the priories by Henry the Eighth, received a grant of the Manor of Sulgrave. This was in 1538. The grandson of this first lord of Sulgrave had many children. Two of them—John and Laurence Washington—emigrated to Virginia about the year 1657, and settled at Bridges Creek, Westmoreland County, on the Potomac River. Here they bought lands and became successful planters. The son of John, one of these boys, married Mildred Warner, of Gloucester

County, and from this union came Augustine, the father of our illustrious General. The mother of the Washington boys, who emigrated to Virginia in the seventeenth century, was Eleanor Hastings, daughter and heiress of John Hastings, who was grandson to Francis, second Earl of Huntingdon. Through Lady Huntingdon she was the descendant of George, Duke of Clarence, brother to King Edward the Fourth and King Richard Third by Isabel Nevil, daughter and heiress of Richard, Earl of Warwick, the king-maker. It has been affirmed that the pedigree of the Hastings branch goes back to the great Danish sea-king, whose sails were long the terror of both coasts of the British Channel. One branch wore, in the fourteenth century, the coronet of Pembroke. From another branch sprang Chamberlain, the faithful adherent of the White Rose. The Earldom of Huntingdon was received by this family from the Tudors, which, after a long dispossession, has been quite recently regained. If this lineage is correct, Washington was entitled to quarter, on his escutcheon, the arms of Hastings, Pole, Earl of Salisbury, Plantagenet, Scotland, Mortimer, Earl of March, Nevil, Montagu, Beauchamp and Devereaux. But his brightest armorial blazonry, his chiefest patents of nobility, were his unpretentious virtues, his humility, his probity; whereby a nation was led through many struggles to a free existence. These are insignia of rank which cannot be taken from him.

First, then, we are to speak of him as the boy-man.

In the year 1732 there stood on the banks of Bridges Creek one of those primitive farm-houses of Virginia, with roof steep and sloping down into low, projecting eaves, which was then in the prevailing style. It had four rooms on the ground-floor, other rooms in the attic, and an immense chimney at each end. The site commanded a magnificent view over many miles of the Potomac and the opposite Maryland shore. Here lived the family of Augustine Washington, and here, in the forenoon of February twenty-second, was born the infant boy who was destined, in his single person, to reflect more glory on his name than the whole line, for ten generations back, had conferred on him. The record, still preserved in the family Bible, says that he "was baptized the third of April following," and that "Mr. Beverly Whiting and Captain Christopher Brooks" acted as godfathers, and "Mrs. Mildred Gregory" as godmother. Not long after this event his father moved from the ancestral acres to the banks of the Rappahannock, nearly opposite what is now Fredericksburg. History tells us that from infancy this boy developed a noble character. His childhood—if it could be called such—was happy; his youth—looking back on it from this distance—seemed a training school, especially adapted to his future career. He was said to have been handsome in features, with well-proportioned physique and gentle manners. He had great moral courage, frankness, integrity, and a keen sense of honor. In brief, the boy was father to the man. At twelve years of age he was left without a father. At fifteen and a-half he had finished school. His bent was towards mathematical and scientific pursuits, and he therefore fitted himself for the profession of a civil engineer. At thirteen he had made a manuscript collection of sixty-nine rules for the government of conduct, which might be said to constitute of themselves a code of moral philosophy. When he had just passed sixteen, in March of the year 1748, he was engaged by Lord Fairfax to survey his immense possessions of land just purchased in that then wild region. With an Indian guide and a few woodsmen, the fearless boy set out on this hardy mission. It occupied the year. In performing it, he faced all the difficulties, dangers and hardships of the explorer—sleeping at night on a bearskin or some straw before the fire, and, for months, not taking off his clothes. At nineteen, he had so grown in the regard of Virginians that he was appointed major over one of the military districts, into which the province was divided for defence against the Indians.

Then began the bloody struggle between England and France for the possession of America. A commissioner was to be sent across the Alleghenies on a perilous, six-hundred-mile journey, bearing remonstances from Great Britain to one of the French posts there stationed. Who, in all the colony, was there to undertake this daring enterprise? The Scotch Governor Dinwiddie looked around him inquiringly. George Washington, twenty years old, volunteered his services. This was regarded by all, as heroic to a high degree. He started from Williamsburg, Virginia, November fourteenth, 1753, with eight men, including two Indian guides. They went to the headwaters of the Monongahela, from there to the Ohio, and in birch canoes, paddled down that stream for nearly three hundred miles, to the point now occupied by Pittsburg. The party reached the end of their journey in forty-one days. The mission was performed, and through many perils by flood and field, the returning party reached Williamsburg again the sixteenth of January, 1754. Washington made his report to the governor, which was published and read eagerly in the colonies and England, and established the fact that the French meant to defend their rights of discovery, and that they had the hearty co-operation of the Indians. The Legislature of Virginia was then in session, and Washington one day mingled with the crowd in the gallery to witness the proceedings of the House. The speaker saw him, and rose from his chair. "I propose," said he, "that the thanks of this House be given to Major Washington, who now sits in the gallery, for the gallant manner in which he has executed the important trust lately reposed in him by his Excellency, the Governor."

The applause and enthusiasm was universal. Every one rose to do him homage, and Washington was conducted, blushing, to the speaker's desk. Then a hushed silence fell on the waiting crowd to hear what might fall from his lips. But the young Major, thus taken by surprise, was speechless. The speaker saw the situation and hastened to his relief. Directing him to a chair, he said: "Sit down, Major Washington, sit down! Your modesty is alone equal to your merit."

An army of four hundred men was raised by command of Governor Dinwiddie, and Washington was appointed colonel of the regiment. The avowed object was to subjugate the French and compel recognition of the right of the British Crown to this continent.

When the little band was within a few days' march of Fort Du Quesne (the site of Pittsburg), they were thrown into consternation by learning the superior force and position of the French. M. De Villiers, who had been thoroughly posted on the movements of the English from the outset, sent a peace commission of thirty-four men, under Jumonville, a civilian, to advise Colonel Washington to return. Learning of the approach of this party, Washington, with a strong detachment commanded by himself, on a night of Egyptian darkness, surprised the sleeping camp, killed Jumonville and ten men and captured the remainder. It is generally agreed that Washington *supposed* this party intended to attack him, though their small numbers would seem to contradict the theory. Be this as it may, the result proved a firebrand which kindled the flames of war between France and England.

A battle immediately followed, at a place named Fort Necessity, on the banks of the Monongahela, in which the little army had no choice but to surrender to the French commander at Fort Du Quesne.

It is unnecessary to give, in detail, a description of the long war for mastery between the French and English powers. Our aim is not that of the historian, but rather the artist, who uses events as the background against which character reveals itself, in more or less striking outlines.

England sent to these shores, as commander of her army, General Braddock, a man conspicuously unfitted for the work committed to his care. Colonial affairs were treated with contempt by court and cabinet. Governor Dinwiddie reduced Washington to the rank of captain, placing over him officers whom he had commanded. Washington immediately resigned, but accepted a position as *aide* on Braddock's staff, which was then offered him, with his former rank. The march of Braddock's army into the valley of death despite the warnings and advice of Washington, their bloody annihilation, the death of their leader, the march back with the remnant of British soldiers that escaped—these all followed in rapid sequence. Then we see the young colonel at the head of seven hundred men, raised by Virginia, for frontier defence. In 1756 he was called to Boston, and travelled the entire five hundred miles on horseback, with two aides and black servants in livery. After his return to Winchester, where a central fort was established, he was so assailed and thwarted in his plans that "nothing" he said, "but the imminent danger of the times prevented him from resigning his command." People everywhere looked to Washington to protect them. They came to him with supplications—women with children—men from the halls of legislation. All this touched him deeply. In 1758 an expedition was organized to march against Fort Du Quesne, under command of General Forbes. Two thousand men raised by Virginia were commanded by Washington. They set out early in July. The whole force consisted of six thousand men. When the "provincials," as they were called, gathered at Winchester, it was found that they were in need of everything necessary to such an exploit: arms, ammunition, field-equipage, etc. Washington went at once to Williamsburg to ask aid of the Council.

While on this journey, just after crossing the Pamunky river, he met at the house of a wealthy Virginia gentleman the beautiful young widow, Martha Custis. He seems to have been fascinated by her from the first moment of meeting, and when, on the following morning, he left the house of his host, his troth was plighted to this charming lady and he had received hers in return. They were to be married at the termination of the Fort Du Quesne campaign. On the march thitherward a similar fate to that of Braddock's army met some of the commands. They were hemmed in by narrow ravines, surprised by the superior strategy of Indians, and killed remorselessly. But the Virginia troops, led by Washington, reached the fort only to find it a smouldering heap of ashes. For, on the previous night, the French commander had blown up the magazine, burned the defences, and embarked his troops—five hundred in number—on the Ohio. The English victories in Canada had cut off reinforcements and supplies to the lonely fort, and left them unprepared to meet their opponents. They had, therefore, no choice but retreat. Another fort was erected on the site of the ancient Du Quesne and named Fort Pitt.

Washington returned to Virginia, and on the sixth of January was married to Mrs. Custis at the "White House," the home of the beautiful and wealthy bride. This place was not far from Williamsburg, in New Kent County. He remained here for three months, and then took his seat in the House of Burgesses at Williamsburg. At the close of the session he removed, with his family, to Mount Vernon, and believed himself, as he expressed it, "fixed for life."

During these halcyon days we have a pleasant little picture of his domestic life as it passed on this princely estate—a picture in happy contrast with the dark scenes of war which had shadowed his previous experience, and which were to be a part of his future.

He rose at five o'clock in the morning, read or wrote

until seven, breakfasted on two small cups of tea and some hoe-cake, and afterwards mounted one of his superb horses and made the "rounds" of his broad acres. He dined at two o'clock, retired at about nine; was fond of athletic sports and the hunt. A lovely barge on the Potomac, manned by six negroes in uniform, was one of his possessions. He dispensed a large hospitality, his house being frequented by troops of guests.

Meanwhile, he was appointed Judge of the County Court and had undertaken a project to explore the Dismal Swamp.

In 1763 the peace of Fontainebleau was signed. The French had been driven from these shores and England sheathed the sword of conquest.

The passage of the "Stamp Act" in 1764 incensed the people and called forth that patriotic burst of eloquence from Patrick Henry which afterwards became so renowned. Washington felt the approach of the gathering war-cloud, and returned to Mount Vernon from the House of Burgesses filled with gloomy forebodings. The British government became alarmed at the temper of America, and, as a matter of conciliation, repealed the "Stamp Act." This was in March, 1766. But the tax on tea and other merchandise followed, and two regiments of English regulars were sent across the water to intimidate the colonists. This was adding insult to injury. The Virginia Assembly denounced Parliament for imposing taxes without allowing representation, and bold resolves were made, declaring that the taxing power should be vested alone in the colonists. Lord Botetort, the new governor, who had set up his court in great splendor in Virginia, heard of these daring denunciations. He summoned the council to his audience chamber, and, in a haughty manner, dissolved the State Assembly. They then convened in a private dwelling, and at this meeting Washington presented a "draft of an association to discountenance the use of all British merchandise taxed by Parliament to raise a revenue in America." Every member signed it, and a printed copy of the draft was scattered broadcast over the country. It was everywhere applauded. "Non-Importation Associations" sprang up in all the colonies. British commerce felt this action, and petitions from British merchants, for the repeal of the taxes, poured into Parliament. Lord North, at this time England's prime minister, removed the importation duties on all articles except tea. That, he said, must be continued, in order to establish "the authority of the mother country."

In vain did earnest and eloquent men in the English Parliament plead for the rights of the colonists. In vain were petitions—in vain remonstrances. Every one who dared to make an appeal to British power, in favor of justice, fell at once into disfavor. George the Third and his court were deaf to all save selfish considerations.

Thus events drifted forward, bringing in their wake the birth-throes of a great nation. The Boston Tea Party, disguised as Indians, boarded the English ships at night and emptied the tea-chests into Boston harbor. In return, insulting decrees were fulminated from the throne, declaring that Massachusetts should no longer have a voice in the selection of her rulers, and that the port at Boston should be closed. In Virginia, the House of Burgesses was broken up by Lord Dunmore,

3

the colonial governor appointed by the crown. Public
indignation against these tyrannies flamed forth everywhere. Letters came from Boston to Williamsburg
recommending a league of the colonies and the suspension of trade with England. The day on which the
"Boston Port Bill" was to be enforced was observed
with fasting and prayer. Flags were at half-mast and
funeral bells were tolled. The colonists became rapidly convinced that nothing would satisfy the cruel
despotism of George the Third save their slavish sub-
mission. This could not be given.

And so the war crisis approached nearer and more
near. Patriot brows grew thoughtful and patriot hearts
resolute as the danger defined itself. The first Continental Congress met in Philadelphia, September fifth,
1774, and Washington was a delegate from Virginia.
He had come there on horseback from Mount Vernon
in company with Patrick Henry and Edmund Pendle-
ton. In that time of sublime fusion of souls, when all
were drawn into concerted action by a common, heroic
purpose, no one, among that distinguished assembly of
great minds, exhibited a loftier patriotism, a nobler
enthusiasm, or more self-sacrificing spirit than the
country's future beloved General. He who had said
to the Virginia Assembly when Boston was menaced,
"I am ready to raise one thousand men, subsist them
at my own expense, and march at their head to the
relief of Boston," could not certainly be accused of selfish or mercenary motives. When, after a session of
fifty-one days, Congress disbanded, Patrick Henry said
of him, "If you speak of solid information, and sound
judgment, Colonel Washington is unquestionably the
greatest man on that floor."

"It is useless," said this prince of orators afterwards, at the Richmond convention, "to address further petitions to the British government, or to await the effect of those already addressed to the throne. We must fight! I repeat it, we must fight! An appeal to arms and to the God of hosts is all that is left us."

In April, 1775, the first patriot blood was spilled at Lexington and all the country was stung to indignation. "To arms!" was the cry which echoed from colony to colony.

The second Congress met in May, 1775, and formed a military confederacy vested with legislative powers for their own defence. Washington was appointed chairman of committee on military affairs.

The question which now swept Congress and hovered with anxious portent on all lips was, "Who shall be commander-in-chief of the united armies?"

John Adams had the honor to first propose George Washington for this position. "A gentleman," he said, "whose skill and experience as an officer, whose independent fortune, great talents and excellent universal character would command the approbation of all America, and unite the cordial exertions of all the colonies, better than any other person in the Union." The vote, which was given by ballot, was found to be unanimous for Washington.

Congress, therefore, on May fifteenth, adopted the "Continental Army" and fixed the pay of the Commander-in-chief at five hundred dollars per month. This salary Washington declined, asking only that Congress defray his expenses.

He received his commission on the 20th of June, and the next day set out from Philadelphia for the army. He was accompanied by Generals Lee and Schuyler and an escort of Philadelphia troops. Twenty miles outside the city they were met by a flying courier with news of the battle of Bunker Hill. Anxiously, every particular of the action was gleaned. Washington listened breathlessly, and when told of the heroic behavior of the Americans, exclaimed, with emotion, "The liberties of our country are safe!"

As he journeyed onward towards Cambridge, volunteer escorts of citizens and soldiers went with him from town to town. Every one was anxious to see him, and everywhere he produced the same favorable effect on the minds of the people. On the third of July, the army, drawn up on Cambridge common, formally received its commander, and his presence imparted to it a wonderful access of enthusiasm.

From this time onward, for eight long, suffering years, until April, 1783, the war of the American Revolution dragged its slow length along; and the history of General Washington is so interwoven with the struggle, that one could not be written without the other. Space can be given to only a few striking illustrations of this great man's generalship.

The manner in which the siege of Boston was conducted, terminating in Howe's precipitate retreat, has been regarded by military judges as a masterly achievement. On the fourth of July, 1776, the great *Declaration* was adopted, and the army received it with wild demonstrations of joy.

Washington's retreat through the Jerseys was unquestionably a piece of splendid generalship. "With a mere handful of freezing, starving, ragged men, he retreated more than a hundred miles before a powerful

WASHINGTON CROSSING THE DELAWARE.

foe flushed with victory and strengthened with abundance. He baffled all their endeavors to cut him off, preserved all his field-pieces, ammunition, and nearly all his stores. There was grandeur in this achievement which far surpassed any ordinary victory."

After crossing the Delaware, he stationed his troops on the western bank, with the broad river flowing between him and his foe. The forces of Cornwallis faced the American lines on the other side. On Christmas night, when the German soldiers were indulging in their convivial holiday customs, Washington, with twenty-five hundred of his best troops and twenty pieces of artillery, made the passage of the Delaware, through floating blocks of ice. He effected a landing nine miles above Trenton, and advanced in two divisions upon the town. Their attack was simultaneous, and the result was a surprise and a victory. It was more: for this piece of military strategy turned the war current in their favor and swept them towards success. Panic seized the British troops and they fled, dismayed. Such superior generalship was not looked for. Arms and stores were captured, besides a thousand prisoners. Washington, took his army back over the Delaware on the same day, and after a brief rest, re-crossed it on the twenty-ninth.

The enemy were concentrating at Princeton. Cornwallis, to whose relief General Howe was marching, supposed he had the American army entrapped, since it was impossible for them to retreat with the Delaware in their rear. But once more Washington rose superior to the occasion, and executed a marvellous feat of skilful daring. On that night the American watch-fires were piled high; bands of sappers and miners were heard noisily at work, and sentinels went their accustomed rounds. But a rapid and circuitous march round the British encampment was conducted in the silence of the night, and morning revealed the unwelcome truth to Cornwallis that he had been again outgeneralled. The American army had slipped from his grasp. They had reached Princeton without discovery, and, attacking the three British regiments stationed there, put them to flight, and won a decisive victory.

The capture of Burgoyne, the battle at Germantown, and the winter at Valley Forge only served to illustrate one of the most illustrious of commanders. The evacuation of Philadelphia by the British was followed, June twenty-eighth, 1779, by the brilliant battle of Monmouth, N. J. The tired soldiers slept upon the field, and Washington, wrapped in his cloak, slept in their midst, with the young French Marquis De Lafayette by his side. During the summer of this campaign occurred the savage massacres of Cherry Valley and Wyoming—horrible blots on the page of history, which can be charged to British instigation. With a skill and judgment which amounted to inspiration, Washington held the fleets and armies of England at bay, baffled the efforts of their ablest leaders, and closed the year's campaign, if not a victor, yet not vanquished. The surrender of Yorktown in October, 1781—the news of which was shouted in the streets of Philadelphia at midnight—echoed over the continent, and awoke the responsive enthusiasm of a liberated people. This culminated, at length, in the treaty of peace, signed at Paris in April, 1783. December fourth, Washington took leave of his brother officers. His eyes were full of tears, and his voice trembling with emotion as the words of affectionate farewell were spoken. "With a heart full of love and gratitude," he said, "I now take leave of you. I most devoutly wish that your latter days may be as prosperous and happy as your former have been glorious and honorable. I cannot come to you to take my leave, but shall be obliged if each of you will come and take me by the hand." Tears choked his utterance. Without a spoken word —in silence more eloquent than any speech, each of them grasped the hand of the man they so loved and venerated. The scene is described as affecting in the extreme.

December twenty-third, he resigned his commission to the Continental Congress at Annapolis. A convention, held soon after, at Philadelphia, fused the Confederacy of States into a nation, and created its constitution. The choice of the new nation was unanimous for Washington as its first President, and his installation took place April thirtieth, 1789.

How he guided the affairs of state into peaceful and wise and successful channels, for two terms of four years each, history records. How America loved him as its father, history records. He retired, a conqueror: not alone on the battle-field and in the chair of state, but in the wide realm of a grateful people's affection. His conquests were more glorious than those of Cæsar, more grand in their results than those of Napoleon. It is questionable whether Napoleon I. or any of the world's military leaders have displayed rarer generalship or greater military genius. More dazzling and meteoric they certainly have been, but hardly more able. Nor have they exhibited sublimer heroism. Nor has any life ever radiated a purer patriotism. He rose beyond the General, and became merged in the Ruler. "He gained the independence of his country by war—maintained it by peace—established it as a free government in the name of order, and law, and justice"—two of the greatest things, says Guizot, which, in politics, man can have the privilege of attempting.

Such laurels as he won, crown only the brows of those heroes sent of Heaven to be the special saviours of special epochs, and to lead the nations and peoples of earth up to higher levels of thought and action.

CHAPTER II.
JOSEPH WARREN.

Birthplace of Warren.—School Days.—Graduation at Harvard.—Studying Medicine.—Warren as a Physician.—The "Sons of Liberty."—Warren's Activity in Politics.—Boston Massacre.—Oration at the Old South Church.—Liberty's Advocate.—The Tea Party.—Faneuil Hall Meeting.—Fourth Anniversary of Boston Massacre.—Second Oration.—Fears of Assassination.—The Crisis Met.—Paul Revere's Ride.—Warren's Presentiment.—Battle of Bunker Hill.—Death of Warren.—"'Tis Sweet for One's Country to Die."—Honors to his Memory.—Bunker Hill Monument.

NO brighter name illumines our country's Roll of Honor than that of Joseph Warren, the hero of Bunker Hill. When the heel of British tyranny would have crushed to earth the sacred liberties of the American people, this young patriot, distinguished already in the councils of state, sprang to the defence of his country, and willingly laid down his life for the principles he had so fearlessly advocated. The Tree of Liberty grew apace, watered by such martyr-blood as that of Warren, and a grateful people hold his name in immortal memory.

When a man thus makes himself the exponent of an idea, when life itself becomes a secondary consideration to justice and to right, the world—always a hero-worshipper—is anxious to learn every detail of that life, to penetrate, if possible, the hidden springs of its action, and discover, if it may, out of what soil the hero took his growth.

Joseph Warren was born in Roxbury, Massachusetts, in 1740, but the accounts we have of his childhood days are too meagre to furnish any hint of the boy that was "father to the man.". It is supposed that he attended the grammar school of Master Lovell, where our forefathers received the training which prepared them for Harvard. When only fifteen years old he entered college, and graduated with honor in 1759.

During his university days he was looked upon as a boy of talent, and also acquired the reputation of great personal bravery. After leaving college young Warren began the study of medicine, and soon became distinguished in his profession. He was especially active during the year 1764, when the small-pox spread throughout Boston. At this time he is described as an accomplished gentleman, of fine presence and engaging address, winning favor alike from the learned and the humble. But his energies were not confined to the limits of his profession. He soon became known as a fine writer and an eloquent speaker.

From the year of the Stamp Act to the final breaking out of hostilities between the colonies and Great Britain, he did not cease to advocate by pen and voice the rights of the colonies—fearlessly condemning taxation as tyranny, and openly advocating resistance to it.

During these years, when the seeds of the Revolution were being sown, a secret society, called the "Sons of Liberty," flourished in Boston, which wielded a powerful influence in politics. From the year 1768 Dr. Warren was among its principal members, and there formed an intimacy with Samuel Adams, which was almost romantic in its strength. "Many of the members of this club filled public offices, and few in the outside world knew from whence the public measures of resistance to British tyranny originated."

In 1772 their numbers were increased, and they met in a house near the "North Battery," where over sixty persons were present at their first meeting. Dr. Warren drew up the society regulations, and it is recorded that "no important measures were taken without first consulting him and his particular friends." Here were matured those plans of defence, which saw their first fulfilment at Lexington and Bunker Hill.

After the tea was destroyed in Boston Harbor, the meetings of this society were no longer secret, but their place of rendezvous was changed in the spring of 1775 from the "North Battery" to the "Green Dragon." No member of this organization was more zealous than Dr. Warren, no one more active in patriotic measures. After the bloody scenes of the Boston Massacre, he was a prominent leader in the efforts made by the town to effect the removal of the troops, and was appointed by the town one of a committee of three to prepare an account of the affair, "that a full and just representation may be made thereof." The account was published, and sent to England in a vessel chartered especially for that purpose.

Dr. Warren was elected member of the State Legislature from Boston for the term of 1770, and his name figures conspicuously in the controversies of the times, and on committees appointed to draft important state papers. In 1773 he was re-elected, and served his term with distinguished success. In March of the year previous he delivered the anniversary oration on the Boston Massacre of 1770, to a large audience in the Old South Church. It was delivered on invitation of the town committee, and was said to be a brilliant effort. In this address he fearlessly charged Great Britain with an invasion of colonial rights, and called on his hearers to resist the torrent of oppression which was being poured upon them. In the course of his oration he gave utterance to the following memorable words:

"The voice of your fathers' blood cries to you from the ground, 'My sons, scorn to be slaves! In vain we met the frowns of tyrants—in vain we crossed the boisterous ocean, found a new world, and prepared it for the happy residence of Liberty—in vain we toiled—in vain we fought—we bled in vain if you, our offspring, want valor to repel the assaults of her invaders!'" The address was printed and widely distributed, and a duly appointed committee returned the thanks of the town to the speaker.

During the exciting years of 1772, 1773 and 1774, Warren seems to have been foremost in every movement looking towards the liberties of the colonies. Then, as now, there was a conservative party in politics, which was afraid to offend the British lion, and which desired reconciliation at almost any price. But if the minions of royalty cried "peace, peace!" Warren told them there was no peace. His voice rung out everywhere, counselling opposition to unjust laws, encouraging the weak, and winning, by force of logic, the faltering.

In 1772 he was one of the celebrated Committee of Correspondence which, November twentieth, handed in its famous report of grievances. This important document was arranged under three heads: First, "A Statement of the Rights of the Colonists;" Second, "A List of the Infringements of those Rights;" and Third, "A Letter of Correspondence with other Towns." Dr. Warren was the author of the second paper, and Mr. Barry sums up the "formidable array of complaints" as follows:

"The assumption of absolute legislative powers; the imposition of taxes without the consent of the people; the appointment of officers unknown to the charter, supported by income derived from such taxes; the investing these officers with unconstitutional powers, especially the 'Commissioners of his Majesty's Customs;' the annulment of laws enacted by the court after the time limited for their rejection had expired; the introduction of fleets and armies into the colonies; the support of the executive and the judiciary independently of the people; the oppressive instructions sent to the governor; the extension of the powers of the Court of Vice-Admiralty; the restriction of manufactures; the act relating to dock-yards and stores which deprived the people of the right of trial by peers in their own vicinage; the attempt to establish the American episcopate; and the alteration of the bounds of colonies by decisions before the King and Council." The paper was a masterly production, and its statements were clear and forcible.

Thus the march of events went forward until a crisis was precipitated on the colonies by the arrival of the celebrated tea in Boston Harbor. Immediately, the country was filled with excitement. "The Committee of Correspondence and the select men of the towns summoned meetings; and every friend of his country was urged to make a united and successful resistance to this 'last, worst, and most destructive measure of the administration.'"

November twenty-ninth, 1773, a meeting was held at Faneuil Hall which, for want of room, adjourned to the Old South Church, where Warren and John Hancock and others were the leading spirits of the occasion.

Of this meeting was born the Boston Tea Party, the first Congress, and, eventually, American independence.

In 1774 Dr. Warren was chosen a delegate from Suffolk County to the General Assembly of Massachusetts, and became thenceforward the leading man of the province. At this time John Hancock was President of the Provincial Congress, but when he went to the Continental Congress at Philadelphia, Warren was elected to fill his place. Meantime, the fourth anniversary of the Boston Massacre was at hand, and some of the British officers had threatened that "they would take the life of any man who should dare to speak on that occasion." Warren, hearing of the threat, solicited the privilege of delivering the anniversary address.

On the day appointed, the Old South Church was filled with an expectant throng. Large numbers of British soldiers crowded the aisles, stairways, and even the pulpit. An ominous silence reigned throughout the vast multitude as they waited the arrival of Warren. At last he came, entering the church through a window back of the pulpit. His friends were on the *qui vive* of alarm—fearing his assassination. Though standing ready to avenge such a cowardly act, would *that* atone for the murder of their beloved Warren? But the crisis passed as Warren, commencing his speech in a firm voice, waxed eloquent as he went on. He pictured the wrongs of the colonies; he proclaimed the corner-stone of his faith—" Resistance to tyrants is obedience to God "—he painted the scenes of the Boston Massacre in such colors, and with such pathos of appeal, that the soldiery who had come there to awe him by their presence, shed tears at the sad picture. To the relief of the friends of Warren, no outbreak occurred during the address, though it was frequently interrupted by the groans and hisses of the tories, and the applause of the patriots.

This speech aroused the enthusiasm of the country to the highest pitch, and all hearts beat with the common sentiment which he had proclaimed—" Resistance to tyrants is obedience to God." One of Warren's biographers, speaking of this time, says: " Such another hour has seldom appeared in the history of man, and is not surpassed in the records of nations. The thunders of Demosthenes rolled at a distance from Philip and his host; and Tully poured the fiercest torrent of his invectives when Cataline was at a distance, and his dagger no longer to be feared; but Warren's speech was made to proud oppressors, resting on their arms, whose errand it was to overawe, and whose business it was to fight. If the deed of Brutus deserves to be commemorated, should not this instance of patriotism and bravery be held in lasting remembrance?"

Samuel Adams was moderator of this meeting, and notwithstanding some disturbance at the close of the oration, succeeded in finishing the business on hand and dispersing the audience peaceably.

On the fifteenth of April the Provincial Congress adjourned—warned probably of the approach of General Gage with an armed force. Hancock and Adams, who remained at Lexington, were, it seems, the special objects of British hatred, and a plot was concocted for their seizure. That their lives were saved at this time is no doubt due to the efforts of Dr. Warren. Paul Revere says that "on the evening of April eighteenth, 1775, he was sent for in great haste by Dr. Warren, who begged that he would immediately set off for Lexington and acquaint Adams and Hancock of their danger." But when the impetuous Revere arrived at Warren's house, he found that an express had already preceded him. It is said that Dr. Warren participated in the battle of the next day—April nineteenth—when the first blood was shed in behalf of American independence, and that a ball took off part of his ear-lock.

Warren was a member of the Committee of Safety, and on May nineteenth this committee was delegated full powers by the Provincial Congress to manage the military force of the province. Everywhere, men were flocking around the standard of liberty, and the war of the Revolution was now fully inaugurated.

Warren was commissioned major-general four days previous to the battle of Bunker Hill, but did not assume command on that historic day, choosing rather to fight as a volunteer. The day before the battle, in a conversation with Mr. Gerry, at Cambridge, he discussed "the determination of Congress to take possession of Bunker Hill." He said, that for himself he had been opposed to it, but that the majority had determined upon it, and he would hazard his life to carry that determination into effect. Mr. Gerry expressed his disapprobation of the measure, as he considered it impossible to hold, adding, "but if it must be so, it is not worth while for you to be present; it will be madness for you to expose yourself where your destruction will be almost inevitable." "I know it," he answered, "but I live within the sound of their cannon; how could I hear their roaring in so glorious a cause and not be there?"

Again Mr. Gerry remonstrated, and concluded with saying, "As sure as you go there, you will be slain!"

General Warren replied enthusiastically, "It is sweet to die for one's country!"

That night he was busily engaged with public affairs at Watertown, and did not reach Cambridge until five o'clock next morning. Throwing himself on a bed, he slept until nearly noon, when he was aroused with the news of the approaching battle at Charlestown. Hastily rising, he mounted his horse and rode to the scene of action—reaching Breed's Hill a short time before the opening of the battle. Colonel Prescott rode forward to resign his command and report for orders, but Warren did not choose to take the position at that time, saying that he considered it honor enough to fight under so brave an officer. He borrowed a musket and a cartridge-box, and rushing into the hottest of the fray, encouraged the men by his brave words and braver example. Three times the British charged the redoubt on the hill, and were twice driven back. At the third charge, when the ammunition of the Provincials gave out, and when a terrible enfilading fire swept the inner line of the redoubt, they were obliged to fall back. Warren was killed after the retreat began—one of the last to leave the redoubt. The fatal bullet pierced his brain, producing almost instant death. He was buried on the spot where he fell.

> "And thus Warren fell—happy death, noble fall,
> To perish for country at liberty's call!"

His presentiment had been fulfilled. His life had been freely given for the cause he held dearer than life.

In April of the following year, after the British troops had left Boston, the "remains were disinterred and borne in solemn procession from the Representatives' Chamber to King's Chapel, and buried with full military and Masonic honors. Perez Morton, one of the most impressive orators of his time, pronounced an oration on the occasion, and the patriot divine, Dr. Samuel Cooper, conducted the funeral services. The orphan children of Warren and his aged mother were there, and the sad silence was broken by her sobs. His remains have since been removed by his family from King's Chapel to St. Paul's Church."

In 1794 a monument was raised to his memory by the Masonic lodge of Charlestown. "It consisted of a brick pedestal, eight feet square, rising ten feet from the ground, and supporting a Tuscan pillar of wood, eighteen feet high. This was surmounted by a gilt urn, bearing the inscription: 'J. W., aged 35.' The simple epitaph was entwined with Masonic emblems." After standing forty years, the monument gave place to the present granite obelisk, which rises to the height of one hundred and fifty feet above the historic hill, and in which is enclosed a statue of General Warren.

In 1777 a resolution was passed by Congress to erect

BATTLE OF BUNKER HILL.

a monument to Warren in the town of Boston, bearing this inscription:

"In Honor of
JOSEPH WARREN,
Major-General of Massachusetts Bay.
He devoted his life to the liberties
of his country;
And in bravely defending them, fell
an early victim,
In the Battle of Bunker Hill,
June 17, 1775.
The Congress of the United States
As an acknowledgment of his services,
Have erected this monument
To his memory."

But the patriotic order was never executed. His truest monument is in the hearts of his countrymen, where, after the lapse of a century, the glory that crowns his name shines as brightly as on the day of his heroic death.

CHAPTER III.
NATHANIEL GREENE.

Birthplace and Ancestry.—Work at the Plough and the Anvil.—Studying Euclid over the Forge.—Education under Disadvantages.—Lindley Murray and Dr. Styles.—Love of the Dance.—Ingenious Shingle Device.—Marriage.—On the Road to Lexington.—Made a Major-General.—Expelled from the Quakers.—Sick in Camp.—At Trenton.—The Brandywine.—Greene's Bravery.—Germantown.—The Fight through the Fog.—Valley Forge and Monmouth.—The Army of the South.—The Long Chase of Cornwallis.—Siege of Ninety-six.—Retirement.

THIS scion of a Quaker stock was one of the strongest characters brought out by the Revolution. His moral worth, sound mind and good generalship were second only to those of Washington, and side by side with that great patriot he breasted the wave of tyranny which rolled over from the mother country.

On the twenty-seventh of May, 1742, in Warwick, Rhode Island, Nathaniel Greene first saw the light. His remote ancestors were English, his father a strict Quaker preacher. The paternal purse not being filled to overflowing, the boyhood of young Nathaniel was one of almost constant toil. But his energies could not be confined to the work of the anvil or the plough, and he found his way to books despite every obstacle. He became acquainted with Lindley Murray and Dr. Styles, and made them contributors to his stock of knowledge. He read Horace and Cæsar, worked the problems of Euclid over his forge, dipped into metaphysics and logic, and even Blackstone and law dictionaries did not escape his craving mind. He was also fond of field sports and other kinds of exhilarating exercise, and, contrary to the strictures of his Quaker father, indulged a very un-Quakerlike love for the mazy dance.

Discovered in the indulgence of this species of amusement, he prepared for the expected horsewhipping by lining his jacket with strips of shingle, and thus escaped unhurt from the parental flagellation.

At twenty he was vigorous in body, bold in mind, and took an active part in the political discussions of the day. The passage of the Stamp Act decided his course of action, and at once he was enrolled among the patriot band of the Revolution. In 1770 he was elected to the General Assembly of the colony, and four years later his marriage with Miss Littlefield took place. In the spring of 1775 he was on his way to Lexington, and with the rank of major-general, was placed in command of sixteen hundred Rhode Island men. His love for the military brought down on him the displeasure of the Quakers, and he was formally expelled from that society during this same eventful year.

Greene entered upon the duties of the drill with vigor, and had soon put his Rhode Island troops in good condition for the field. After the battle of Bunker Hill his command was removed to Cambridge, and here he gained the lasting esteem and confidence of Washington.

After the evacuation of Boston by the British, Greene was placed in command of Long Island, at which point an attack was hourly anticipated. His head-quarters were established at Brooklyn, and the surrounding woods and roads were explored and guarded at all points of access. Every precaution was taken to insure success to the patriot band. But while this defensive work went forward, Greene was seized with fever, and for days lay hovering between life and death. While in this helpless condition, the cannon of the enemy thundered in his front, and defeat to the American arms followed. This disaster was a source of bitter grief to General Greene, and the result was no doubt due to his absence from the field. As soon as he was able to ride, his troops were summoned to the defence of New York, which was threatened by the enemy. At Harlem a stand was made and a brilliant fight ensued, General Greene behaving with great bravery in this his first battle. When the enemy pushed forward from Fort Washington on Staten Island towards Fort Lee, Greene, who had been stationed at that point, succeeded by superior strategy in cutting off their retreat to the Hackensack. He threw himself across their track and kept them at bay until Washington came to his relief. In the retreat through the Jerseys, Greene was the companion of Washington, and shared his glory and his vicissitudes. The brilliant surprise of Trenton was planned in part by his strategy, and the night of its caputre he commanded the division with which Washington marched in person.

In the winter of 1777 Greene was in command of a division stationed at Baskingridge, New Jersey, where a series of skirmishes occupied the winter. To aid in the reorganization of the army for the next campaign and hasten the action of Congress in the matter,

Greene was despatched to Philadelphia as the fittest person for such a mission, and the one most likely to succeed in influencing that body towards a favorable result.

On the tenth of September of that year the Americans were encamped on the banks of the Brandywine, and the next day witnessed the battle which made this ground historic. The Americans were massed at the ford, and stubbornly contested the enemy's advance. But a heavy force under Howe and Cornwallis had crossed the river by a circuitous route and were rapidly marching upon the American rear. At this unexpected manœuvre the patriot ranks were thrown into confusion and were flying in disorder, when Greene with two fresh brigades came to their rescue. His field-pieces were planted in the path of the enemy, and by their well-directed fire arrested the headlong advance of the British. The flight which had begun in panic was now converted into a well-ordered retreat, and, halting in a narrow defile, Greene drew up his troops in line of battle. This gave them the advantage of position, and they awaited the onset of the foe. The British came on in a wild charge, only to be hurled back by the death-dealing fire of the patriot troops. Again and again did the enemy endeavor to take this strong position, but without avail. Greene and his invincible men held their ground without wavering until night brought the conflict to a close. The enemy then retired, leaving the American forces in victorious possession of the field.

When Howe occupied Philadelphia, and Washington had determined upon making an attack on the enemy at Germantown, Greene was intrusted with the command of the left wing of the American army. The battle commenced at daybreak on the fourth of October, and the contending armies were veiled from each other's view by a thick fog. The long blaze of musketry fire flashing out from the gloom was the only guide which directed the aim of the patriot forces. But they rushed forward into the village driving the enemy before them, when suddenly, in the confusion and gloom of the morning, the division of Stevens became panic-stricken, and Cornwallis arriving with fresh troops, the patriot forces were compelled to fall back. General Greene conducted this retreat in a masterly manner. A running fight was kept up for five miles, and the day closed in disappointment to the Americans. But reverses sometimes only serve to give greater strength, and the lessons of this day were neither lost nor fruitless.

During the winter at Valley Forge, Greene was of great service in reorganizing the army, especially in the quarter-master and commissary departments, which it seems were sadly in need of a wholesome change. At the urgent desire of Washington and Congress, he had accepted the position of quarter-master-general, and the result proved the wisdom of their choice, as an immediate reform in those departments amply demonstrated.

Greene stood with Washington in counselling the battle of Monmouth, while a majority of officers opposed it, and to his services on that field the victory was largely due. After twenty-four hours of fighting and constant exercise and anxiety, discharging the double duties of his two offices, he was at last enabled to throw himself down at the foot of a tree, wrapped in his cloak, to snatch a few hours of needed rest.

Afterwards, when the attack on Newport, Rhode Island, was planned, Greene's command constituted a portion of the force under Sullivan, which was marched northward for that purpose. The misfortune which rendered powerless the aid of D'Estaing's fleet, defeated their well-laid plans, and a retreat was rendered necessary. Greene's "coolness and judgment" on this occasion were conspicuous.

After the burning of Elizabethtown by Clinton, an interval of inaction and inactivity followed. The slow current of affairs was suddenly broken by the treason of Arnold and the arrest of Andre. Greene presided over the court of inquiry which convicted that brave young officer; but neither his sympathies nor his regrets were allowed to interfere with the solemn execution of his duty in this important trust. Afterwards he was appointed to the command of the armies of the South, and his presence and good generalship revealed themselves in the most encouraging results. Marion, Sumter, Pickens, Morgan, Howard, Lee and Carrington were the leaders under his command, and with such brave material, his achievements were brilliant in the extreme. The superior strategy of Greene and his fine tact were illustrated during his campaign in the South by the sorry chase he led Cornwallis. For nearly a month that general kept up his pursuit of Greene without being able to entrap him or out-general his masterly manœuvres, and the retreat ended only when the Americans were landed safely on the northern banks of the River Dan. In the subsequent battle of Guilford Court-House, Greene took an active part, as also in the field at Camden, and the sharply contested siege of Fort Ninety-Six.

The execution by the British of Colonel Hayne in Charleston as a spy, greatly exasperated Greene, who threatened retaliation—a promise likely enough to have been fulfilled had the war continued. At the battle of Eutaw Springs, Greene's losses were severe, though in this engagement he took five hundred prisoners.

The campaign of 1781 closed, leaving South Carolina again in possession of its rightful owners.

The State Assembly, in 1782, voted General Greene an address of thanks for his distinguished services, to which was added a gift of ten thousand guineas. After the evacuation of Charleston, Greene made a triumphal entry into that city on the fourteenth of December, accompanied by a civil and military escort, the governor riding by his side. After the war he removed to a plantation at Mulberry Grove, on the Savannah River, in Georgia, where he lived until his death. At the age of forty-four his life was cut short by an unhappy exposure to the rays of a southern sun. On June nineteenth, 1786, he breathed his last and received his promotion to a higher sphere. His memory lives, entwined with that of Washington and all the patriot dead whose precious services gave to us a country and with it transmitted the sacred heritage of freedom.

CHAPTER IV.
LAFAYETTE.

Noble Lineage of the Marquis.—Early Surroundings.—A Member of the King's Regiment.—Commissioned at Fifteen.—Marriage.—The Dinner at Metz.—Noble Resolve.—Preparations to Sail for America.—Obstacles Everywhere.—Voyage of the "Victory."—Arrival.—Home of Benjamin Huger.—Journey to Philadelphia.—Fighting for Liberty.—Battle of Brandywine.—Services in the Revolution.—Arnold and Lafayette.—Return to France.—Visit to the United States.—Terrors of the French Revolution.—Flight and Imprisonment.—The Magdeburg Dungeon.—Liberated by Napoleon.—Visit to the United States in 1824.—Joyful Welcome.—The Citizen King of the French.—Last Days of Lafayette.

THE Marquis de Lafayette, of glorious memory, was descended from a long line of noble ancestry. His father, also a marquis and a chevalier of the order of St. Louis, bravely fought and fell on the field of Minden, Germany, under the leadership of the Duke de Broglie, two months before Lafayette was born. His mother came of the noble house of Lusignan.

At the family chateau of the ancient line, in Chavagniac, province of Auvergne, France, on September sixth, 1757, Lafayette was born. All the luxury that wealth could give, all the advantages which titled rank could confer, awaited him. His childhood was a pathway of flowers. No adverse circumstances arose like mountains, in the road down which he was to walk. Not then, nor afterwards, until he deliberately *chose* the rugged way, because liberty was found in it, and he preferred hardship with liberty to luxury without it.

When he had arrived at the age of twelve, he was sent to the Plessis college at Paris, where he became a favorite at the royal court of Louis the Grand, and received the appointment of one of the queen's pages. Having also joined the king's regiment of musketeers, the queen obtained for him a commission when he was only fifteen years old. At sixteen he was married to a daughter of the Duke D'Ayen, a young lady fourteen years old; and though the alliance was favored and promoted by relatives on both sides, it was said to be purely a love-affair between the young marquis and his girlish bride. For once, at least, the old adage was contradicted, and the course of true love seemed to run smooth. After his marriage the new relatives of Lafayette endeavored to obtain a position in the establishment of the king, for the marquis, but their plans were defeated by Lafayette himself, who had no relish for the favors of royalty. The negotiations regarding the matter were pending a long time, and before they were concluded an event occurred which changed the whole current of Lafayette's life, and gave him to future fame as the champion of American liberty.

Near the close of the year 1776, about two years after his marriage, Lafayette, who was at that time an officer in the French army stationed at Metz, met the Duke of Gloucester, brother of King George the Third, at the head-quarters of the commandant of the place. A dinner was given to the distinguished guest, and Lafayette was among the number invited to be present. At table the leading topic of conversation was the struggle then going on in America, and there was at least *one* deeply interested listener. Many of the details of the contest across the water, Lafayette now heard for the first time, and he took part in the conversation with great earnestness. He seemed to comprehend the situation at a glance, and saw that the cause of the American colonies was the cause of "justice, of liberty, of heaven."

Before he rose from the table his resolution was taken. Henceforward he would identify himself with the struggling colonists on the soil of the new world. Speaking of this time he says: "When I first learned the subject of this quarrel my heart espoused warmly the cause of liberty, and I thought of nothing but adding also the aid of my banner. . . . . Such a glorious cause had never before attracted the attention of mankind."

With Lafayette, to resolve was to act, and he made preparations at once to go to America. His friends and relatives strongly opposed him in the step he was about to take, and discouragements sprang up in his path everywhere. But his young enthusiasm and dauntless courage were not to be thus overcome. Endless difficulties confronted him before he could leave the ports of France on his outward-bound voyage, and at last he was driven to the extreme of purchasing a ship of his own, since all other means of transportation had been denied him. With sublime courage he conquered every obstacle which stood between him and the achievement of his glorious purpose to enroll himself among the defenders of American liberty. At last, after having run the gauntlet of exposure a long time, he set sail for the shores of the new world. His ship was named the "Victory." As soon as it was known that he had gone, the French court despatched orders to the West Indies to arrest his progress, as it was customary for all French cruisers to take that route. But Lafayette, anticipating pursuit, sailed directly for an American port, and after a tedious voyage of seven weeks landed on the South Carolina coast, near Georgetown, at the mouth of the Pedee River. "Entering the river about dark, they went ashore with their boats, and attracted by a light approached the house of Major Benjamin Huger. The furious barking of the dogs promised them anything but a warm reception." The family of Mr. Huger at first supposed them to be a marauding party, but when their character was made known by Baron DeKalb, who was with them and acted as interpreter, they were received with cordial welcome. With the hospitality characteristic of the South, everything was provided for the comfort of the generous foreigners who had come to aid them in their struggle for liberty. Lafayette was agreeably impressed with the new country and with the unaffected simplicity of the inhabitants, and his zeal for the cause he had espoused continued unabated.

Writing from Charleston on the nineteenth of June, he says: "The country and its inhabitants are as agreeable as my enthusiasm had led me to imagine. Simplicity of manner, kindness of heart, love of country and of liberty, and a delightful state of equality are met with universally." At Charleston he received the respect and attention due his high standing and his noble devotion to principle. He had left that city by carriage for Philadelphia, where Congress was then assembled, to ask the privilege of joining the American army. He had before him a journey of nine hundred miles over rough roads, the greater part of which was accomplished on horseback. He was a month on the road; but he arrived at last at Philadelphia, while Washington was encamped at Germantown, ten miles from the city, after having made his historic passage of the Delaware. On the thirty-first of July, Congress conferred on Lafayette the rank of major-general. It was entirely unsolicited on his part, as he had asked simply to serve as a volunteer at his own expense.

When Washington arrived at Philadelphia he met Lafayette at a dinner party, and having been made acquainted with the circumstances of his coming to America, complimented him upon his zeal and sacrifices and invited him to consider the head-quarters of the army his home. This was the beginning of an intimate and lifelong friendship between Lafayette and Washington.

When the Continental army marched through the streets of Philadelphia on its way to Delaware, Lafayette was at the side of the commanding general, and shortly afterwards, at the battle of Brandywine, distinguished himself for his bravery, covering the retreat of the American forces in a masterly manner. During the action he received a severe wound in his leg, but fought gallantly on, unheeding the stream of blood which flowed over his boot-top. He was afterwards laid up for six weeks with this first wound in liberty's cause. In the battle of Brandywine Lafayette fought as a volunteer, not having yet obtained a command, though his commission had been received some time previous. When Congress conferred on him the rank of major-general he lacked one month of being twenty years of age, and he had already entered upon a career of almost unparalleled brightness.

In the winter of 1777–78 a party conspiracy was

formed, whose object was to displace Washington and give the chief command to General Gates. With a view to detaching Lafayette from his interest, an expedition against Canada was planned and Lafayette appointed to the chief command. But with a noble integrity he refused to accept the position unless he could be considered as acting under Washington and subject to his orders. But the ambitious designs of the cabal proved abortive, and the expedition to Canada was abandoned.

In May following, he conducted a retreat from Barren Hill, in the face of superior numbers, with a skill which won the admiration of the army, and his gallant services at the battle of Monmouth in the succeeding month elicited the thanks of Congress. At the close of the campaign of 1778 he addressed a letter to Congress, enclosing one from Washington. In this letter, among other things, he says: "As long as I thought I could dispose of myself, I made it my pride and pleasure to fight under American colors in defence of a cause which I dare more particularly call *ours*, because I had the good fortune of bleeding for her. Now that France is involved in a war, I am urged by a sense of my duty as well as by the love of my country, to present myself before the king and know in what manner he judges proper to employ my services." He then asks permission of Congress to return to France as a soldier on furlough, and tenders his services in behalf of the American cause in his own country. Congress granted the permission he asked, giving him unlimited leave of absence and instructing the president to write him a letter of thanks for his zeal in the cause of American independence. A sword was also presented him in the name of the United States as a token of gratitude and esteem.

He landed on the French coast February twelfth, 1779, and met with a warm reception among his enthusiastic countrymen. The court, at first cold and distant, afterwards appointed him to a command in the king's regiment, where he served with his usual activity during the year.

In March, 1780, Lafayette returned to the United States and again tendered his services to Congress. They were gratefully accepted; and from that time until the close of hostilities he took an active part in the colonial struggle for independence. He succeeded in infusing into his men some of his own enthusiasm for the cause in which he was engaged, and prevented desertions by appeals to the honor of his troops, instead of adopting the usual harsh code. He defended Virginia against the invasion of Cornwallis with masterly skill, and in Baltimore raised means from his own credit with the merchants of that city, to obtain much needed supplies of clothing.

In the trying times of Arnold's treason, when the question, " Whom can we trust now?" was anxiously asked, Lafayette was the bosom-friend of Washington, and his counsel and advice were ever relied upon. When an accident threw upon Arnold the command of the entire British force in Virginia, Lafayette refused to hold any correspondence whatever with him. He returned a letter, sent by flag of truce, unopened, with the reply that if any of the British officers had written to him he would have been happy to receive their communications, and extend to them the courtesy rendered necessary by the death of their commander,

General Phillips—an event which had just occurred and which was the occasion of Arnold's position.

After the surrender of Cornwallis, Lafayette again petitioned Congress for leave of absence to visit his family in France, and thus terminated his connection with the Revolutionary war. "From Congress, from the several States, from literary institutions and from assemblies of the people on every side, he received the most ample testimonials of the high sense universally entertained of his disinterested sacrifices in the cause of American freedom and of the distinguished ability and success with which he had consecrated to it the flower of his manhood." Prayers and blessings followed him across the Atlantic. Congress intrusted him with confidential powers to his government, and wrote a letter recommending him to his king "in words of unequivocal praise." France received him with demonstrations of joy, and the king conferred on him the rank of field-marshal.

After the fall of Yorktown another year was occupied by turbulent conferences and negotiations for peace. Lafayette, as confidential agent of the United States in the old world, was largely instrumental in securing the happy termination of the negotiations, and was the first one to send the joyful tidings to America. In his eagerness, he chartered a ship especially for that purpose. Through his influence also, Spain the more speedily recognized the independence of the United States.

When everything in his power had been done for the furtherance of the interest of America in Europe, Lafayette accepted the urgent invitation of Washington to visit the country for whose freedom he had so freely expended blood and treasure. He was also prompted by his own strong desire to meet once more his comrades-in-arms. He embarked at Havre on July first, 1784, and arrived in New York on August fourth. His journey through the United States was an ovation. Universal welcome greeted him, and the "triumph accorded by the heart of a nation to one of its deliverers" was his. In every town and village through which he passed, the mothers and daughters and widows of the land, as well as his comrades-in-arms, gathered around him with heartfelt welcome. "Congress appointed committees to receive him and to bid him adieu; and in every way a grateful nation showered upon him the most gratifying marks of their love and respect."

On the twenty-fifth of January, 1785, he was again in Paris. He found France in the state of confusion which immediately preceded the Revolution, and at once endeavored to obtain for the people a liberal basis of government. Through him a convocation of nobles was called at which he sought to obtain for his countrymen "personal liberty, religious liberty, and a representative assembly of the people."

Through strenuous and long-continued efforts the power of the throne was at last limited, and the people found voice through a legislature. But the lower classes, so long held under despotic rule, were swept in the reactionary wave of the Revolution, and the terrors of that time were now inaugurated. Kings, princes and nobles were beheaded at the bloody shrine of which Robespierre was high priest, and the streets of Paris ran red with the best blood of France.

Through all these times of terror, Lafayette walked

with steady purpose. Every position which the power of the monarchy could offer was tendered him, but he refused them all. He would accept no pecuniary compensation for his services. His aim was far higher than mere personal aggrandizement.

"Finding himself, after the execution of the king, no longer able to command the army he had created, beset by enemies, denounced in the assembly as a traitor, and by that assembly ordered to be arrested, Lafayette had but two alternatives, either to yield himself to their authority, or to fly. He chose the latter course, but in the territory of Liege fell into the hands of the Austrians, who treated him as a prisoner of war." Austria finally gave him into the custody of the Prussian government, and after being dragged about for some time from one prison to another, he was at last taken to the fortress of Magdeburg, where he suffered the tortures of a living tomb. Nothing could excuse this inhuman treatment received at the hands of the Austrian and Prussian governments.

"When, after the first victory of the arms of Brunswick, an exchange of prisoners was about to take place, he was transferred to the Emperor of Germany, to avoid his being included in the cartel, and was placed in the dungeons of Olmutz, in Moravia." In this prison he was cut off from all communication with the outside world. Even his jailers were forbidden to speak his name, and neither knife nor fork was allowed him, on account of a fear that he might be tempted to put an end to so wretched an existence.

His health failed to such a degree under this cruel treatment that his physician repeatedly declared him unable to recover without the aid of fresh air. The court of Vienna listened unmoved to these appeals, until at last, alarmed by the execrations of the world, Lafayette was permitted exercise abroad under an armed guard. At this time his rescue was attempted by Colonel Huger and Dr. Bollman, which resulted disastrously in their capture and imprisonment for six months.

The noble wife of Lafayette, escaping the fate of her relatives upon the scaffold only through the fall of Robespierre, sought the imperial presence of the German Emperor and plead for the release of her husband. Denied this boon, she then asked permission to share his imprisonment. The request was granted, but her health gave way under the close confinement, and her petition for a leave of absence was refused. "She was told that she might go if she would, but that she could never return." With heroic devotion she remained; but her system never recovered the shock here incurred. Wilberforce, Fox, General Fitzpatrick and Washington all plead in vain for the release of Lafayette; but at last Napoleon came to ask the same favor with a determination which would brook no denial. " Napoleon restored Lafayette to liberty, but scarcely to life, for his constitution was shattered and his estates had been wasted by the convulsions which had shaken his country." After the downfall of the Directory he revisited France, now so changed, and sought the quietude of his home at Lagrange. He refused the favors which Napoleon heaped upon him, and remained true to his Republican principles through all conflicts. He rejected even the cross of the Legion of Honor; and the position of Governor of Louisiana, which Mr. Jefferson offered, failed to allure him. He wanted neither titles nor advancements. In the seclusion of his family circle he watched the progress of events, and when the empire of Napoleon crumbled and France was again in danger, he appeared once more in the political arena, advocating the cause of the people. All his influence was used to restore tranquillity, but he did not fail to urge the representative system.

During these troublous times his course had been eagerly watched by the people of the United States, and after the restoration of Louis VIII. both Houses of Congress passed a resolution inviting him to this continent. His second visit of 1824 was the result. He was hailed by the Nation with joy and gratitude, and the blessings and prayers of old and young followed him. He returned to France to enter the Revolution of 1830. In this hour of his country's need he was looked to for counsel. "The nation confided to him its fate, and, like Washington, he had the privilege of refusing a crown. He felt that France was not ripe for the institutions of the United States; but he desired to secure to the people an acknowledgment of their rights, though with a king." The supreme object of his life was ended when he had presented to the people the *citizen king* in the person of the Duke of Orleans, Louis Phillippe, a man tried in adversity and found true. Here terminated his great career.

He sleeps his last sleep in a cemetery near Paris by the side of his faithful wife and daughter. On the morning of the twentieth of May, 1834, his great spirit took its flight, leaving behind an example of the purest integrity, the loftiest virtue. Worldly power did not tempt him; crowns or kingdoms could not allure him. He belonged not alone to France, but to America, to the world. He was the champion of Liberty, the advocate of the people. To France he was the high priest of the new Republic, inaugurating free thought, and a representative system. The words which fell from his lips were the electric sparks which fired the minds of the people and caused an empire to tremble to its fall. His aspirations were to elevate the condition of his fellow-men. His aims were liberty and justice. France loved him, and America reveres his memory.

CHAPTER V.
ISRAEL PUTNAM.

Ancestry of Putnam.—Boyhood Days.—Marriage.—Removal to Pomfret.—Adventure with the Wolf.—Seven Years' War.—Putnam in Command of a Company.—Adventures along the Hudson. —Surprised by Indians.—Down the Rapids.—Indian Superstition. —Putnam at the Stake.—The Rescue.—The Guns of Lexington. —The Plow Exchanged for the Sword.—Murray Hill and the Quakeress.—Putnam's Rapid Rise in the Army.—*Ruse* at Princeton.—Escape at Horseneck.—Paralysis.—The Last of Earth.— Eulogiums.

ISRAEL PUTNAM was one of the most gallant and daring officers of the revolutionary war. He was renowned for his keen strategy and intrepid bravery, which served him many a good turn in the adverse fortunes of war, and certainly no more skilful or patriotic general ever served his country under the glorious leadership of Washington.

The boy Putnam first saw the light in Salem, Massachusetts, and was ushered into the affairs of this world just seven days after the new year of 1718 had spoken once and parted forever with the old year of 1717. His paternal grandfather was one of the Pilgrims who came over in the "Mayflower" and landed at Plymouth Rock. The name of this ancestor was John Putnam, who with two brothers emigrated from the south of England and settled in Salem.

Of the early days of Putnam there are few incidents to relate. He was a plain farmer's boy, full of sturdy health and brought up in the simple, industrious habits of the times. When he had arrived at the age of twenty-one he married a girl of Salem, and the next year—1740—removed to the town of Pomfret, in Connecticut, where he settled down into the steady life of a farmer. It is of these days that the well-known story of Putnam's adventure with the wolf is told—a story which has been disputed in some particulars by several writers on the subject.

During the fifteen years which succeeded his removal to Pomfret, he was occupied exclusively with his farm and accumulated a handsome property. Then came the Seven Years' War between England and France, and Putnam was placed in command of a company in a regiment of Connecticut Provincials. The vast continent of North America was the rich prize contended for, and the long war was inaugurated by Braddock's expedition against Fort Du Quesne, while the battles at Fort Niagara and Fort Edward were enacted in the early part of the same campaign.

In this expedition Captain Putnam and his company performed the duty of rangers and were sent on special and perilous service, reconnoitering the enemy's camp and capturing their outposts and supplies. It was during this first campaign that Captain Putnam saved the life of Major Rogers of New Hampshire.

At the close of the campaign Captain Putnam returned to his home, but re-entered the service the next year—1756—having had his commission as captain renewed.

An incident illustrating his bravery and bold spirit is told, respecting his recapture of provisions taken by the enemy. They had been captured at Halfway Brook, between Fort Edward and Lake George, by a force six hundred strong. Putnam and Rogers went in pursuit, having about one hundred men in boats and two "wall-pieces and two blunderbusses." They proceeded down the lake and took a line across the land to the narrows, in order to cut off any possible retreat. "They succeeded in reaching the spot before the French with their bateau, now laden with plunder, had gained it. Unexpectedly they opened a tremendous fire upon them, killed many of the boatmen and sank several of the boats. The rest by a strong wind were swept into South Bay, and thus escaped to bear the news to Ticonderoga. Anticipating their return with reinforcements, Putnam and Rogers hastened to their boats, and at Sabbath-day Point they found their expectations had not deceived them, for the French, about three hundred strong, were approaching on the lake. When the enemy had come within pistol-shot, the wall-pieces and blunderbusses were unmasked and opened upon them, aided by musketry, producing the most dreadful carnage, and leaving the further retreat of the rangers unmolested."

It was such adventure as this that gave to Putnam a wide reputation for bravery and strategic skill, and in 1757 the Legislature of Connecticut conferred on him a major's commission. If there was a hazardous enterprise to be performed, or a difficult feat to be accomplished, Putnam was the man selected to do it. Once, while lying on the Hudson in his bateau, near the rapids at Fort Miller, he was surprised by the sudden appearance of a party of Indians on the bank. Putnam had with him only five men, and to land would have been certain destruction. His decision was instantly taken, and wheeling his boat amid stream he

PUTNAM RESCUED BY MOLANG.

glided swiftly towards the rapids. The dusky sons of the forest watched him in amazement from the shore as his boat swept down the dangerous rapids, making the passage safely and gliding out into the smooth waters below. The red men thought him favored of the Great Spirit.

Once, however, his guiding star of good fortune seemed to have forsaken him. While reconnoitering the enemy's position at Ticonderoga, he was surprised and captured by a detachment of Indians under the leadership of the French officer Molang. He was tied to a tree and forced to remain there while a hot struggle ensued between the provincials and the French allies, leaving the provincials in possession of the field. In their retreat the Indians took their prisoner with them. "He was dragged onward by his foes, who stripped him of his clothes, his shoes and hat, and forced him to bear the most cruel burdens, while his flesh was incessantly lacerated by the thorns and briers of the woods. One of these savages had struck him with the but-end of his musket and fractured his jaw, causing excruciating pain, and another had wounded him with a tomahawk in the neck. His sufferings were not ended with this treatment. He had been destined to perish at the stake, and the brutal conquerors had already determined upon inflicting the most cruel torture to add to the bitterness of death. They bound their victim to a tree, naked and covered with wounds, and had already lighted the fagots that were to consume him, when one of them, more humane than the rest, informed Molang of his danger, and this officer rushed to his rescue. . . . Putnam was carried to Ticonderoga, where he was made known to Montcalm, who had him transferred to Montreal. In this city there were several American prisoners, and among them Colonel Peter Schuyler. This gallant officer was very much overcome" on seeing Putnam stripped of his clothing, and exhibiting marks of such cruel treatment, and succeeded in getting him exchanged with others, when the transfer of prisoners took place.

In 1759 Putnam received the rank of lieutenant-colonel, and in 1762, when war broke out between England and Spain, he went to Cuba in command of a Connecticut regiment. After contributing to the success of the English in subduing Havana, he returned to his home in Connecticut.

Ten years of his life had thus far been spent in warfare, and with the respite of another decade, the war of the Revolution furnished an opportunity for the continuance of his military career.

When the guns of Lexington, on the memorable nineteenth of April, 1775, announced the contest for liberty on the soil of the New World begun, Putnam was at his plow in the field. When the news reached him, he mounted his horse and galloped to the scene of action. On the twenty-first a council of war was held at which Putnam was present, and the Assembly of Connecticut conferred upon him the commission of brigadier-general.

During the month of May, General Putnam assisted by Warren succeeded in removing the cattle from the islands in Boston Harbor, thus cutting off the supplies of the enemy. General Putnam also accompanied the detachment of one thousand men that on the night of the sixteenth of June took possession of the heights of Bunker Hill and Breed's Hill. The history of the next day's battle is too well known to need recital here. While Warren was bravely fighting behind the redoubt on Breed's Hill, Putnam was also leading his men in the action with his customary fearlessness. "On the evacuation of Boston by the British, Putnam was placed in command of the city, where he remained until the twenty-ninth of March of the next year, when he was ordered to take command of New York, and to complete the defences of the city commenced by General Lee." On August twenty-third Putnam received the chief command, and on September twelfth New York was evacuated by our forces. "Soon after this, some British ships ascended the Hudson as far as Bloomingdale, while Sir Henry Clinton landed four thousand troops on the eastern side of the island at Kipp's Bay." If these two forces should effect a junction across the island, Putnam saw that his division would be entrapped, and set himself to work to escape the enclosing meshes before his retreat could be cut off. As the enemy were obliged to pass under Murray Hill, where resided a patriotic Quakeress, Putnam despatched his aide to the lady, requesting her to offer refreshments to the army of Sir Henry Clinton, and to detain them as long as possible. It proved a very successful piece of strategy. One hour of precious time was lost to the enemy and gained by the forces under Putnam. When the British general resumed his march, he saw to his surprise that Putnam had escaped him and was advancing into the Bloomingdale plains.

In December, 1776, when Washington had crossed the Delaware to prevent the enemy from entering Philadelphia, Putnam was placed in command at that post. This was a high compliment to his generalship, as Philadelphia was considered a point of vital importance to hold. In 1777 he received orders to go to New Jersey, where the enemy were occupying winter quarters at New Brunswick and Amboy. His object having been accomplished of forcing a concentration of the enemy's forces, he went to Princeton, where he spent the remainder of the winter. At this time he had but a handful of troops to oppose to the British legions, his whole command numbering only a few hundred men. Great strategy and skill was therefore required to conceal his scarcity of troops from the enemy. An incident occurred which taxed his powers in this direction to the utmost. A Scotch captain, wounded at the battle of Princeton, was lying at the point of death in his camp, and asked permission to "send for a friend in the British army at Brunswick, that some testamentary matters of great importance might be confided to him." It was cruel to refuse, it was dangerous to grant the request. In this dilemma Putnam finally consented that the Scotchman might receive his friend from the British army if he would come at night. "An officer was despatched to Brunswick to conduct him to McPherson's chamber. It was after dark before they reached Princeton. General Putnam had the College hall and all vacant houses lighted up, and while the two friends were closeted had his men marched rapidly before the house and around the quarters of the captain with great pomp and bustle, repeating the manœuvre several times to give an impression of a strong force." The *ruse* succeeded, and the Scotchman's friend, when he went back, reported a large force at Putnam's camp.

After this Putnam was ordered to the Highlands, and made his head-quarters at Peekskill from the month of May until October.

During the winter of 1778 Putnam was busily engaged rebuilding the demolished forts in the Highlands, and made the selection of West Point for the site of a fortification, which was begun in January of that year. The celebrated escape at Horseneck is also chronicled of this year. Some writers record this event as occurring in the winter, others make the time in July. Rogers, who was with Putnam, says it was July, and it is natural to suppose that his authority is the best. General Putnam, it seems, was visiting one of his outposts at West Greenwich, against which Governor Tryon was marching with a force of fifteen hundred men. Putnam with his small force made a stand near a church which stood on the edge of a precipitous hill, and sent a volley from his artillery into the ranks of the advancing foe. But the British cavalry was forming for a charge, and Putnam, knowing the hopelessness of resistance by his little company of fifty men, ordered a retreat to a swamp behind the hill inaccessible to cavalry, while he urged his own horse directly down the steep face of the hill. His pursuers galloped to the edge of the bluff, and paused in amazement, not daring to follow such a breakneck plunge down the rocks. A volley was fired after Putnam, but the shot passed harmlessly over his head. The perilous descent was safely made, and after obtaining reinforcements, Putnam returned in pursuit of Governor Tryon.

The fortifications in the Highlands occupied General Putnam until the winter of 1779, when on returning from a visit to his family he was attacked with paralysis, from which he never recovered, though his death did not take place until May of 1790. The manner of his attack is related. He had started on a journey to Morristown in the month of December. While on the road between Pomfret and Hartford, he felt the stealthy approach of the paralytic stroke. A gradual numbness crept through his right hand and foot until he was deprived in a great measure of the use of his limbs on that side. He reached the house of his friend, Colonel Wadsworth, with difficulty. He did not recover, as he expected, but remained in this half-paralytic condition, though enabled to walk and ride moderately, until the seventeenth of May, 1790, when he was violently attacked with an inflammatory disease, and two days later the patriotic life went out, to be rekindled no more on earth. The farewell volleys of the infantry were discharged over the hero's grave, and the minute guns of the artillery sounded like signals of distress.

The Grenadiers of the Eleventh Regiment, a corps of artillerists and various military companies of the neighborhood, besides the Masonic fraternity, moved in the sad funeral *cortege*.

Dr. Waldo pronounced the following eulogium over his grave:

"Those venerable relics once delighted in the endearing domestic virtues which constitute the excellent neighbor, husband, parent and worthy brother! Liberal and substantial in his friendship, unsuspicious, open and generous, just and sincere in dealing, a benevolent citizen of the world—he concentrated in his bosom the noble qualities of an HONEST MAN.

"Born a hero, whom nature taught and cherished in the lap of innumerable toils and dangers, he was terrible in battle! But, from the amiableness of his heart, when carnage ceased his humanity spread over the field like the refreshing zephyrs of a summer's evening. The prisoner, the wounded, the sick, the forlorn experienced the delicate sympathy of this soldier's pillow. The poor and the needy of every description received the charitable bounties of this CHRISTIAN SOLDIER.

"He pitied littleness, loved goodness, admired greatness, and ever aspired to its glorious summit! The friend, the servant, and almost unparalleled lover of his country, worn with age and the former trials of war, PUTNAM rests from his labors,

> "Till mouldering worlds and tumbling systems burst
> When the last trump shall renovate his dust;
> Still by the mandate of eternal truth
> His soul will flourish in immortal youth!'

"This, all who knew him know,—this, all who loved him tell."

Rev. Dr. Dwight, President of Yale College, an intimate friend of Putnam, wrote the following inscription, which was engraven on his tomb:

> "Sacred be this Monument
> to the memory
> of
> ISRAEL PUTNAM, ESQUIRE,
> Senior Major-General in the Armies
> of
> The United States of America,
> who
> was born at Salem,
> in the Province of Massachusetts,
> on the seventh day of January,
> A. D. 1718,
> and died
> on the nineteenth day of May,
> A. D. 1790.

HEROES OF THREE WARS.

Passenger,
if thou art a Soldier,
drop a tear over the dust of a Hero,
who,
ever attentive
to the lives and happiness of his men,
dared to lead
where any dared to follow:
if a Patriot,
remember the distinguished and gallant services
rendered thy country
by the Patriot who sleeps beneath this marble;
if thou art honest, generous and worthy
tender a cheerful tribute of respect
to a man
whose generosity was singular,
whose honesty was proverbial,
who
raised himself to universal esteem
and offices of eminent distinction
by personal worth
and a
useful life."

CHAPTER VI.

ETHAN ALLEN.

Birthplace of Allen.—The New Hampshire Grants.—The Green Mountain Boys.—Ethan Allen a Leader.—Price on his Head.—Allen's Fearlessness.—The Revolution.—Capture of Ticonderoga.—Benedict Arnold's Part in the Affair.—Allen in Canada.—The Army of Invasion.—Plans for the Capture of Montreal.—The Fatal Snare.—Allen a Prisoner.—Brutal Treatment by British Officers.—In Falmouth, England.—The Gentlemen of Cork.—Exchanged.—Liberty and the Green Mountains Once More.—Joyful Welcome.—Allen Again Fighting the Battles of Young Vermont.—Review of his Character.

IT has been said that no one man contributed more, by his personal efforts, to the independence of our country than did that bold knight of Liberty, Ethan Allen.

He first comes to our notice as the leader of the renowned Green Mountain Boys, in the troublous times when the land-owners of Vermont, under the New Hampshire Grants, defended their homesteads and property against the false claims of the British Governor Tryon of the New York Colony.

Ethan Allen was born in Litchfield, Connecticut, January tenth, 1737. His father, Joseph Allen, was a native of Coventry, of the same State, from whence he emigrated to Litchfield, and afterwards to Cornwall, where he raised a large family of children. Four or five of the boys settled in the land west of the Green Mountains, and did much towards shaping the destiny of the infant State, Vermont. The passion for liberty seems to have been inborn with the whole family, and though none of them became so distinguished as Ethan, they were all staunch pioneers in freedom's cause, and battled nobly against injustice and oppression.

About the year 1772 the hero of Ticonderoga removed to Bennington, Vermont, and it is from this date that we begin to hear of him as a conspicuous leader among the bold mountaineers of the Green Mountains.

A difficulty arose between the States of New York, Connecticut, Massachusetts and New Hampshire, owing to conflicting boundary lines as granted by the charters of the several States, or colonies. The original grant of King Charles the Second to the Duke of York, his brother, made the Connecticut River the eastern boundary line of the Colony of New York, which interfered directly with the Massachusetts and Connecticut charters. A compromise of claims, however, was settled upon between the three States of Massachusetts, Connecticut and New York, and all remained in a condition of comparative quiet until Benning Wentworth became Governor of New Hampshire, with authority from the king to "issue patents for unimproved lands within the limits of his province." Application being made for grants west of the Connecticut River, and even beyond the Green Mountains, Governor Wentworth gave a patent for a township six miles square, near the northwest boundary of Massachusetts, which was named Bennington. A remonstrance went up from New York against this measure, that colony claiming for itself the territory north of Massachusetts and east of the Connecticut River. But Governor Wentworth, by all accounts, ignored the claims of New York, and went steadily forward in the work of granting patents, until in four years' time he had issued patents for one hundred and thirty-eight townships. This territory was known by the name of the "New Hampshire Grants," and did not take its present name, Vermont, until the breaking out of the Revolution. The government of New York appealed to the arbitration of the Crown, and a royal decree was issued, stating that the Connecticut River was the dividing line between New York and New Hampshire. This decree, according to New York jurisprudence, forced the settlers under the New Hampshire Grants to purchase their lands over again or submit to writs of ejectment in favor of newer claimants who had obtained grants of the New York government. Ethan Allen, who was already a leader among the sturdy yeomanry of the Green Mountains, became noted for his zeal in opposing this injustice, and was chosen to represent their claims at the Albany courts. The trial was little more than a farce, and the case, as might have been expected, was decided against Allen's constituency.

He went home and reported the condition of affairs to the excited and indignant mountain pioneers, and a meeting was immediately held by the people of Bennington, at which a formal determination was expressed to defend their property by force. They agreed to unite in resisting all encroachments on lands purchased from the government of New Hampshire. Open war was now inaugurated between the Green Mountain Boys and the officers who came to enforce the king's decision. Forces of armed men successfully drove away sheriffs and their posse coming to serve writs of ejectment on the settlers, and in some instances the intruders were caught and administered a whipping with the "twigs of the wilderness."

Ethan Allen was the head and front of this resistance in the name of justice: the chief leader and adviser of the Green Mountain faction. The force thus taking the law into their own hands was regularly organized, and Ethan Allen was appointed colonel commanding, with several captains under him, chief among whom were Seth Warner and Remember Baker. "Committees of safety were likewise chosen, and intrusted with powers for regulating social affairs. Conventions of delegates representing the people assembled from time to time, and passed resolves and adopted measures which tended to harmonize their sentiments and concentrate their efforts." In this manner affairs went on until Governor Tryon issued a proclamation offering a reward of one hundred and fifty pounds for the capture of Allen, and fifty pounds each for the capture of Seth Warner and five others. Not recognizing the authority of New York in this matter, Allen and his friends sent out a counter-proclamation, offering a reward of five pounds to any person who would take and deliver the Attorney-General of the Colony of New York to any officer in the military association of the Green Mountain Boys. That gentleman had been particularly active in the warfare against them, and was in consequence an object of special dislike.

Allen, seeing only his duty in thus setting at defiance the authority of New York, went forward perfectly regardless of threats and faithful in the execution of the trust reposed in him by his brother pioneers. The settlers acted strictly on the defensive, but, nevertheless, commotions, mobs and riots were the order of the day. Manifestoes were published defending the outlaws and condemning the New York proclamation. Thus the course of events went on from bad to worse, the hostilities growing more determined, the enmity deeper.

How long this state of things would have continued, or to what pitch it would have been carried, no one can tell, had not a common cause united the people in resistance to a common enemy. The smaller feud was eclipsed by the greater. Ominous clouds of tyranny on one hand and opposition to it on the other were slowly gathering in the political horizon of the young colonies, and the battle of Lexington announced the first thunder-burst of the Revolution. Vermont, now recognized as an independent State, boldly stepped to the front in the contest for liberty, and Ethan Allen was her standard-bearer.

Eight days after the battle of Lexington a plan was on foot for the capture of Fort Ticonderoga, on Lake George, and the seizure of its cannon for the Provincial army at Boston. This fort, together with Crown Point, constituted the key of all communication between New York and Canada, and was consequently a point of great strategic importance.

The scheme for its capture was a private one, although it originated with several members of the Assembly then in session at Hartford, Connecticut.

A committee, at the head of which was Edward Mott and Noah Phelps, went through the frontier towns raising men for the project, and a thousand dollars was loaned from the treasury of the State to carry the plan into execution.

Sixteen men were collected in Connecticut, and in Pittsfield, Massachusetts, Colonel Easton added some of his militia to the force, enlisting volunteers as he went forward. About fifty of these reached Bennington, where a council of war was immediately held, and parties were sent to secure the roads to the northward, thus preventing intelligence of their approach from reaching the enemy.

Colonel Allen and his Green Mountain Boys joined the force here, and the whole party reached Castleton on the evening of the seventh of May. "Here a second council of war was held, at which Allen was appointed commander of the expedition, James Easton the second in command, and Seth Warner the third." The force now consisted of over two hundred men, and they marched directly to a place called Shoreham, on the bank of the lake opposite Ticonderoga. It now became necessary to have a guide who was familiar with the fort and its places of access. Accordingly, Nathan Beman, a young boy, whose father lived near the shore of the lake, was induced to lend his services to the occasion.

The number of boats being exceedingly deficient, only eighty-three men had crossed when the day began to dawn.

The moment was critical. The fort, if taken at all, must be surprised before daybreak. There was no time to be lost. In this dilemma Colonel Allen resolved to march on the fort at once, without waiting for the rear-guard to cross the lake. Accordingly, Colonel Allen drew up his mountaineers in three ranks and first made a little speech to them, reminding them that they had come to fight in the cause of liberty, and offering any who chose to avail themselves of it an opportunity to retire. No one retired. The order to advance was then given, and the force marched in silence up the heights to the fort. They passed the sentinels, one of whom retreated to his bomb-proof after discharging his piece, and another contented himself with wounding an officer in the head. The men, after forming inside the fort, gave vent to loud huzzas, which startled the sleeping inmates of the barracks. Colonel Allen then demanded to be shown the apartment of Captain Delaplace, the officer commanding, and, mounting the steps leading to the officer's room, ordered him, in a voice of thunder, to come forth instantly or the whole garrison would be sacrificed.

Captain Delaplace, startled from sleep by the unexpected summons, sprang to the door with his pants in his hand, and his pretty wife peering over his shoulder behind him.

There stood Ethan Allen, like another Ajax, stern and thunderous, and demanded the immediate surrender of the fort.

"By what authority," asked Captain Delaplace, "do you presume to make such a demand?"

"In the name of the Great Jehovah and the Continental Congress!" thundered Allen, in return.

The authority of the Continental Congress not being exactly clear to Delaplace, he began speaking in reply. But his speech was cut short by the uplifted sword of Allen, as the demand for immediate surrender was sternly reiterated. Thinking further parley of no avail, Delaplace surrendered the garrison, ordering his men to parade without arms, and Allen with his brave boys took possession of the captured fort. When the day dawned on that immortal tenth of May, it seemed to flood the earth with unusual splendor—so wrote Ethan Allen in his autobiography concerning this eventful time. Perhaps the beauty of the morning took a shade of brightness from the rosy flush of the victory he had just achieved. One hundred and twenty pieces of cannon, besides swivels, mortars, small arms and stores, were captured with the fort.

In a few days after the seizure of Ticonderoga, Colonel Allen sent Captain Seth Warner to Crown Point with a detachment of men, and the surrender of the garrison at that post followed. Captain Remember Baker on his way to Ticonderoga reached Crown Point just in time to join Warner in taking possession.

Benedict Arnold had arrived from Massachusetts just before the expedition for Ticonderoga set out, commissioned by the Committee of Safety of that colony to raise men for the same purpose. Finding an organization already under way, having in view the same object, he endeavored to assume command, and lead them to the fortress himself. But the Green Mountain Boys would not permit their beloved commander to be supplanted by a stranger, and to prevent disturbance Arnold submitted to the dictation of the majority, and went as a volunteer. His conduct on the occasion was brave. He had marched by the side of Allen, and entered the fort with him. After the surrender he again attempted to assume command, but his orders were not obeyed, and he was once more obliged to look to Allen as his ranking officer.

A scheme was entered into at this time between Allen and Arnold for the purpose of seizing the garrison at St. Johns, and taking possession of a royal sloop

ETHAN ALLEN AT TICONDEROGA.

which lay there. The beginning of the enterprise was successful, but reinforcements arriving for the enemy from Montreal, Allen was attacked, and driven to his boats. After this adventure he remained at Ticonderoga as commander-in-chief, while Arnold held Crown Point. Meantime, Colonel Allen was busy planning new successes, and on June second, 1775, he addressed Congress a long letter asking permission to make an advance into Canada with a force of two or three thousand men, confidently asserting his power to conquer this province of Britain. He said that with fifteen hundred men he could take Montreal. This project met with little favor from Congress at the time, that body having resolved only the day before the date of Allen's letter that no invasion of Canada ought to be countenanced.

Three months later an expedition into Canada, seconded by the voice of the whole nation, met with disastrous results. Had Congress listened to Allen when he first proposed his plan, there is little doubt that the invasion would have been successful.

Allen was now relieved of his command at Ticonderoga, Colonel Hinman with his Connecticut troops having arrived from that State. The majority of Allen's men returned to their homes, their term of service having expired. Afterwards, Colonel Allen and Seth Warner went to the Continental Congress to procure pay for the soldiers who had served under them, and also to obtain permission to raise a new regiment in the New Hampshire Grants. They succeeded in both objects. When the new regiment was raised, Seth Warner was chosen its lieutenant-colonel, and Samuel Safford, major. It is not clear why Colonel

Allen was not connected with this organization in an official capacity, but in a few days afterwards he joined General Schuyler as a volunteer, and that officer sent him on a mission to Canada to ascertain the temper of the people there on the question of uniting with Americans in shaking off the shackles of British rule, and achieving for themselves the enjoyments of freedom. He was the bearer of an address to the people of Canada from General Schuyler, then at Isle-aux-Noix, which was intended to convince them that the invasion was not against the rights of the citizens of Canada, but against British tyranny exclusively. Allen went first to Chamblee on his dangerous mission, and found many citizens friendly to the American cause. He was attended by an armed escort, furnished by the citizens, which accompanied him constantly in his journeys through the woods. For eight days he was traversing the country on this mission, at the end of which time he returned to General Schuyler's army at Isle-aux-Noix.

General Montgomery was in command of the Canada expedition, and was at this time besieging the garrison at St. Johns. Colonel Allen was immediately sent back to raise as large a force as he could to unite with the American army at that place. In a week thereafter he wrote to General Montgomery from the parish of St. Ours, saying that he had two hundred and fifty Canadians under arms, and that in three days he intended to be at St. Johns with five hundred Canadian volunteers. But unfortunately Colonel Allen was led to change his plans, and a long array of evils followed in natural sequence.

When nearly opposite Montreal, on his way to St.

Johns, he fell in with Major Brown, who was at the head of an advance party of Americans and Canadians. This officer represented the defenceless condition of Montreal, and proposed a joint attack to take the city by surprise. A plan was entered into at once, by which a simultaneous assault was to be made by the two parties at opposite points. On the evening of the twenty-fourth of September, Allen crossed the river with eighty Canadians and thirty Americans, and landed them undiscovered before dawn, where he waited the signal of Major Brown. Daylight came but Major Brown did not, and it was now too late to retreat. Soon, about forty British regulars and two or three hundred Canadians advanced to attack the handful of men under Colonel Allen, and after a skirmish of an hour and three-quarters Allen agreed to surrender upon promise of honorable terms. He was conducted to the presence of Colonel Prescott in Montreal. Was this the same Allen who had taken Fort Ticonderoga? that officer inquired. It was.

Then the valiant Colonel Prescott burst into a towering passion, threatened Allen with a halter at Tyburn, and ordered him to be bound hand and foot on board the "Gaspee," schooner of war. Allen wrote a letter to Prescott, protesting against this inhuman treatment. His only reply was a continuation of the brutality meted out to the worst criminals instead of to honorable prisoners of war. Allen's companions-in-arms suffered a like fate with their brave leader. During several consecutive months Allen was transferred from one vessel to another, where the degree of kindness or cruelty with which he was treated depended on the disposition of the captain of the craft. At last he was taken to England, where he was regarded as quite an object of interest. The fame of his Ticonderoga exploit had preceded him there, and many came to see the distinguished prisoner. He was confined at Falmouth. His dress at this time consisted of a short fawn-skin double-breasted jacket, a vest and breeches of sagathy, worsted stockings, a plain shirt and a red worsted cap, materials which had been gathered during his Canada invasion.

Though in bondage he did not cease to advocate the claims of his country, or to grow eloquent on the theme of liberty.

At last his exchange was ordered, and in company with his fellow-prisoners, he was conducted on board the "Solebay," a ship in the harbor of Cork. When it was known in Cork that Colonel Allen and the American prisoners were on board the "Solebay," several gentlemen of the city sent to them generous gifts in the shape of clothes, choice food and money, to the indignant disgust of the captain commanding the vessel.

After many wanderings and much adventure, Colonel Allen arrived off Staten Island, and was conducted to a sloop in the harbor, where he awaited the arrival of Lieutenant-Colonel Campbell, for whom he was to be exchanged. The two prisoners met on the fifth of May, 1778, and drank a glass of wine together in celebration of their mutual happiness. Colonel Allen had been a prisoner of war for two years and seven months. After his release he at once reported to Washington at Valley Forge before turning his face towards home in the Green Mountains. His welcome home was an ovation. Cannon were fired in honor of the event, and demonstrations of joy were universal. After his return Congress conferred on him the commission of brevet-colonel in the Continental army, and it was voted that he should receive the pay of a lieutenant-colonel during the time of his imprisonment.

The controversy for the independence of Vermont was renewed on Allen's return, and he entered into it with all his wonted spirit. Young Vermont, in gratitude for past services, appointed him general and commander of the State militia. No stronger proof of their confidence in him could have been given at this time by the hardy yeomanry of the Green Mountains. During the progress of the disputes there was an attempt made to gain Allen's influence in a project to unite Vermont with the British provinces in Canada. As might be supposed, this attempt was a total failure. At last the difficulties were settled, and Vermont, chiefly through the efforts of Allen, was accorded the place of independence she claimed. At the next election after his return from captivity, General Allen was chosen a representative to the Assembly of his State, and after the restoration of peace he devoted himself to the pursuit of agriculture. At this time his thoughts seemed to set in a new channel, and he wrote a book entitled "Reason the only Oracle of Man, or a Compendious System of Natural Religion." It was published at Bennington in the year 1784.

A good many stories are told of Allen which are characteristic of the man, and throw out in bold relief the strong points of his nature. Perhaps these incidents are more indicative of character than anything else. At one time during Allen's imprisonment he was released on parole in New York. An incident is told of this time by one of the actors in the affair: "Rivington, the King's printer, a forcible and venomous writer, had incurred Allen's enmity by his caustic allusions to him, and the hero of Ticonderoga swore he 'would lick Rivington the very first opportunity he had.'"

This is how he escaped the threatened castigation: "I was sitting," says Rivington, "after a good dinner, alone, with my bottle of Madeira before me, when I heard an unusual noise in the street and a huzza from the boys. I was in the second story, and stepping to the window, saw a tall figure in tarnished regimentals, with a large cocked hat and an enormous long sword, followed by a crowd of boys who occasionally cheered him with huzzas of which he seemed insensible. He came up to my door and stopped. I could see no more. My heart told me it was Ethan Allen. I shut my window and retired behind my table and my bottle. I was certain the hour of reckoning had come. There was no retreat. Mr. Staples, my clerk, came in paler than ever, and clasping his hands said:

"'Master, he has come.'

"'I know it.'

"'He entered the store and asked if James Rivington lived there. I answered, Yes, sir. Is he at home? I will go and see, sir, I said; and now, master, what is to be done? There he is in the store, and the boys peeping at him from the street.'

"I had made up my mind. I looked at the Madeira—possibly took a glass.

"'Show him up,' said I, 'and if such Madeira cannot mollify him, he must be harder than adamant.'

"There was a fearful moment of suspense. I heard

him on the stairs, his long sword clanking at every step. In he stalked.

"'Is your name James Rivington?'

"'It is, sir; and no man could be more happy than I am to see Colonel Ethan Allen.'

"'Sir, I have come—'

"'Not another word, my dear Colonel, until you have taken a seat and a glass of old Madeira.'

"'But, sir, I don't think it proper—'

"'Not another word, Colonel. Taste this wine I have had in glass for ten years. Old wine, you know, unless it is originally sound, never improves by age.'

"He took the glass, swallowed the wine, smacked his lips and shook his head approvingly.

"'Sir, I am come—'

"'Not another word until you have taken another glass, and then, my dear Colonel, we will talk of old affairs, and I have some queer events to detail.'

"In short, we finished two bottles of Madeira and parted as good friends as if we had never had cause to be otherwise."

Allen's kindness of heart was proverbial. It takes a brave man to be kind. "At one time two little girls, daughters of one of the pioneers of Vermont, wandered into the woods and were lost. The distressed parents with a few neighbors commenced a search, which was continued through the night without success. The next day a large number of persons from the neighboring towns joined them, and the search was continued until the afternoon of the third day, when it was relinquished, and the people who had been out were about to return to their homes. Among them, however, was one who thought the search should not be abandoned.

"That one was Ethan Allen.

"He mounted a stump, and soon all eyes were fixed upon him. In his laconic manner he pointed to the father and mother of the lost children, now petrified with grief and despair, bade each individual present make the case of these parents their own, and then say whether they could go contentedly to their homes without one effort further to save those dear little ones who were probably now alive but perishing with hunger, and spending their last strength in crying to father and mother to give them something to eat. As he spoke his giant frame was agitated, the tears rolled down his cheeks, and in the assembly of several hundred men but few eyes were dry.

"'I'll go! I'll go!' was at length heard from every part of the crowd. They betook themselves to the woods, and before night the lost children were restored to the arms of their parents."

Here is an incident illustrative of his incorruptible honesty:

"On one occasion, an individual to whom he was indebted commenced a suit against him. Allen, being unable to pay the debt, employed a lawyer to have the execution of legal process against him postponed for a short period. As an easy measure to effect this and throw the case over to the next session of the court, the lawyer denied the genuineness of the signature. Allen, who was present, stepped angrily forward, and exclaimed to his astonished counsel: 'Sir, I did not employ you to come here and lie! I wish you to tell the truth. The note is a good one—the signature is mine; all I want is for the court to grant me sufficient time to make the payment.' It is needless to add that the plaintiff acceded to his wishes."

Allen was twice married. His first wife died in Connecticut. His second courtship was somewhat out of the usual line of business in the traffic matrimonial. It was during a session of the court at Westminster, that "Allen appeared with a magnificent pair of horses and a black driver. Chief Justice Robinson and Steven R. Bradley, an eminent lawyer, were there, and as their breakfast was on the table, they asked Allen to join them. He replied that he had breakfasted, and while they were at table he would go in and see Mrs. Buchanan, a handsome widow who was at the house. He entered the sitting-room and at once said to Mrs. Buchanan:

"' Well, Fanny, if we are to be married let us be about it.'

"' Very well,' she promptly replied, 'give me time to fix up.'

"In a few minutes she was ready, and Judge Robinson was at once called upon by them to perform the ceremony.

"Said Allen, 'Judge, Mrs. Buchanan and I have concluded to be married; I don't care much about the ceremony, and as near as I can find out, Fanny cares as little for it as I do; but as a decent respect for the customs of society requires it of us, we are willing to have the ceremony performed.'

"The gentlemen present were much surprised, and Judge Robinson replied,

"' General Allen, this is an important matter: have you thought seriously of it?'

"' Yes, yes,' exclaimed Allen, looking at Mrs. Buchanan, "but it don't require much thought.'

"Judge Robinson then rose from his seat and said:

"'Join your hands together. Ethan Allen, you take this woman to be your lawful and wedded wife; you promise to love and protect her according to the law of God—'

"'Stop, stop, Judge—the law of God,' said Allen, looking forth upon the fields, 'all nature is full of it. Yes, go on. My team is at the door.'

"As soon as the ceremony was ended General Allen and his bride entered the carriage and drove off."

A son of one of the governors of Vermont vouches for the truth of the following:

"While Allen was on his way to lay his schemes for the invasion of Canada before the Continental Congress, he attended church at Bennington, where the Rev. Mr. Dewey preached a sermon on the capture of Fort Ticonderoga. In his prayer Mr. Dewey thanked the Lord for having given the possession of this important fortress into the hands of a people struggling for the defence of their dearest rights. Allen was displeased, and as the preacher continued in this strain of thanksgiving, the bluff old hero cried out:

"'Parson Dewey!'

"The preacher prayed on, not heeding the interruption.

"Allen exclaimed, still louder:

"'Parson Dewey!'

"No response. At last Allen was exasperated, and sprang to his feet while he fairly roared out, for the third time:

"'Parson Dewey!'

"At last the praying clergyman opened his eyes and gazed in astonishment at Allen. Allen then said, with energy:

"'Parson Dewey! please make mention of *my* being there.'"

Before the close of the war General Allen removed from Bennington, and finally settled himself in the vicinity of the Onion River, where in partnership with his brothers he purchased large tracts of land.

His constitution, which was strong and robust, at last gave way under an attack of apoplexy, and he died at Burlington in the year 1789.

We are not given an account of the closing chapters in the life of this disciple of liberty, but his example while living is radiant with the glow of heroism. "Few have suffered more in the cause of freedom, few have borne their sufferings with a firmer constancy or a loftier spirit." He went forward fearlessly in the cause of right, through whatever dangers threatened, with a sublime courage which compels our deepest admiration. His personal presence was commanding in the extreme, and he carried about him a consciousness of nobility, a kind of high-born pride in his own worth and character, which embodied the highest form of self-respect. His figure, when arrayed in the Continental dress of the times, showed to excellent advantage, and with his armor buckled on and his sword clanking at his heels, he looked every inch the commander. Vermont owes more to the clear, powerful brain and strong right arm of Ethan Allen, for the foundation of her State in liberty and equity, than to any other man, or any other one influence. Such names as his well deserve the lasting remembrance which a grateful posterity accords them.

CHAPTER VII.
FRANCIS MARION.

The Huguenot Blood of Marion.—Boyhood Days.—Early Adventures.—The Shipwreck.—Battle with Cherokee Indians.—Marion Leads the Forlorn Hope.—The Bloody Pass.—He Leaves Congress for the Army.—Fame of Marion's Men.—Battle around Savannah.—The Williamsburg Band.—Marion's Brigade.—The Camp in the Swamp.—Successful Surprises.—The Dinner in the Woods.—Tarleton and the *Swamp-Fox*.—Song of Marion's Men.—Fighting for Liberty without Clothes or Food.—Marriage.—Closing Scenes.

IF the old aphorism that "blood tells" be true, then we need not wonder that the glorious Huguenot blood of Francis Marion responded so warmly to the alarum drums of Liberty, calling all true sons of the soil to her aid, in the hour of danger.

The fame of Marion's men has come down to us in song and story, glorified by poet and historian, and encircled with a light which the world will not willingly let die.

Francis Marion was born at Winyah, near Georgetown, South Carolina, in 1732—the birth year of Washington. His grandfather fled from France, in 1685, in company with other Huguenots, who sought on the shores of the New World the freedom denied them at home. The same heroic love of liberty was transmitted to his grandson, who braved all dangers in her cause.

The early boyhood of Marion was one of physical weakness, his constitution being so feeble, until his twelfth ye:r, as to excite the apprehension of his relatives concerning his chances for life. But a love of athletic sports came to his aid at this time, and, though always small of stature, he gradually acquired a hardiness of frame and a power of endurance, which was a fitting school of preparation for the work of after years, when frequently the earth was his only pillow and the sky his only covering. At fifteen he tried the sea, embarking on a small schooner engaged in trade with the West Indies. But the sea illy recompensed him, and gave him only accident and shipwreck. On his first voyage out, a plank torn from the bottom of the vessel by a whale caused the ship to founder, and the crew floated out to sea in a little life-boat, where for six days their only food was a small dog which had come to them from the sinking schooner. In consequence of this disaster the crew nearly perished with famine and thirst, and four of the party died. At last a big ship came to their aid, and they were taken aboard. This adventure seems to have cured young Marion of all further desire for the sea, and for the next thirteen years he remained at home an humble tiller of the soil, cultivating quiet virtues and winning the esteem of all who knew him. His first experience in military life began in 1761. In that year the Cherokee Indians, living on the frontiers of the Carolinas, commenced hostilities against the whites, and a force of twelve hundred regulars was soon marching upon them. Marion offered himself as a volunteer, and the governor gave him a lieutenancy in a provincial regiment. It was June the seventh when the army marched from Fort Prince George against the hostile Cherokees, who had made a stand in a narrow mountain defile, near the Indian village of Etchoee. The pass was dangerous, and the concealed foe had all the advantage of position. Who would volunteer to lead the advance guard into this wily trap of the red warriors? Who but Marion? At the head of thirty men he fearlessly advanced into the narrow mountain pass. A savage war-whoop and a blazing rifle-blast greeted their entrance to the dangerous glen, and twenty-one out of the thirty fell mortally hurt. But Marion was saved to the future. The battle soon became general, and after a bloody time of it the whites were victorious. The Indian village of Etchoee was wantonly burned, and the corn-fields of the tribe laid waste. Marion's description of this act reveals the pathos, the poetry and the deep sympathy of his nature. In a letter to a friend he says: "I saw everywhere around the footsteps of the little Indian children, where they had lately played under the shade of this rustling corn. No doubt they had often looked up with joy to the swelling shocks, and gladdened when they thought of their abundant cakes for the coming winter. When we are gone, thought I, they will return, and peeping through the weeds with tearful eyes will mark the ghastly ruin poured over their homes and happy fields, where they had so often played. 'Who did this?' they will ask their mothers. 'The white people did it,' the mothers reply; 'the Christians did it.'" What a world of sarcasm there is in the last sentence!

The Cherokees were conquered, and Marion returned to his farm. In the year 1775, when the struggle for American independence began, Marion was a member of the Provincial Congress of South Carolina from Berkeley County; but he was not content to remain inactive when his country stood imperilled, and entered the patriot army as captain. In company with his friend Captain Horry he started on a recruiting expedition, and they succeeded in raising two companies of sixty men each, to join the regiment under Colonel Moultrie. Marion was a master of tactics, and soon had his men under thorough drill. His leadership seemed to inspire them, and Marion's name soon became their rallying cry.

The capture of Fort Johnson, on an island in Charleston Harbor, was the first military duty in which Marion was engaged; but as most of the garrison had gone to the ships, it proved an easy conquest. Soon after this Marion was commissioned major, and distinguished himself in the defence of Fort Moultrie on Sullivan's Island. In 1779 our French allies, under Count D'Estaing, anchored off Savannah, and demanded a surrender of the English garrison at that point. To the amazement of Marion, twenty-four hours was granted the British officer in command of the fort in which to determine whether he would accede to the demand of the French count. As might have been anticipated, it was a fatal delay. The enemy were enabled to intrench, and when the Americans attacked the works around Savannah, they were met with repulse. In this battle the Polish Count Pulaski was killed. Marion was in the thickest of the fight, but escaped uninjured.

In 1780, when General Lincoln, after a stubborn defence of Charleston, was forced to surrender the city, Marion was not made a prisoner of war with the others on account of a fractured ankle, which had necessitated his removal from Charleston before the surrender took place. At Camden the American army again suffered defeat, and here the brave Baron DeKalb was killed. The words of Washington, standing over his grave, have been recorded. "There lies the brave DeKalb," said he, "the generous stranger who came from a distant land to water with his blood the tree of our liberty. Would to God he had lived to share with us its fruits!"

The cause of freedom at this time seemed almost hopeless. The outlook on every side was gloomy, and the most ardent patriots were well-nigh despairing. But Marion went bravely and hopefully forward in the struggle for independence, undeterred by the threatening aspect of affairs.

Somewhere near the twelfth of August, 1780, he received a summons from a brave band of patriots near Williamsburg to join them and become their leader. Accepting the invitation he went to Linch's Creek, where the force was encamped. Governor Rutledge, of South Carolina, conferred on him a general's commission, and placed him in command of that part of the State. The band numbered not more than thirty men at first, but after Marion's arrival it increased, and soon became famous as Marion's Brigade. The force was mounted, and was soon put in excellent shape for service. They became renowned for their skill in the use of the rifle, and their daring deeds were the admiration of the patriots and the dread of the Tories. Saw-mills were plundered of their saws to furnish sabres for these bold troopers, and blacksmiths were employed to convert them from their original uses into rude swords. The men were good riders, were active and hardy, and well adapted to the life they led. "To join Marion, to be one of Marion's men, was esteemed the highest privilege to which a young man could aspire who wished to serve his country." Thus "Marion commenced the forest warfare which was his only hope." His refuge was the swamp fastness, from whose gloomy depths he would sally forth at the head of his troopers and strike the enemy a blow which never failed of success, and retreating to his swamp remain secure until ready for another attack. "No vigilance could guard against his attacks; no persevering efforts could force him to a conflict when the chances of war were against him. At one time he would appear at one point, and after sweeping a troop of Tories before him and securing their munitions, in an incredibly short period he would strike another point far distant from them."

The liberties of America were indeed well defended at the hands of Marion's men. Right away after taking command of this force Marion captured the squadron of Major Gainey, coming upon them by surprise and taking the whole force prisoners. Another success more brilliant soon followed. Two hundred American prisoners taken at Camden were being conducted to Charleston across the country, under a guard of ninety British soldiers. They passed near Nelson's ferry, and Marion and his men concealed themselves on the other side awaiting their approach. When the English had crossed they sought a public house near by, and after spending some time in drinking and carousing, threw themselves down to sleep in a spacious arbor in front of the house. Seizing the favorable moment Marion's bold troopers rushed upon the sentinels, and with shouts and demands for surrender, surprised and captured the British soldiery. The American prisoners they had with them were set at liberty. Other equally bold exploits followed these in rapid succession, until a special force of the enemy was set on track of Marion with the determination to crush him by overwhelming numbers. But Marion was not destined to be thus easily crushed. "With more than two hundred British regulars in his front and about five hundred Tories in his rear, he commenced a retreat which was conducted with consummate skill and success." Many of his men were dismissed to their houses after pledging themselves to return when called for, promises which were never known to be disregarded. Then, at the head of about sixty men, he would enter the swamps where the enemy dared not follow, and lying concealed, wait until the immediate danger was over. His style of living at this time was hardly suggestive of luxury, much less comfort. Judge Janes describes a dinner with General Marion in one of these swamp camps as follows: "The dinner was set before the company by the general's servant Oscar, partly on a pine log and partly on the ground. It consisted of lean beef without salt, and sweet potatoes. The author had left a small pot of hominy in his camp, and requested leave of his host to send for it. The proposal was gladly acquiesced in. The hominy had salt in it and proved, though eaten out of the pot, a very acceptable repast. . . . We had nothing to drink but bad water, and all the company appeared to be rather grave."

At last the enemy abandoned the pursuit, and Marion left North Carolina and again advanced southward. Information reached him that a large force of Tories was stationed at Shepherd's Ferry, on the Black Mingo

River, and he determined to surprise and capture their camp. The only approach to it was over a plank bridge about a mile below the ferry. Unfortunately the galloping hoofs of the horses as they crossed the bridge was heard through the stillness of the night by the enemy, and an alarm gun was sounded which warned the sleeping Tories of his approach. Marion then ordered a charge, and the patriots swept down upon the enemy with irresistible fury. The Tories fled in confusion, and their commander was killed. The surprise and capture was complete. It was said that after this conflict Marion never crossed a bridge at night without spreading blankets upon it to deaden the sound. Some time after this event Marion learned that one Colonel Tynes was raising a body of Tories in the forks of the Black River, and that he had in his possession a full supply of saddles, blankets, pistols, powder and ball, which he had brought from Charleston. These were the very articles which Marion's men wanted, and a midnight attack was planned. The result was all they had hoped for. Colonel Tynes and a large part of his force were taken prisoners, and the coveted spoils fell into Marion's hands. Thus he made himself the terror of the Tories far and wide wherever his bold warriors rode. Renewed efforts were made by the British to crush him, but without success. At one time, after a fruitless chase by Colonel Tarleton, this officer is reported to have said to his men, "Come, boys, let us go back. We will soon find the game-cock"—meaning General Sumter—"but as for this swamp-fox the devil himself could not catch him!" Marion was in the habit of calling his men by imitating the cry of the swamp-fox, and from this circumstance the name doubtless originated. One of the songs sung by Marion's men also perpetuates this appellation:

"We follow where the Swamp-Fox guides,
  His friends and merry men are we;
And when the troop of Tarleton rides
  We burrow in the cypress tree.
The turfy tussock is our bed,
  Our home is in the red deer's den,
Our roof the tree-top overhead,
  For we are wild and hunted men.

. . . . .

"We fly by day and shun its light,
  But prompt to strike the sudden blow,
We mount and start with early night
  And through the forest track our foe;
And soon he hears our chargers leap,
  The flashing sabre blinds his eyes,
And ere he drives away his sleep
  And rushes from his camp, he dies.

. . . . .

"Now stir the fire and lie at ease,
  The scouts are gone, and on the brush
I see the colonel bend his knees
  To take his slumbers too—but hush!
He's praying, comrades: 'tis not strange;
  The man that's fighting day by day
May well when night comes take a change,
  And down upon his knees to pray.

. . . . .

"Now pile the brush, and roll the log—
  Hard pillow, but a soldier's head,
That's half the time in brake and bog,
  Must never think of softer bed.
The owl is hooting to the night,
  The cooter crawling o'er the bank,
And in that pond the plashing light
  Tells where the alligator sank.

. . . . .

"But courage, comrades, Marion leads;
  The Swamp-Fox takes us out to-night,
So clear your swords, and coax your steeds,
  There's goodly chance I think of fight.

> We follow where the Swamp-Fox guides,
> We leave the swamp and cypress tree;
> Our spurs are in our coursers' sides,
> And ready for the strife are we.
> The Tory camp is now in sight,
> And there he cowers within his den;
> He hears our shout, he dreads the fight,
> He fears and flies from Marion's men."

While lying at Snow's Island, an exchange of prisoners having been agreed upon, a young British officer was sent from Georgetown to complete the arrangements with Marion. He was conducted into the camp blindfolded. When his eyes were unbandaged a forest scene greeted his gaze. Tall trees surrounded him. Groups of rudely-costumed soldiers were lying under their shadow, and horses stood near by ready to be mounted at a moment's notice. "Before him stood Marion himself, small in stature, slight in person, dark and swarthy in complexion, with a quiet manner, but a brilliant and searching eye." The young English officer was struck with astonishment. Was this the man whose name had become so famous, and were these the soldiers who had filled with terror the hearts of the Tories? After business was over, the officer was asked to remain to dinner. He did so. "Sweet potatoes smoking from the ashes were placed upon a piece of bark, and set before the general and his guest."

"Doubtless this is an accidental meal," said the bewildered officer; "you live better in general?"

"No," was the reply, "we often fare much worse."

"Then I hope at least you draw noble pay to compensate?"

"Not a cent, sir," replied Marion, "not a cent."

The officer reported at Georgetown that he had seen an American general and his officers, without pay and almost without clothes, living on roots, and drinking water—all for liberty. "What chance have we against such men?" said he. This officer resigned his commission, and never afterwards served during the war. In 1781 General Greene sent the celebrated command of Lieutenant-Colonel Henry Lee—"Light-Horse Harry"—to join Marion, but they were baffled in their efforts by want of strict co-operation in their forces.

Major McIlraith, an English officer, once reproached Marion for his Indian mode of warfare, and proposed a conflict on open ground. Marion sent back word that if Major McIlraith thought proper, a pitched battle might take place between twenty picked men on both sides. The offer was accepted, but as the hour for the conflict drew near, McIlraith abandoned the project, and escaped with his entire force.

After this there came a time of despondency to the patriot band, who were so closely and so constantly pursued by the enemy. But Marion kept up their spirits by patriotic speeches, and "so wrought upon them, that those who were with him declared they would rather die than desert him." Harry Lee again joined Marion, and Fort Watson, on the Santee River, was invested, and speedily capitulated. Fort Motte next surrendered, and Marion's activity continued in this unremitting way until the close of hostilities in South Carolina.

Some time after the surrender of Cornwallis at Yorktown, Marion left his brigade, and returned to his plantation in St. John's parish, where he set himself to work to repair the damages done his property by the fortunes of war. Once more he was sent to the Senate of South Carolina as the member from St.

John's. "On the twenty-sixth of February, 1783, the following resolutions were unanimously adopted by the Senate of his native State:

"*Resolved*, That the thanks of this House be given to Brigadier-General Marion in his place, as a member of this House, for his eminent and conspicuous services to his country.

"*Resolved*, That a gold medal be given to Brigadier-General Marion as a mark of public approbation for his great, glorious and meritorious conduct."

In 1784 Marion was appointed to the command of Fort Johnson, in Charleston Harbor, with a salary of five hundred pounds. He was now fifty years old, and yet unmarried. But at this time Cupid came to his rescue. Miss Mary Videau, "a maiden lady of Huguenot descent, of considerable wealth and most estimable character," was the person upon whom his choice fell, and who was the constant companion of his declining years. Her deep admiration for this hero of a hundred battles grew into a more tender feeling, and their mutual friends were instrumental in bringing about the happy result. They lived a quiet, peaceful life together during the rest of Marion's life. On February twenty-seventh, 1795, the brave soul of Marion passed to the spirit world. He took with him the consciousness of noble actions and pure motives.

"Thank God!" he exclaimed, "I can lay my hand on my heart, and say that since I came to man's estate I have never intentionally done wrong to any."

Marion left to posterity the noblest of examples— an example which will, no doubt, be a source of inspiration to many a youth in this generation, and in generations to come, inciting them to purity and strength and splendid endeavor.

CHAPTER VIII.
JOHN PAUL JONES.

The Sailor-Boy of Solway Frith.—Ancestry.—Boyish Pursuits.—His First Voyage.—Rapid Rise in the Marine Service.—In Virginia.—America his Adopted Country.—Created an Officer of the United States.—Adventures on the Sea.—The Terror of the English.—Action of the "Bon Homme Richard" and "Serapis."—Glorious Generalship.—Surrender of the English Ship.—Fame of the Chevalier Paul Jones.—The Gold Sword and the Cross of Merit.—American Prisoners Liberated.—At the Courts of Denmark and Russia.—Medals and Honor.—Last Days of the Hero.

OF Chevalier John Paul Jones, the Americanized Scotchman, I write as of one whose remarkable exploits are worthy of being recorded; whose name, blazing suddenly out from the unnoticed atmosphere of private life into the lustre of fame in a noble cause, deserves to be placed upon the nation's roll of honor. His birthplace was Arbigland, parish of Kirkbean, stewartry of Kirkcudbright, Scotland. The time of his arrival bears date of July sixth, 1747. Though some writers have endeavored to trace the lineage of this hero of the seas to noble blood, there is no authentic record to sustain the theory. His father and his grandfather pursued the humble occupation of gardeners. The family maintained a reputation for great respectability and intelligence, but no lord, or earl, or noble duke can be truthfully accredited to their genealogical tree. The mother of the embryo chevalier, before marriage, bore the name of McDuff—a name which the genius of Shakspeare has duly immortalized;

but she also was of humble birth, being only the daughter of a small farmer in the neighboring parish of New Abbey, though some of her family had been small landed proprietors in the parish of Kirkbean from time out of mind.

The very pronounced liking of young John Paul for the ocean, was shown at an early age, and the favorite occupation of his boyhood was prophetic of his after career. He lived near the shores of the Solway, in one of the most beautiful points of the Frith, and it was his delight to launch his little boat on the waters, and shout his orders to an imaginary crew. "At this time the town of Dumfries carried on a considerable trade in tobacco with America, the cargoes of which were unshipped at the Carse-thorn, near the mouth of the River Nith, which was not then navigable by foreign vessels. His daily intercourse with seamen here tended of course to strengthen and confirm his nascent passion." He began his career on the ocean when he was twelve years old. At that time he was apprenticed to Mr. Younger, a merchant trading with America, who resided at Whitehaven, on the opposite side of Solway Frith. During his apprenticeship he applied himself to the study of navigation at intervals when he was off duty. He kept up a systematic course of midnight toil, where he learned the French language in addition to his seafaring studies, and attained such proficiency that afterwards his correspondence was partly carried on in well-written French. Before he was thirteen he sailed for the Rappahannock in the "Friendship," of Whitehaven, Captain Benson commanding. It was his first voyage out, and it laid the foundation for his subsequent attachment to America, the country of his adoption. While in port on the Rappahannock, he stayed at the home of his elder brother William, in Virginia. Here was fostered that deep sympathy for the cause of American independence for which, in after years, he drew his sword, and in whose behalf he performed such valiant deeds.

Soon after this date, Mr. Younger, owing to embarrassments in business affairs, released young John Paul from his apprenticeship. Thus the responsibility of the young hero's future career was taken upon himself. He did not go straight to ruin, as might have been reasonably anticipated, as under the circumstances nine boys out of ten would have done. On the contrary, he rose rapidly to the position of master of a ship. In the first place, after being thrown upon his own resources, he obtained the appointment of third mate in the "King George"—a vessel engaged in the slave trade, hailing from Whitehaven. "In 1766 he shipped as chief mate on board the brigantine 'Two Friends,' of Kingston, Jamaica." This vessel was also engaged in the slave traffic, but it is recorded that the prospective chevalier became so disgusted with the business of stealing human beings, that he left the ship on her arrival in the West Indies. Returning to Scotland, a passenger on another vessel, the captain and mate died of fever on the way, and Paul took command of the brigantine, bringing her safely into port—a service for which he was rewarded by receiving the appointment of master and supercargo of the vessel. In the employment of this firm he afterwards made two voyages, and some time during the year 1770, commanded the "Betsy," of London, a vessel engaged in the West India trade. Here he entered into large and successful financial speculations. In 1771, he left Scotland, as his home, forever. In 1773, he was called again to Virginia to settle the estate of his brother William, who had died childless, and whose property, therefore, fell to John Paul. At this time, if we may judge from his letters, he contemplated a life of quiet seclusion and peaceful pursuits on the estate to which he had fallen heir. In a letter to the Countess of Selkirk at this time, his theme was the retirement of domestic life, its joys, its quietude, its "calm contemplation and poetic ease."

But Nature moulded him for other purposes. His was destined to be no life of calm sailing on unruffled seas. A stirring epoch awaited him. The struggle for American independence drew on apace, and great circumstances claimed him as their master. His adopted country—the land of his affections and friendships—needed her hero of the seas, and he was not deaf to her call. In the beginning of the year 1775, John Paul sailed from Boston, commissioned by the Continental Congress an officer of the United States. He was of great service on the high seas to the young colonies, and soon became the leading man in the American navy. He gave to the American flag in foreign waters a reputation which it never afterwards lost. With a seemingly insignificant force he became the terror of the British coast.

On the eighth of August, 1776, John Paul received a captain's commission from the President of the Provincial Congress. The document read as follows:

"*The Delegates of the United States of New Hampshire, Massachusetts Bay, Rhode Island, Connecticut, New York,*

New Jersey, Pennsylvania, Delaware, Maryland, Virginia, North Carolina, South Carolina and Georgia, To

"JOHN PAUL JONES, ESQ.

"WE, reposing especial trust and confidence in your patriotism, valor, conduct and fidelity, do by these Presents, constitute and appoint you to be Captain in the navy of the United States of North America, fitted out for the defence of American Liberty, and for repelling every hostile invasion thereof. You are, therefore, carefully and diligently to discharge the duty of Captain, by doing and performing all manner of things thereunto belonging. And we do strictly charge and require all officers, marines and seamen under your command, to be obedient to your orders as Captain. And you are to observe and follow such orders and directions from time to time as you shall receive from this or a future Congress of the United States, or committee of Congress for that purpose appointed, or commander-in-chief for the time being of the navy of the United States, or any other your superior officer, according to the rules and discipline of war, the usage of the sea, and the instructions herewith given you, in pursuance of the trust reposed in you. This commission to continue in force until revoked by this or a future Congress.

"Dated at Philadelphia, October 10th, 1776.
"By order of the Congress:
"JOHN HANCOCK, *President.*
"Attest, CHARLES THOMPSON, *Secretary.*"

In command of the sloop "Providence," Captain Jones went out on a cruise against the enemy. His orders did not limit him to any particular place or service. The "Providence" mounted twelve four-pounders, and when he set sail from the Delaware, August twenty-first, he had only seventy men. He arrived at Rhode Island, October seventh, 1776. "Near the latitude of Bermudas he had a very narrow escape from the enemy's frigate, the 'Solebay,' after a chase and an engagement of six hours within cannon-shot, and part of the time within pistol-shot. Afterwards, near the Isle of Sable, Captain Jones had a running fight with the enemy's frigate, the 'Milford,' and the firing between them lasted from ten in the morning until after sunset. The next day Captain Jones entered the harbor of Canso, where he recruited several men, took the Tory flags, destroyed all the fisheries and burned the shipping, sailing again next morning on an expedition against the island of Madam. He made two descents at the principal ports of that island at the same time; surprised, burned and destroyed all their shipping and fishery, though the place abounded with armed men." This series of achievements occupied six weeks and five days, in which time Captain Jones made sixteen prizes and destroyed a great number of small vessels and fisheries.

On the second of November, 1776, he started on an expedition in command of the "Providence" and "Alfred"—the last ship mustering only one hundred and forty men. That night he anchored at Tarpawling Cove, near Nantucket, and the next day proceeded on his conquering voyage. During this cruise, which lasted until the fifteenth of December, when he anchored in Boston Harbor, he captured five prize-ships and brought back one hundred and fifty prisoners on board the "Alfred." While making trips between Newport and New York transporting stores and troops, Captain Jones had several rencounters with the "Cerberus" frigate and with others. In a memorial to the President of Congress he speaks of this time as follows:

"The first service I performed in the 'Providence' was to transport a number of soldiers from Providence to New York, which General Washington had lent us at New London to inspire us with courage to venture round to Rhode Island. The commodore employed me afterwards for some time to escort vessels from Rhode Island into the Sound, etc., while the 'Cerberus' and other vessels cruised round Block Island. At last I received orders to proceed to Boston to take under convoy some vessels laden with coal for Philadelphia. I performed that service about the time when Lord Howe arrived at Sandy Hook." After this he sailed from the Delaware with "unlimited orders" in command of a little squadron—a trust to which he never failed to do honor. The list of prize-ships he captured was always large, and at times his skill was taxed to the utmost to convoy the prizes safely into a home port. Many were the hair-breadth escapes, many the skilful manœuvres, and many the deeds of daring performed by the valiant Captain John Paul during these years of war for glorious liberty. He took the sea against the British flag with a success which amply proved both his patriotism and his signal ability. His letters during this time written to the American Commissioners and others, contain full descriptions of his adventures.

On the twenty-second of February, 1778, he wrote to the Marine Committee as follows:

"I have in contemplation several enterprises of some importance.... When an enemy thinks a design against him improbable, he can always be surprised and attacked with advantage. It is true, I must run great risk; but no gallant action was ever performed without danger. Therefore, though I cannot ensure success, I will endeavor to deserve it."

Captain Jones now began to excite some attention in England, as the following extract from a London paper of February twenty-second, 1778, will show:

"Paul Jones is about thirty-six years of age, of a middling stature, well proportioned, with an agreeable countenance; his conversation shows him a man of talents, and that he has got a liberal education. His letters in foreign gazettes show he can fight with the pen as well as the sword. The famous Captain Cunningham is with him, who escaped out of an English prison."

In command of the American Continental ship "Ranger," he engaged the "Drake," an English vessel, in a sharp fight off the Scotch shore, near Whitehaven. He was victorious as usual, and made a successful descent upon Whitehaven. "The surprise produced in Great Britain by this daring attempt upon her coasts must have been as great as the latter was unexpected. His objects were, distinctly to make some bold stroke which should inspire fear of the American arms, to retaliate for the burning of towns and destruction of private property, to destroy as much public property as he could, and to secure a number of prisoners as hostages for the better treatment of the captured Americans, who were suffering miserably in the jails and hulks of the enemy." The success of the

Chevalier John Paul cannot fail to excite astonishment. "It was one of the most impudent attacks since the time of the sea-kings, and it is no wonder that those whose eyes were so rudely opened to a discovery of their weakness, stigmatized it as inglorious and its conductor as a pirate." Jones' vessel was not a privateer, but a United States vessel of war, under the command of a fully commissioned officer of the United States.

In this descent upon Whitehaven, the family plate of the Countess of Selkirk was taken by his men. When afterwards it was sold by the prize agents, Captain Jones became its purchaser and returned it to its owners. On his return to Brest, May eighth, 1778, he wrote a letter to the countess on the subject, which was very widely published. The letter was characterized by Dr. Franklin as a "gallant letter which must give her ladyship a high opinion of his generosity and nobleness of mind." Part of the letter is quoted below. Its language is indeed full of gallantry.

"MADAM:

"It cannot be too much lamented that in the profession of arms the officer of fine feeling and of real sensibility should be under the necessity of winking at any action of persons under his command, which his heart cannot approve; but the reflection is doubly severe when he finds himself obliged, in appearance, to countenance such actions by his authority.

"This hard case was mine when, on the twenty-third of April last, I landed on St. Mary's Isle. Knowing Lord Selkirk's interest with his king, and esteeming as I do his private character, I wish to make him the happy instrument of alleviating the horrors of hopeless captivity, when the brave are overpowered and made prisoners of war. . . . It was my intention to have taken him on board the 'Ranger,' and to have detained him until, through his means, a general and fair exchange of prisoners, as well in Europe as in America, had been effected."

In this vein of politeness the letter continues—telling the fair countess that he would undertake to redeem the family plate, captured against his wishes. It was fortunate for Lord Selkirk that he was absent from home. Otherwise he would have been "detained," as the chevalier expresses it, as a hostage for fair treatment.

Lord Selkirk wrote a letter in reply to that addressed to his countess, intimating that he would accept the return of the plate if made by order of Congress, but not if redeemed by individual generosity. The letter was delayed some months in the general post-office in London, and it was not until the beginning of 1780 that Jones was enabled to get the plate from the prize agents into whose hands it had fallen. It was at last returned in the same condition in which it had been removed, after no end of difficulty and trouble on the part of Jones.

The hostile attitude of England and France at this time, and the sympathy of the nation of Lafayette for America, rendered the news of John Paul's expedition "gratifying and inspiring to the French Court." Praises were heaped upon him, and promises were plentiful.

After this the Chevalier Paul remained at Brest for

many months of inglorious inactivity, waiting for a ship to be got ready for him, concerning which there was an unaccountable delay. A great deal of diplomatic correspondence supplemented the impatient waiting, until at last he was tendered the command of a squadron with *carte-blanche* orders, and the limitless field of the high seas for his theatre of action. The armament consisted of the "Bon Homme Richard," the "Alliance," the "Pallas," the brig "Vengeance," and the "Cerf," a fine cutter. The "Bon Homme Richard," commanded by the chevalier himself, mounted only one hundred and forty guns, but it was destined soon after to win deathless laurels as the successful participant in one of the most famous naval battles then on record. The prowess of iron-clad "Merrimacs" and turreted "Monitors" had not yet claimed the attention of the world.

The engagement between the "Bon Homme Richard" and the British ship of war "Serapis," took place on the evening of September twenty-third, 1779. The desperate conflict was witnessed by thousands of spectators along the English coast off Flamborough Head, near Scarboro, and the light of a beautiful harvest moon shed its peaceful radiance across the waters in striking contrast to the bloody scene going on below. At about noon of that historic day, Captain Jones discovered a fleet of forty-one sail rounding Flamborough Head, and immediately hoisted the signal for a general chase. The fleet was protected by two ships of war, the "Serapis" and the "Countess of Scarborough."

When the merchant vessels discovered the squadron of Captain Jones bearing down upon them they

FIGHT BETWEEN THE "SERAPIS" AND "BON HOMME RICHARD."

"crowded sail towards shore" and thus escaped. The Chevalier Jones was unable to come up with the fleet until seven o'clock in the evening, and when he had approached to within pistol-shot of the "Serapis," Captain Pearson, commanding, demanded:

"What ship is that?"

He was answered with, "I can't hear what you say."

The "Serapis" asked again, "What ship is that? Answer immediately or I shall be under the necessity of firing into you."

The answer was a broadside.

Thus the famous battle began, and for between three and four hours it raged with uninterrupted fury. The two ships closed like men in mortal combat, their death-dealing guns touching each other's sides, and their rigging becoming entangled.

As the jib-boom of the "Serapis" ran into the mizzen-rigging of the "Bon Homme Richard" they were made fast by Captain Jones, with a hawser, which afterwards prevented an attempt of the "Serapis" to escape. The batteries of the "Bon Homme Richard" became disabled, until only two nine-pounders were left which could be used, but her brave commander never thought of surrender.

With the gallant craft cut entirely to pieces between decks from the foremast to the stern, with the rudder gone, with five feet of water in her hold and her rigging on fire in several places, she still fought valiantly on, in the face of terrible odds, until the captain of the "Serapis" with his own hand struck the flag of England to the free Stars and Stripes of young America.

The scene of carnage, wreck and ruin on board the two ships surpassed all power of description. Some of the hand-grenades thrown from the "Bon Homme Richard" fell among the powder scattered on the deck of the "Serapis" which had been emptied from broken cartridges, and produced an explosion which was described as awful. More than twenty of the enemy were blown to pieces, and many stood with only the collars of their shirts upon their bodies. In less than an hour afterwards, the surrender of the "Serapis" took place. Captain Pearson struck the flag which was nailed to the mast with his own hand, because none of his men dared venture aloft on this duty. Several times during the conflict the flames on the "Bon Homme Richard" were within a few inches of the magazine, and the men were frequently under the necessity of suspending the combat in order to extinguish the fire.

One of the escaped prisoners on board the "Bon Homme Richard" passed through the port to the "Serapis," and informed Captain Pearson that if he would hold out a little longer the American ship would either strike or sink, and that the prisoners had been released to save their lives. Of course the "Serapis" renewed the battle with added ardor after receiving this piece of intelligence, but it availed them nothing. The Chevalier Paul was not to be thus conquered. And to him alone redounds all the glory of this brilliant action.

The "Bon Homme Richard" fought single-handed, receiving no help from the remaining vessels of the squadron. The "Countess of Scarborough," the other British ship of war in company with the "Serapis," was engaged by one of Captain Jones' fleet, and that, also, surrendered.

"From the commencement to the termination of the action there was not a man on board the 'Bon Homme Richard' ignorant of the superiority of the 'Serapis,' both in weight of metal and in the qualities of the crews. The crew of the 'Serapis' were picked seamen, and the ship itself had been only a few months off the stocks; whereas the crew of the 'Bon Homme Richard' consisted of part American, English and French, and in part of Maltese, Portuguese and Malays; these latter contributing by their want of naval skill and knowledge of the English language," to lessen the chances of success. Neither the consideration of the relative force of the ships, nor the blowing-up of the gun-deck above them, by the bursting of two of the eighteen-pounders, nor the alarm that the ship was sinking, could depress the ardor or change the determination of the heroic Captain Jones to conquer at all hazards. Once, during the action, the enemy attempted to board the "Bon Homme Richard," but on finding Captain Jones in the gangway with a pike in his hand ready to receive them, they retreated, supposing a large force in reserve. It was a fortunate mistake for the brave John Paul, as the reserve force consisted entirely and only of himself.

During this engagement, the heroic Captain Jones not only commanded the "Bon Homme Richard" and its men, directing the skilful strategy which secured his splendid victory, but also worked as a common sailor. With his own hands he lashed the ships together, met the enemy when they attempted to board his vessel, and worked the guns himself when only two remained that were serviceable. He did not escape without wounds. It would have been little less than a miracle otherwise.

Of course this sea-battle created a vast excitement on both continents, and the name of Paul Jones was on every tongue. The press of the day overflowed with accounts of it, and the chevalier was the hero of the hour. The London *Chronicle*, of October seventeenth, 1779, published the following communication from Amsterdam. It is dated October seventh:

"Last Tuesday, Paul Jones, with the prizes, the 'Serapis' and 'Scarboro',' entered the Texel, and this day he appeared on the Exchange, where business gave way to curiosity. The crowd pressing upon him by whom he was styled the terror of the English, he withdrew to a room fronting the public square, where Monsieur Donneville, the French agent, and the Americans, paid him such a volley of compliments and such homage as he could only answer with a bow. He was dressed in the American uniform, with a Scotch bonnet edged with gold, is of a middling stature, stern countenance and swarthy complexion. It was supposed he was going to Paris to receive the congratulations of the Grand Monarque and Dr. Franklin; but I am now informed he is gone to the Hague, to solicit by the French ambassador the repair of his shipping, which, if he should succeed in, he will probably elude the vigilance of a seventy-four gun-ship waiting before the Texel."

A story is told of Captain Jones, who was in Paris a short time after this battle. He was informed that Captain Pearson, of the "Serapis," had been knighted.

"Well," said he, "he deserves it, and if I fall in with him again, I will make a lord of him."

The "Bon Homme Richard" was so disabled, that, despite every effort to tow her into port, she went down on the next day but one after the battle.

In a letter of Dr. Franklin to Jones, written October fifteenth, in reply to despatches from Jones, he says:

"I am uneasy about your prisoners, five hundred and four in number. I wish they were safe in France. You will then have completed the glorious work of giving liberty to all the Americans that have so long languished for it in British prisons." That grand object was at last accomplished, and the Chevalier Jones was the chief instrument in bringing it about. On the first of January, 1780, he escaped from the Texel road, where, for three months, he had been blockaded by the British fleets. Three days afterwards we find him writing poetry to a young lady at the Hague, who had penned a metrical effusion to the chevalier. He cherished a romantic regard for women, and was ever the incarnation of gallantry to them.

During the year 1780, Captain Jones was in France, and his correspondence of that time is voluminous. In one of these letters he says:

"As an American officer and as a man I affectionately love and respect the character and nation of France, and hope the alliance with America may last forever. I owe the greatest obligation to the generous praises of the French nation on my past conduct, and I shall be happy to merit future favor."

While the chevalier remained in Paris he was lionized to an unlimited extent. Everywhere he was greeted with the homage accorded a hero. Men chanted his praises. Women smiled upon him. Court and community united to do him honor. In a brief notice of him published in the Edinburgh Encyclopedia, it was said that he spoke several European languages, was a lover of music and poetry, played on different musical instruments, and used to write verses for the amusement of the Parisian ladies. Of his public reception it was said that he received at Paris and other parts of the kingdom the most flattering applause and public approbation whenever he appeared. Both the great and learned sought his acquaintance in private life, and honored him with particular marks of friendship. At court he was always received with great kindness. His rank at this time was that of commodore, and the French king ordered a gold sword to be presented him, and also the cross of military merit conferred only on those who had distinguished themselves in the service of France. From Dr. Franklin also he received an honorable testimonial of his bravery and conduct.

On the eighteenth of February, 1781, Captain Jones arrived at Philadelphia, having been absent from America three years and three months. On the twenty-seventh, Congress, at that time assembled in Philadelphia, passed resolutions commending Captain Jones for his distinguished bravery and military conduct, and endorsing the action of the King of France in bestowing upon him the cross of merit.

The great object of the brave John Paul had been to effect the liberty and exchange of American citizens confined in the dungeons of England, and this noble purpose, after herculean efforts, had been accomplished.

Having won the admiration of two continents, the gallant chevalier rested for a time from his labors. He afterwards went to Portsmouth to take command of the "America," but on arriving at that place he found the ship unfinished, and was necessitated to remain and superintend its construction. On his way thither he visited Washington and Count Rochambeau at White Plains, wearing on that occasion his cross as Chevalier of the Order of Merit.

After long delays the "America" was at last launched, displaying the stars and stripes and the flag of France at her masthead. The chevalier was the chief actor in the ceremony attending the launching, and after the affair was over, he delivered her to the Chevalier De Martigne and returned to Philadelphia.

Captain Jones afterwards wrote to the minister of the marine, requesting that, unless Congress had some service of greater consequence for him, he might be ordered back to Boston to embark as a volunteer in pursuit of military marine knowledge, to enable him to better serve his country when America should increase her navy.

The chevalier never married, notwithstanding his extravagant admiration for women. Some of his letters reveal the fact that he sometimes indulged in dreams of domestic happiness, which were never realized.

He wrote to a friend in the United States just before the close of the war that "if peace should be concluded he wished to establish himself on a place of his own, and offer his hand to some fair daughter of liberty." But this dream was destined to remain only a dream.

The chevalier went to Philadelphia soon after peace was restored, remaining from May until November, when he again sailed for France. Meantime, in addition to the gold sword and cross of the French King Louis, he had been presented with a gold medal from Congress. Loaded with honors and in the height of his popularity he went to Denmark and Russia, and was received at the royal courts of these countries with great distinction. He afterwards entered into the Russian service, and the queen conferred on him the grade of rear admiral. In a letter to Lafayette at this time, Jones said he was detained a fortnight against his will, and continually feasted in court and the first society. He was lionized at St. Petersburg as he had been at Paris. A St. Petersburg letter of this date chronicles his arrival, and says that "he was presented to the sovereign by the French ambassador, and immediately promoted to the rank of admiral. He is to take command of a squadron in the Black Sea. . . . He wears the French uniform with the cross of St. Louis, and a Danish order which he received at Copenhagen, where he had the honor to dine with the king. He has also received since he came here one of the first orders of merit in this country." His visit to the court of Denmark was of a political nature.

During all these years of adventure and daring service on the high seas, he kept a detailed account of his doings in an elegantly bound journal. At last we find him again in Paris, where on the eighteenth of July, 1792, he died of dropsy. His health had been gradually failing for a long time previous, and at length his heroic soul passed to the spirit land. He was surrounded by friends to the end. His funeral discourse was pronounced by Mr. Marron, a Protestant clergyman of the city which had heaped upon him such honors.

Noble in his courage, princely in his liberality, and grandest of all in his tender humanity, Paul Jones was every inch a hero. The beloved flag of America had no braver defender during the long struggle for independence in the days of the Revolution, nor had liberty a more ardent lover. He was the champion of justice and right the world over, but America was the country of his affections. His chiefest glory as he often declared was to be a citizen of the United States.

CHAPTER IX.
THADDEUS KOSCIUSZKO.

Early History of Kosciuszko.—Education in the Art of War.—An Affair of the Heart.—Exile.—Position on Washington's Staff.—Siege of Ninety-Six.—Service in Poland.—Dictator and Generalissimo.—Battle of Raczlawice.—Victory Followed by Defeat.—Decisive Battle of Maciejowice.—Overwhelmed by Superior Numbers.—" Finis Polonæ!"—Imprisonment.—Freedom Regained.—Retirement at Fontainebleau.—The Fall from the Precipice.—Closing Scenes.

DURING the struggle of the infant colonies for liberty in the days of the Revolution, the young Polish nobleman, Thaddeus Kosciuszko, was an accession of value to our army and to the staff of Washington. He was born February twelfth, 1756, and was educated in the military school at Warsaw. His family was both ancient and noble, and he proved himself a worthy scion of so honorable a house.

At an early age he seems to have enlisted the sympathies of one of the princes of the reigning house, who conferred on him the rank of lieutenant of cadets and sent him to France to further his military education. On his return to his native country he received a captaincy and was on the high road to promotion, when an unhappy affair of the heart put an end to his fair prospects. He dared to cherish a love for a lady whom Prince Lubomirski also loved, and this was his offence. For such a piece of presumption he was obliged to fly from his native land, and on the arena of the New World, where liberty was struggling for an existence, he sought a field for action. Here he won the lasting renown which is always accorded noble daring. But change of scene did not quench the ardor of his attachment. With beautiful fidelity, through all the eventful years of his life, he remained true to the lady for whose sake he had suffered banishment. No other woman ever took her place. He came to America with the highest credentials and offered his life and services in the cause of liberty. Washington, with keen appreciation, gave him the position of aid on his staff and Kosciuszko did honor to the choice. His conduct in the many engagements in which he participated was always distinguished by a spirited bravery. He received the rank of brigadier, and was on duty as principal engineer of the army. At the siege of Ninety-six all the approaches and besieging operations were planned by him. He behaved with cool indifference under fire, and at the close of the war left America for Europe with the rank of general and as a member of the American order of Cincinnati.

In 1786, he returned to his native land, and the next year received the appointment of major-general. In 1791, he went into service under Prince Joseph Poniatowski, and at the battle of Dubienka repulsed a force of eighteen thousand Russians with less than a quarter of that number.

When Poland yielded allegiance to Catherine of Russia, Kosciuszko left the army and went to Leipsic, where he became a naturalized citizen of France. But the Poles did not easily submit to the domination of a foreign power, and rebellion and war were again inaugurated. When the liberties of his country stood imperilled, Kosciuszko could not longer remain away, and went to Cracow to draw his sword in her behalf. The crisis found him ready to meet it, and on the twenty-fourth of March, 1794, he was proclaimed Dictator and Generalissimo. His rule began with victory. The Russians were driven from Cracow, and the constitution of the Polish people was restored.

On April fourth, the battle of Raczlawice was fought; and Kosciuszko, at the head of four thousand men, met and repulsed twelve thousand Russians. The conflict was desperate and bloody, and three thousand of the enemy's dead were left upon the field. The Polish patriots were encouraged, and Poland once more stood upright with the shackles of slavery shaken from her feet. Law and order were again restored, and Kosciuszko was on the pinnacle of fame and greatness. Up to this time his course had been marked by nothing but victory, but the shadow of defeat was yet to fall upon his future. The patriot band he had gathered around him was confronted by the combined armies of Russia and Prussia, and after bravely contesting the ground he was obliged to retire to his defences before Warsaw. Cracow fell and Warsaw was besieged by sixty thousand men. Two months of daily battle at last brought on a general assault, and the allied armies were ingloriously defeated by a force of only ten thousand men. The siege was raised, and on the bright banner of fame the name of Kosciuszko was immortalized forever. "With an army of but twenty thousand regular troops and twice that number of peasants he had maintained himself successfully through the campaign against four hostile armies, numbering altogether one hundred and fifty thousand men." The hearts of the people were with him and he belonged most truly to the people. With no other object in life, he lived only for his country. Order and peace were restored for the time, and Kosciuszko gave back to the national council the power delegated to him as Dictator.

But the invaders, confident in the ultimate success of their overwhelming numbers, renewed the conflict with an army of over sixty thousand. Kosciuszko had only twenty-one thousand. The battle-ground was at a place named Maciejowice, about fifty miles from Warsaw, and it occurred on October tenth, 1794. The fight was desperate. Three violent assaults were made on the Polish lines without effect, but at the fourth charge the patriot ranks gave way and the brave and valiant and noble Kosciuszko fell from his horse, pierced with wounds.

"This is the last of Poland!" he exclaimed, as he was borne a prisoner to the enemy's camp. His words bore the spell of prophecy, and Poland was indeed lost to him and his countrymen as an independent nation.

The successor of Catherine of Russia liberated the captives whom she had imprisoned, and Kosciuszko received many marks of favor and esteem. The emperor even presented his sword to the Polish chieftain —an honor which Kosciuszko declined, saying that "he who no longer had a country, no longer had need of a weapon." Other gifts were offered him by the emperor, but Kosciuszko declined them all. He again visited France and England—last of all America. In this country he was received with the honor due to one of the heroes of the Revolution and the bosom-friend of Washington. In 1798, he again went to France from America. His countrymen in the army of Napoleon presented him with the sword of John Sobieski, and Napoleon endeavored to interest him in his own ambitious schemes by promises of freedom for Poland. But he was not to be deceived by such illusive hopes. Never afterwards did he wear a sword. He bought an estate near Fontainebleau, and lived in seclusion for many years. In 1814, he made an appeal to the Emperor Alexander to give a free constitution to Poland and to grant amnesty to his countrymen in foreign lands. The next year he travelled in Italy, and the year after settled at Solcur, Switzerland. Here he lived in quiet retirement until his death, which took place on October sixteenth, 1817. This event was brought about by a fall from his horse over a precipice near Vevay. In 1818, his body was deposited in the tombs of the kings at Cracow, at the request of the Senate.

Thus passed into death's dark eclipse one of the bravest spirits that ever suffered exile and martyrdom for liberty. Personal ambition and selfish indulgence were alike forgotten in a grand and absorbing love for country, and through all time the name of this noble patriot will shine bright and clear on the world's roll of honor.

CHAPTER X.
HUGH MERCER.

The Moors of Culloden.—The Assistant-Surgeon of the Highland Army.—Emigration to Pennsylvania.—Indian Wars.—Wounded and Alone.—Outbreak of the Revolution.—The Fredericksburg Home.—Farewells.—Days of '76.—First Campaign.—A Gloomy Time.—Influence of Washington.—Across the Delaware.—Affairs in Philadelphia.—Putnam's Order.—Hasty Adjournment of Congress.—Change of Policy.—Attack on Trenton.—Victory.—The Night March on Princeton.—Desperate Fighting.—Ten to One.—Mercer Mortally Wounded.—The Farm-House Scene.—Last Moments.—Victory and Death.

HUGH MERCER first appears among the dramatis personæ of history, fighting under the standard of the Scottish prince, Charles Edward, on the moors of Culloden. Colonel Wolfe, of Quebec fame, fought in the English ranks against him, and Fraser, afterwards major-general, was also there. The bloody defeat of that day, April sixteenth, 1746, is known to history. Of the exiled prince and his band of devoted followers, it concerns us to trace the career of only one of them, the young assistant-surgeon of the Highland army, who afterwards crossed the ocean and identified himself with the patriot ranks struggling for liberty. After emigrating to Pennsylvania, and making a home on what was then the lonely, western frontier, he became captain in the Provincial army at the outbreak of the Indian wars of 1755. He fought under the leadership of that brave old Scotch Covenanter, Colonel John Armstrong, whose son afterwards bore him mortally hurt from the battle-field of Princeton. At the assault on Kittanning, an Indian stronghold, which was successfully carried, Mercer received a severe wound, and in the confusion of the fight, got separated from his company and was reported "missing." Alone, with his shattered arm, he wandered through the forest for weeks, living on roots and berries, until at last he reached Fort Cumberland exhausted.

In 1758, Mercer, as lieutenant-colonel, was left in charge of Fort Du Quesne, after its reduction by the army of General Forbes, a post which it was considered important to hold. During this time he became acquainted with young Colonel Washington, from Virginia, and a warm friendship sprang up between them.

During the succeeding contest for colonial independence, Hugh Mercer was foremost among the defenders of American rights. A few months after George Washington was chosen commander-in-chief of our armies, Mercer was honored by Congress with a commission as brigadier-general. Soon afterwards he left his home in Fredericksburg, Virginia, and joined the Continental forces at New York. The farewells uttered at this time to his wife and little ones were final farewells, though he knew it not. He never again returned to the Virginia home where he had planted his roof-tree. His life had been risked for the defence of the country of his adoption, and the noble sacrifice was made on the field of Princeton.

General Mercer's first campaign was crowded with events which were of vital interest to the country. "The battle on Long Island, the retreat to New York, the evacuation of that city contrary to the advice of Mercer, who was perhaps wisely overruled, and of Greene, whose bold counsel it was to burn the city to the ground, the battle of White Plains, the fall of Fort Washington, the projected attack on Staten Island confided to Mercer, and the retreat through New Jersey, were the prominent incidents of this eventful period. Throughout it all, Mercer was in active service under the immediate orders of the commander-in-chief, to whose effections he was closely endeared."

In the early part of December, 1776, the banks of the Delaware were reached by our dispirited army, pursued by the well-regulated troops of the British. A cloud of gloom seemed to hover over the country which pervaded alike the army and Congress, then on the point of leaving Philadelphia for a safer retreat at Baltimore. This was the darkest period of the Revolution, and the influence of Washington, at this time, is said to have been sublimely felt. He was a pillar of flame by night, and a pillar of cloud by day, to the desponding hopes of the patriot army, and the anxious, waiting hearts at home. Calmly resolute, he went forward, Congress having put upon him the entire responsibility of the issue at stake. The trust was grandly executed, as history knows, and Fame, in gratitude, encircled his brow with her purest rays of light.

In a letter written by Washington, General Lee, at Basken Ridge, was implored to come at once, and unite his forces with the main army, but just as the letter reached him, Lee was made a prisoner by a party of British dragoons, and *that* hope was cut off. With large bodies of Hessian and British troops within a few miles of Philadelphia, and with a British frigate and sloop of war lying at anchor in the Delaware, the state of affairs in the Quaker city may be imagined. The effect is described by one who witnessed it at the time. "It was just dark," he says, "when we entered Front street, and it appeared as if we were riding through a city of the dead. Such was the silence and stillness which prevailed that the dropping of a stone would have been heard for several squares, and the hoofs of our horses resounded in all directions." But General Putnam, the lion-hearted Richard of our Revolution, held the command of the city, and that of itself was an element of success. The following order, issued by him, vividly portrays the unsettled and threatening state of affairs at the time:

"The late advances of the enemy oblige the general to request the inhabitants of this city not to appear in the streets after ten o'clock at night, as he has given orders to the picket-guard to arrest and confine all persons who may be found in the streets after that hour. Physicians and others, having essential business after that hour, are directed to call at head-quarters for passes.

"The general has been informed that some weak or wicked men have maliciously reported that it is the design and wish of the officers and men in the Continental army to burn and destroy the city of Philadelphia. To counteract such a false and scandalous report, he thinks it necessary to inform the inhabitants who propose to remain in the city, that he has received positive orders from the honorable Continental Congress, and from his excellency, General Washington, to secure and protect the city of Philadelphia against all invaders and enemies. The general will consider any attempt to burn the city as a crime of the blackest dye, and will, without ceremony, punish capitally any incendiary who shall have the hardiness and cruelty to attempt it. The general commands all able-bodied men who are not conscientiously scrupulous about bearing arms, and who have not been known heretofore to have entertained such scruples, to appear in the State House yard, at ten o'clock, with their arms and accoutrements. This order must be complied with, the general being resolutely determined that no person shall remain in the city an idle spectator of the present contest who has it in his power to injure the American cause, or who may refuse to lend his aid in support of it; persons under conscientious scruples alone excepted."

On the eleventh of December, Congress passed a resolution denouncing a current rumor that they intended to leave Philadelphia, and on the very next day they hastily adjourned to Baltimore, leaving Washington with *carte-blanche* orders as to the conduct of the war. But his faith in the right and in the belief that liberty would triumph, remained unshaken, though the means of attaining this end seemed shrouded in gloom. At this crisis a suggestion was made to change the war policy from defensive to offensive operations, and attack the enemy's outposts through New Jersey. General Mercer seems to have been among the first to propose this offensive movement, and it was decided between himself and his aid, Mayor Armstrong, to speak of the subject in turn to the commander-in-chief. The suggestion met with the cordial support of such men as Greene, among others of Washington's most valued advisers, and a plan of attack on Trenton was quickly arranged. The troops were to cross the Delaware in two places, and attack the enemy from two points at once. With Washington's small and illy-equipped force the move was a desperate one, and the fate of a nation trembled on the issue. "For God's sake, hurry on the clothing to my suffering men," he wrote to Robert Morris, two days previous to the attack. "Leave no arms or valuable papers in the city, for sure I am that the enemy wait for two events alone to begin their operations on Philadelphia—ice for a passage over the Delaware, and the dissolution of the poor remains of my debilitated army."

In the winter darkness of that Christmas night, an hour before dawn, the momentous attack was made, and the tide of reverse and disaster was turned by the splendid victory which followed. Mercer led the column of attack on the main street coming in from Princeton, and effectually cut off the enemy's retreat.

After this glorious achievement the American forces recrossed the Delaware and waited until the last of the month before resuming offensive operations. On the night of January second, 1777, the patriot camp in New Jersey held a council of war, at which Mercer proposed the bold idea of a night attack on Princeton, for the purpose of capturing two regiments of the enemy stationed at that point, and then continuing the advance to Brunswick to destroy the magazines there. The proposition was at once agreed to by all present, and before dawn the movement was put into execution. They had pitched their tents that night not far from the British camp—a small stream flowing between the two hostile armies.

An attack was to have been made on the Americans next morning, by the enemy, but Lord Cornwallis woke to find his intended victims flown. The thunder of the guns at Princeton, heard in the distance, first announced to him the fact that the foe no longer confronted him, and that the British forces at Princeton were being attacked.

Mercer, at the head of his brigade, threw himself between the main body of the enemy and their reserves, thus precipitating a general action. Colonel Hazlet fell, mortally hurt, and Mercer's horse was shot under him. Disdaining to fly or to surrender in the confusion which this occasioned, he fought dismounted single-handed and alone against the on-rushing hordes of the enemy. But the terrible odds were too great and he was trampled to the earth, pierced by the bayonets of overwhelming numbers. The struggle was sharp and bloody, the victory glorious, but what brave blood consecrated the sacrifice! What heroic lives went out that liberty might live!

Major Armstrong found his general lying insensible on the field and carried him to a neighboring farmhouse, where he lingered a few days in mortal agony before the expiring flame of life went out. He died in the arms of Major George Lewis—a nephew of Washington—with a prayer on his lips for his fatherless family and his suffering country.

This last sad scene in the drama of Hugh Mercer's life was not unrelieved by the presence of woman. The two who lived under that humble roof did not fly from the rain of leaden death which fell around them, while the duty of watching by the bedside of this dying soldier claimed their service. As woman alone could, they soothed his last moments, and their tears fell over his pallid form as the spirit took its final flight. Let us draw the curtain gently over this sorrowful picture, and stand with hushed pulses in the presence of the memory of this soldier of the Revolution, who died in defence of liberty.

CHAPTER XI.

ANTHONY WAYNE.

Birth and Ancestry.—Youthful Bent Towards Military Studies.—Marriage.—Beginning of Public Life.—In the Legislature.—Commissioned as Colonel.—Expedition to Canada.—At Brandywine.—Engagement of Germantown.—Service at Valley Forge.—Monmouth.—Storming of Stony Point.—Splendid Victory.—Revolt of the Pennsylvania Line.—Investment of Yorktown.—War with the Indians.—Peace Commissioner.—Death at Presque Isle.—Monument of the Cincinnati.

ANTHONY WAYNE was a son of Pennsylvania, of whom that State is justly proud and whose glorious career adds a lustre to her history. He and the new year of 1745 were born together, and he proved to be a valuable New Year's gift to the young American nation which afterwards emerged from the darkness of servile subjection to the English crown, into the light of independence. His father belonged to Erin's green isle—the land of poetry and song, of generous impulses and Irish wit, the land of Moore and Emmet.

As a boy, young Wayne is said to have displayed a taste for military studies. The Revolution gave this faculty its direction. Otherwise, perhaps, he might never have been known to the world or to these pages. But when a great crisis convulses a nation, the leading spirits rise to the top of the tide of events and take their places. Anthony Wayne was one of these. His boyhood, uneventful, save in the routine of daily toil, merged slowly into manhood, and at twenty-two he was married. This was in 1767, and for the succeeding two years he was occupied as a farmer and land-surveyor in his native county of Chester. In 1774, he was elected a member of the Pennsylvania Legislature, and in 1775, was on the Committee of Public Safety. He now began a course of military study in anticipation of approaching events, and in September resigned his seat in the Legislature to raise a regiment of volunteers. On January third, 1776, he received from Congress the commission of colonel, and at the beginning of the campaign of that year was ordered to the field of operations in New York and Canada. His regiment was with General Sullivan at the defeat of Three Rivers, in Canada, and during the well-ordered retreat which he conducted at that place, he received his first wound in the cause of freedom.

From Canada he went to take charge of Fort Ticonderoga for a time, and afterwards, in May, 1777, joined the army of Washington in New Jersey. In February previous, Congress had conferred on him the rank of brigadier-general, and the commander-in-chief had also testified to his distinguished bravery and skill.

At the famous battle of Brandywine, the brigade of Wayne was one of the most conspicuous on the field and covered itself with glory and fame.

At Germantown he was in command of one of the divisions on the right, taking the Chestnut-Hill road. They advanced with fixed bayonets and the action soon became general. Every student of history knows the unhappy termination of this action and the lamentable mistakes caused by the fog of that October morning. The roan horse of General Wayne was shot dead under

him within a few yards of the enemy's front, and himself received several slight wounds. In a letter written at the time concerning the engagement he says:
"Upon the whole, it was a glorious day. Our men are in high spirits, and I am confident we shall give them a total defeat the next action, which is at no great distance."

In this battle General Wayne covered the retreat of the American army, compelling the enemy to give up pursuit by the very effective fire of a battery planted on an eminence which commanded their line of advance.

During the severe winter at Valley Forge in 1777, when the patriot ranks were suffering from want of proper clothing and food, General Wayne was appointed commander of a foraging expedition, whose efforts were soon apparent in hundreds of fat cattle, horses and rations. It was a grateful relief to the starved and shivering army in their huts at Valley Forge, and furnished the solution to a most important problem.

Of General Wayne's part in the battle of Monmouth, Washington, in his official report to Congress, says: "The catalogue of those who distinguished themselves is too long to admit of particularizing individuals. I cannot, however, forbear to mention Brigadier-General Wayne, whose good conduct and bravery throughout the action deserves particular commendation."

At the storming of Stony Point, Wayne especially distinguished himself. This bold and brilliant enterprise—one of the most hazardous of the Revolution—was confided entirely to the generalship of the brave Pennsylvanian, and the trust was nobly executed.

Stony Point was a strongly fortified post on the Hudson River, commanding King's Ferry, the principal avenue of communication between the Eastern and Middle States. Through this point the enemy could easily strike the Highlands, should that be desired, and it was therefore of great strategic importance. Surrounded by the river on two sides and a deep morass on the third, it was made still more difficult of access by two rows of *abatis* besides the usual breastworks and artillery, covering the summit of the hill. It was garrisoned by six hundred men under Lieutenant-Colonel Johnson, and was regarded as impregnable.

General Wayne set himself to the task of taking this nearly inaccessible post, with undaunted courage. His troops started from Sandy Beach, fourteen miles away, on July fifteenth, 1779, and reached the vicinity of the fort in the evening of that day. As they came up they were formed into two columns, headed by a forlorn hope of twenty men each, under Lieutenant Gibbon of the sixth, and Lieutenant Knox of the ninth Pennsylvania regiments. At twenty minutes after midnight the assault was made. The advance guard rushed forward up the hill with bristling bayonets, undeterred by a galling fire of grape and musketry which was poured into their ranks from the enemy. But they succeeded in gaining the crest despite the formidable array of obstructions placed in their way, and the two columns met in the centre of the works. It was a splendid victory, eliciting the thanks of Congress and the praise of the people.

The attacking party lost only about one hundred men in the assault, including killed and wounded. During the action General Wayne fell to the earth, stunned by a wound in the head, but speedily recovering, he led his troops into the fort. Letters of congratulation were received by him from civilians and army officers alike, and his name was on the lips of the people as one of its saviors.

When the "Pennsylvania Line" came back to duty after their unhappy revolt, they put themselves under General Wayne's command, and offered to repel the troops of Sir Henry Clinton, which had been sent out to give them the assistance they had demanded of their own country. They *had* suffered wrongs which were unredressed, but it was not their patriotism that gave way in this stress of events, as the sequel proved. When their country's enemy offered them all they asked if they would come over to him, the proposition was indignantly repelled; and then it was that the old Pennsylvania Line put itself under the leadership of its beloved general, to drive out the troops of Clinton, who had been sent to receive them. Congress at last listened to their complaints, and by according them the long-delayed justice they sought, put an end to the unhappy mutiny.

At the investment and capture of Yorktown, General Wayne was actively engaged—the attacks of his brave troops contributing effectively to the work. Afterwards he was sent to the aid of General Greene, in Georgia, where his services were of the most important character. "He brought back to their allegiance many of the disaffected, made Whigs of Tories, and contrived to produce a spirit of discontent, which extended to the British army itself." He defeated the efforts of the British general to use Indian troops against him—capturing and repulsing large bodies of

Creek and Choctaw warriors, on their way to join the enemy. Their savage leader was slain and the force dispersed.

Charlestown was evacuated by the British and taken possession of by Wayne on December fourteenth, 1782, and this was his last military service in the Revolution. In July of 1783, he returned to civil life in his native State. The next year he was elected to the General Assembly from Chester county, and served two sessions. But General Wayne's military life was not yet at an end. In the Indian war which followed the war for Independence, he was appointed by Washington to the command of the armies of the United States, and executed his high trust with such masterly skill that the contest was concluded by the Treaty of Greeneville, and a long peace with the red men of America ensued.

General Wayne was afterwards appointed commissioner to treat with the Indians of the north-west, and while on his way down Lake Erie from Detroit, died from an attack of gout. The melancholy event took place at Presque Isle, December fifteenth, 1796. He was buried on the shore of the lake, but his remains were afterwards taken to his native county, where the State Society of Cincinnati erected a monument to his memory.

One of the inscriptions on the commemorative marble was as follows:

Major-General
ANTHONY WAYNE,
Was born at Waynesborough,
in Chester county,
State of Pennsylvania,
A. D. 1745.

After a life of honor and usefulness
he died in December, 1796,
at a military post
on the shores of Lake Erie,
Commander-in-Chief of the army of
the United States.
His military achievements
are consecrated
in the history of his country,
and in
the hearts of his countrymen.
His remains
are here deposited.

Men who have freely bestowed their services in glorious and unselfish causes, as did this noble patriot, must live while heroes are remembered or their brave deeds emulated.

CHAPTER XII.

JOHN STARK.

Chivalrous Character of Stark.—Incident of Bunker Hill.—Birthplace and Early Life.—The Young Hunter.—On a Trapping Excursion.—Captured by the Indians.—On the Way to St. Francis.—Running the Gauntlet.—Admiration of the Tribe for the White Hunter.—He is made a Chief.—Seven Years' War.—New Hampshire Rangers.—Battle in the Snow.—Brilliant Fighting of Stark.—Promoted.—The Guns of Lexington.—The Muster at Medford.—Advance on Trenton.—Princeton.—Re-enlistment.—Popularity of Stark.—Under a Cloud.—Defence of Vermont.—Battle of Bennington.—Close of War.—1812.—The Warrior's Last Sleep.

THERE is a peculiar kind of heroism about the character of John Stark as it is handed down to us by the historian. A dash of romance interthreads it which suggests the noble pioneers of Cooper's stories. It is the heroism of a strongly-marked individuality —of a gentle nature covered over by a rough exterior. There is a kind of latter-day chivalry enveloping the accounts we have of him, which, in the times of tournament and spear, would have passed current as the true gold of knighthood. Had he lived in the days of English King Alfred, he would have been numbered among the band of the Round Table, beside such stars as Sir Launcelot, the brave, and Sir Galahad, the pure. But no knight of ancient or modern days ever drew lance or sword in nobler cause than did John Stark, and the grandeur of it filled him—inspired him, as one incident related of him alone will testify: At the battle of Bunker Hill, a courier in haste came to him with the news (afterwards discovered to be false) that his son had fallen on the field. The Spartan reply was:—

"Is this a time for *private grief* with the foe in our face?" and the courier was ordered back to duty.

Not until he had reached his twenty-fifth year did John Stark appear as an actor on the public stage. He had previously lived the simple, sturdy life of a New England pioneer farmer, having been born in Londonderry, New Hampshire, August twenty-eighth, 1728. He was descended from Scotch ancestry. His avocations besides that of tilling the glebe were hunting and trapping, and for these last adventurous pursuits he held the true frontiersman's love. During this period, in company with three others, he went on a hunting excursion into the almost unexplored wilderness of the northwestern portion of the State. The tract was known to be infested with wild beasts and hostile tribes of Indians, but neither the one nor the other deterred the young woodsman from setting out on his perilous journey. After being out two days the party struck an Indian trail which they were bold enough to follow. Stark was somewhat in advance of his companions for the purpose of collecting traps, and was the first victim of the St. Francis Indians, who seized him and demanded the whereabouts of his companions. Stark pointed in the opposite direction, but the others were soon overtaken just as they were getting into a boat on Baker's River. The young trapper called to his companions to pull for the opposite shore, and, as the savages drew their pieces to fire on them, he struck the weapons out of his captors' hands. This boldness in their white victim excited the admiration of the Indians, although they chastised young Stark severely for his temerity. His skill in hunting and trapping was put to the test at once, and, becoming of use to them, he thus made another long stride in their favor. He was taken with the tribe on their way to St. Francis, and was allowed the rights of property in the capture of game.

After his arrival at St. Francis, he was condemned to run the gauntlet—a ceremony in vogue among them which is administered as a species of training to their young warriors in order to test and discipline their courage. It consisted of passing through the centre of two lines of armed savages, who delivered each a blow to the flying novice as he rushed down the gauntlet thus formed. Young Stark went through this ordeal in a manner which astonished his red captors, and won their unbounded admiration. As he sprang down the line he seized the club of the foremost among them, and, swinging it vigorously aloft, scattered his foes right and left, leaving them baffled and subdued. Loud was their praise in honor of this act of daring. Afterwards when Stark was set to hoe corn, he tossed his hoe into the river with contempt, saying it was "work for squaws, not warriors." What more did these Indians need to convince them of his entire worthiness to become a brave among their braves? A council was called at once, and Stark was formally created a chief of the tribe.

For many moons he remained among these St. Francis people, and ever afterwards declared that he received more real kindness at their hands than he ever knew prisoners of war to receive from civilized nations. At last he was ransomed by the commissioners of Massachusetts for one hundred and three dollars, though his companion captured at the same time was only valued at sixty dollars.

During the seven years French and Indian war which preceded the Revolution, John Stark was no idle spectator. A corps of Rangers under Robert Rogers was recruited for service, and in this organization Stark received his first commission. He was ever active in recruiting, scouting, and exploring during the pauses in the heat of the long contest. In the middle of January, 1757, on an extremely cold day, with the snow and sleet nearly blinding the eyes of the Rangers, the enemy was encountered midway between Ticonderoga and Crown Point, and a battle ensued. Rogers was wounded, their lieutenant killed, and Stark fougnt desperately on—almost the only officer left unhurt. At last the lock of his gun was broken, and springing forward he seized a weapon from the grasp of a prostrate Frenchman and continued the fight, exciting his men to action. When a retreat was suggested he declared he would shoot the first man who attempted to fly. The fight was kept up from two o'clock in the afternoon until night compelled a cessation of hostilities, when in the cold and snow they commenced a retreat to Fort William Henry, their only succor, forty miles away. Their wounded were soon compelled to halt, unable to continue the difficult march. In this crisis, John Stark and two others set out on snow-shoes to the fort to bring help and relief to their disabled and dying. The long distance was traversed and the return journey made before Stark allowed himself to think of sleep. This battle was the means of promoting him to the rank of captain.

At the downfall of Ticonderoga, the New Hampshire Rangers, foremost in danger and in the brunt of battle, won an enviable reputation for bravery and daring, and afterwards during this protracted struggle, many were the battles fought in which they bore a conspicuous part, and of which history took little note. At the end of the French and Indian war the "Rangers" of Major Rogers and Captain Stark were disbanded, and Stark returned once more to the pursuits of a peaceful life. This interval of peace lasted about twelve years before the guns of Lexington awoke the country with their echoes, and the sons of the soil rushed to her rescue. It is said that within ten minutes after the tidings of the fight at Lexington had reached him, Stark was on his way to the scene of action, armed and equipped for battle. As he went, he called on all lovers of country and liberty to meet him at Medford, and twelve hundred men responded to this alarum call. With these brave boys he was in the hottest of the fight at Bunker Hill, and not only sustained the reputation he had previously won, but added fresh laurels to his chaplet of fame.

As the great wave of the Revolution swept on, Stark was ever found promptly at his post, fearless of danger, alert for the foe.

Before, or about the time the policy of the war had changed from one of defence to an aggressive advance, Stark was prompt with his advice on the subject, even though he counselled so great a general as Washington, himself.

"You must teach your men to rely upon their firearms instead of their pickaxes, if you ever mean to establish the independence of the United States," he wrote to the commander-in-chief, and that general responded quickly enough. "This is what we have agreed upon. We are to march to-morrow upon Trenton. You are to command the right wing of the advance-guard, and General Greene the left."

. . . . The victory of Trenton followed, and that of Princeton tripped closely on its heels. Despair was turned into joy, and the country began to see that her precious blood had not been spilled in vain. Just at this juncture of affairs, when it was necessary to follow up the tide of victory with vigorous work, the term of enlistment of most of the men expired, and the personal popularity and influence of their leaders was thus put to the test. Would the men go, or could they be induced to stay through another term of enlistment before seeking the respite they desired at their homes? John Stark made an appeal to his regiment not in vain, and every man, without exception, re-enlisted for six weeks longer under the banner of their beloved leader. Then he went to New Hampshire for recruits, and scores flocked around his standard.

But at this time there transpired an act of injustice to the heroic Stark, which the faithful chronicler records with a sense of shame. Through some unaccountable stupidity on the part of those in authority, he was superseded in the command of his regiment by novices in war and in years.

Against this insult to his patriotic services his protest was entered in vain. His high spirit could not brook a subordinate position so undeserved, and there was nothing left for him to do but to resign his commission. This he did, and then returned to his New Hampshire farm, to the labor of the furrow and the scythe. He indulged in no petty or personal spite.

Though he suffered under the wrong inflicted on himself, he loved his country and her cause too well not to lend it his hearty support. All, therefore, whom he could influence, were urged to go to the front. His four sons were sent to battle while he stayed behind to work on the farm. When General Schuyler urged him to remain in the service, he replied, that "an officer who could not maintain his own rank and assert his own rights, could not be trusted to vindicate those of his country."

But circumstances did not long permit the veteran soldier to remain merely a spectator of the ever-memorable scenes of the Revolution. The New Hampshire Grants, as Vermont was then called, were threatened by the invading foe who was approaching through the region of Lake Champlain and Ticonderoga. The speaker of the House at Exeter, in the face of the imminent danger which hung over the homes of Vermont, rose in his seat and pledged his money, his plate and his possessions to the support of the contest. He then proposed Stark as the man who should lead the State forces to check the advance of Burgoyne, and protect their beloved boundaries. Thus, once more was the veteran hero forced into the field, and nobly did he execute the trust reposed in him. The battle of Bennington followed. Colonel Gregg had been ordered to the defence of the town, and Stark went to his support. It was a hot day in August when the battle was fought, and the action lasted for two hours, continuously. Stark said it was the sharpest engagement in which he ever participated, and the result, as every student of history knows, was a complete victory. Burgoyne's men and their Indian allies were sent flying in disorderly retreat, and the pursuit was kept up by

Stark until night interposed its darkness between the victorious Vermont boys and the routed foe. Seven hundred prisoners were captured by our forces, besides many hundred stands of arms and other military accoutrements.

A vote of thanks was tendered by Congress to Stark for this brilliant achievement, and he was immediately invested with the rank of brigadier-general in the American army.

It was at the battle of Bennington that Stark prefaced the action with the famous words:

"We must conquer to-day, my boys, or to-night Molly Stark's a widow!"

After this engagement he joined the army under General Gates at head-quarters, and subsequently was stationed at West Point, where he participated in the trial of Andre.

After the surrender of Cornwallis, General Stark returned once more to his home and farm. He had served his country long and faithfully, and retired from his protracted period of active service beloved by the people and full of honors. He lived to be ninety-four years old and consequently witnessed the war of 1812. He sleeps upon the banks of the Merrimac, nor heeds the noisy rush of the river as it speeds on its mission to the sea. No clash of musketry, no roar of cannon will ever waken him more from this last, deep repose. Men call it death, but if it be death, it is that of the body only, for his memory still lives and speaks to us across the years. It bids us be noble and unselfish, and high of purpose and grand of aim. Will the oncoming generations, who con the story of his life, listen to the preaching of such an example in vain?

PART SECOND.

The Mexican War.

SUBJECTS:

Chapter	Page
XIII. WINFIELD SCOTT	173
XIV. ZACHARY TAYLOR	188
XV. WILLIAM JENKINS WORTH	203
XVI. JOHN E. WOOL	209
XVII. SAM HOUSTON	212
XVIII. JAMES SHIELDS	227
XIX. CHARLES MAY	230

CHAPTER XIII.
WINFIELD SCOTT.

Lineage and Early Life.—A Captain of Artillery.—Court-Martialled. — Queenstown Heights. — Tomahawks.—Fort George.— Battle of Chippewa.—Lundy's Lane.—Wounded.—Public Enthusiasm.—Through a Score of Years.—War in Mexico.—Vera Cruz.—"Don't Expose Yourselves, Men!"—Cerro Gordo.—At Puebla.—Churubusco.—Contreras.—Chapultepec.—Molino del Rey.—City of Mexico Taken.—Grand Plaza Scene.—Results.— "Hail to the Chief!"

IN the unsettled period of civil affairs which succeeded the dawn of American Independence, there were many whom the force of circumstances, united to their own strength of character, brought prominently forward as champions of the nation's honor against foreign insult. Among this distinguished group the striking figure of Winfield Scott occupies a commanding position. Of Scottish descent, he was a Virginiàn by birth, and made his first entry on this world's calendar at Petersburg, June thirteenth, 1786. Between this date and his seventeenth year, old Father Time was kind to the growing boy, and with busy power developed the superb physique for which the future general was noted.

Orphaned at seventeen, he studied law, and in 1806 was admitted to the bar. He practised his profession for two terms in Virginia, and the next year went to South Carolina. It is doubtful whether nature ever intended him for a lawyer; but if she gave a hint in that direction, contrary currents of circumstance unshipped the design. For when in 1807-8 Congress enlarged the army, Scott applied for a commission, and through the influence of an Honorable friend, was appointed a captain of light artillery. He was now afloat on the military channel and drifted steadily towards the great ocean of events which surged threateningly around the young nation. In 1809, Scott was ordered to New Orleans, and during the public agitation occasioned by the Burr intrigue and trial, expressed his mind freely concerning General Wilkinson, whose conduct in connection therewith he regarded as traitorous. For this indiscretion and through the machinations of Wilkinson, he was court-martialled and sentenced to suspension from service for a year. The affair seems to have created rather a favorable effect than otherwise, since he was soon after "complimented by a public dinner, given by many officers and citizens of the neighborhood."

During the year of his suspension he was diligent in the pursuit of military studies, and in July, 1812, a month after war was formally declared with Great Britain, he received the appointment of lieutenant-colonel in the Second Artillery. Immediately afterwards he set out for the Niagara frontier and established his post at Black Rock.

The battle of Queenstown Heights occurred on the thirteenth of October, and though unfortunate in its principal results, it exerted a beneficial effect on the country. The daring of many of the officers rose to the pitch of heroism, and the courage, skill and effectiveness of Colonel Scott were especially conspicuous. The people saw that they had men among them who were fully qualified to lead them to ultimate victory.

SCOTT WOUNDED AT THE BATTLE OF LUNDY'S LANE.

While lodged as a prisoner of war, after this action, at a small hotel in the village of Niagara, Scott came near losing his life at the hands of a couple of brawny savages who sent in a message that they wished to see the "tall American." Not knowing who his strange visitors might be, he went into the entry without suspicion. After a moment of parley the Indians drew their knives and tomahawks, declaring they would kill him. Scott snatched up a long sabre from a pile lying in the corner, and for some uncertain seconds, held the red athletes at bay in their desperate endeavors to close in on him together. Nobody, it seems, was within call; but just at this critical instant, a British officer entered from the street, saw the situation, shouted "The guard!" and the sentinels entering, put an end to the treacherous affair.

The campaign of 1813, which opened brilliantly with the capture of York, the capital of Upper Canada, closed in disaster with the abandonment of the expedition down the St. Lawrence. This was brought about by the unexplainable blunders and delays of some of those in command—conspicuously so in the case of General Wilkinson, who refused to descend the river because General Hampton had refused to join him. But Scott had distinguished himself at the battle and capture of Fort George, the key to the peninsula on the British side of Niagara, tearing down the flag of Britain with his own hands, and also in numerous small actions which reflected great credit on his skilful handling of material as well as his power of grasping situations and making the most of them. In July, he had been promoted to the command of a double regiment, and on March ninth, 1814, he received the appointment of brigadier-general. Immediately afterwards he set out for the Niagara frontier from Albany, joining Major-General Brown. A camp of instruction was established at Sackett's Harbor under Scott, the effectiveness of whose discipline was afterwards amply illustrated on the battle-fields which burst from the storm of war that swept the shores of Niagara.

On the morning of July fourth, Scott's brigade was on the march towards Chippewa, and for sixteen miles a running fight was kept up with the British One Hundredth Regiment, under Marquis Tweedale. At nightfall they were driven across Chippewa River, and the next day the famous battle of that name was fought on the plain between this stream and Street's Creek. The American troops were manœuvred with splendid ability, they fought with great bravery, and the rout of the enemy was complete. The best soldiery of Britain marched over Chippewa bridge that day to meet on the battle-plain the regiments of America, and though the latter were numerically inferior, they proved conclusively that they were "the same sort of men as those who captured whole armies under Burgoyne and Cornwallis." A writer in an English periodical of that day says: "Numerous as were the battles of Napoleon and brave as were his soldiers, I do not believe that even he, the greatest warrior that ever lived, can produce an instance of a contest so well maintained, or, in proportion to the numbers engaged, so bloody as that of Chippewa."

General Brown, in his official report of the battle, says: "Brigadier-General Scott is entitled to the highest praise our country can bestow: to him more than any other man am I indebted for the victory of the fifth of July. His brigade covered itself with glory." Scott was, indeed, the actual commander in this action, and justice awards him the chief laurel won on that far distant day.

On the twenty-fifth of the same month, a little below that sublime spot where the wide waste of waters which rush over the falls of Niagara roar and thunder into the gulf below, and where Lundy's Lane meets the rapid river at right angles, was enacted the scene of conflict which took its name from the locality, and is variously called the battle of "Lundy's Lane," or "Niagara." The action began forty minutes before sunset, and it is recorded that the head of the American column, as it advanced, was encircled by a rainbow— one which is often seen there, formed from the rising spray. The happy omen faithfully prefigured the result; for when, under the cloudy sky of midnight, the battle at length terminated, the Americans were in possession of the field and also the enemy's cannon, which had rained such deadly death into their ranks. In this action General Scott had two horses killed under him, and about eleven o'clock at night he was disabled by a musket-ball wound through the left shoulder. He had previously been wounded, and at this juncture was borne from the fray. He had piloted Miller's regiment through the darkness to the height on Lundy's Lane where the enemy's batteries were posted, and upon which the grand charge was made that decided the battle. Throughout the action he was the leading spirit of the occasion, giving personal direction to the movements of his men, and lending the inspiration of his presence to all parts of the field. The plaudits which press and people afterwards showered on him were certainly well deserved.

His recovery from the dangerous wounds inflicted at Niagara was slow and painful, and when, months afterwards, he journeyed by easy stages, to Philadelphia for treatment, he was greeted along the route by public demonstrations of enthusiasm. At Princeton, particularly, the pale and wounded soldier, with his arm in a sling, was especially honored, and the trustees of New Jersey College conferred on him the honorary degree of Master of Arts.

Six months after the battle of Niagara peace was declared and Scott was ordered to Europe, both for the restoration of his health and also as the confidential diplomatic agent of government. On his return in 1816, he was assigned to the command of the seaboard, with head-quarters at New York. In March, 1817, he married Miss Maria Mayo, of Richmond, Virginia, a lady of reputed beauty and culture.

Near the close of the war of 1812, Congress passed a vote of thanks in which General Scott was complimented, not only for his part in the actions of Chippewa and Lundy's Lane, but "for his universal good conduct throughout the war," a higher meed of praise than was paid, by that body, to any other officer.

For the succeeding twenty years General Scott retained the same command, and during that time resided at New York and Elizabethtown, New Jersey. Much concerning the occurrences of these years, as connected with him, must be passed over which it were pleasant to relate; events which were full of public interest at the time, but which our space excludes. Such was the Black Hawk war, and such the mournful interest attached to Scott in connection with the Asiatic cholera, which broke out with so sudden a terror among the troops in 1832, midsummer, after having travelled all over Europe. The ravages of this dread destroyer were more appalling than those of the sword, and the panic produced by it proportionately greater. More than half the troops embarked at Buffalo for Illinois, took their eternal flight to the world of spirits, through this silent but powerful foe. Scott's humane conduct during this crisis, exhibited him, says an eye-witness, "not only as the hero of battles but as the hero of humanity."

We pass rapidly in review the Nullification schemes in South Carolina which almost resulted in open war and the careful and wise conduct of Scott in the midst of this agitation; the "Compromise Act," and then the Seminole war in Florida; also, the trouble which again broke out on the Niagara frontier, the Cherokee controversy, his noble address to those Indians, his call once more to the Northern frontier between Vermont and Canada, where hostile feeling rode rampant over disputed boundary lines, the tranquillizing result of his visit, his reputation as a pacificator, his prospects for the Presidency in 1839, and last, but not least, his entrance upon the theatre of the Mexican war in 1846.

General Scott reached the Rio Grande about the first of January, 1847, and on the seventh of March, embarked his forces, twelve thousand strong, on transports bound for Vera Cruz, at which point they effected a brilliant landing, without accident or loss, a little before sunset on the same day. The entire army occupied its assigned positions by the twelfth, and the investment of the city was complete. The guns of Vera Cruz and the famous castle of San Juan d'Ulloa kept up a constant firing, but without injury to the American troops. For fifteen days the beleaguered city was a theatre of terrible activity. The screech of shells, the roar of cannon, the explosion of shot reverberated through its streets, and poured their fire on the castle. General Landero, commanding the Mexican forces, at last made overtures of surrender, and on the twenty-seventh, articles of capitulation were signed. Five thousand prisoners surrendered on parole and nearly five hundred pieces of artillery were captured. The environment had been skilful in plan and decisive in strength. On the morning of the twenty-ninth, America's flag, blown by the winds of the gulf, floated from the renowned castle of d'Ulloa, land of the Aztecs! It is said that, during this siege, when Scott was once walking along the trenches, he observed that the soldiers would frequently rise up and look over the parapet. "Down, down, men!" he cried, "don't expose yourselves!" "But, general," said one, "*you* are exposed." "Oh," replied Scott, "generals, now-a-days, can be made out of anybody, but *men* can't be had."

Ten days after the surrender of Vera Cruz, the division of Twiggs, which had been detached from Taylor's command, was marching towards the mountain heights of Cerro Gordo, defended by Santa Anna with fifteen thousand men. Scott, with skilful foresight, after inspecting the position, ordered a road to be cut to the left of the Cerro Gordo crest, which by winding around the base of the mountain, would ascend in rear of the Mexican forts and behind the entire Mexican position. "The labor, the courage of American soldiers accomplished it." Nor did the Mexicans discover it for three days.

On the seventeenth, Twiggs, under fire of grape and musketry, had carried the hill below Cerro Gordo, above the new road. On that day, too, the prophetic order of Scott was issued, containing the movements of attack, battle and victory, as, with one exception, they were the next day carried out. "The enemy's position, on the night of the seventeenth, seemed impregnable. On their right, rolled a deep river. From its sides rose a chain of mountains one thousand feet high, crowned with heavy batteries, and over all, the tower of Cerro Gordo." Behind these fortressed ramparts fifteen thousand troops were in waiting to defend the position. Under cover of darkness, one thousand men from the brave division of Twiggs, divided into relief-parties of five hundred each, dragged by hand, a battery up the steep sides of the captured hill below Cerro Gordo, a position commanding every defence of the enemy except the fortress of Cerro Gordo itself. *That* must be stormed. And the next morning, in the teeth of its belching guns, the gallant Harney led the storming party. Nor stopped, though the front ranks sank under a withering blaze, until with shouts that echoed from the mountain sides, those heroic men entered the citadel, tore down the Mexican banner and reqlaced it with their own conquering ensign. The army of Santa Anna were flying in all directions and the pursuit was kept up until noon. That general made his escape by way of the Jalapa road. "Three thousand prisoners, forty-three pieces of bronze artillery, five thousand stand of arms and five generals, with the munitions and materials of war" were captured in this single battle. The masterly manner in which the strength and defences of the enemy's position were overcome, reflects undying lustre on the generalship of Scott; but not more than does his humane treatment of and sympathy with his wounded soldiery, after the battle. He visited them in person and saw that they had the best attendance.

"From the field of Cerro Gordo, the rout of the Mexican army was complete." The city of Jalapa was taken, the town of Perote captured and Puebla occupied. From the shores of the Mexican Gulf, the invading army had marched two hundred miles into the heart of the Aztec land.

On the tenth of August, the American forces set out on their advance from Puebla to the city of Mexico. They followed the stage route through and over the Cordilleras, leading down into the far-famed and beautiful valley of Mexico. On the eighteenth, they were concentrated in that valley and Scott had established his head-quarters at San Augustine. The crisis of the campaign—the capture of the city of the Montezumas—was now the problem presented. Santa Anna was there with a well-appointed army and two strong lines of defences. Near the city was *Churubusco*, with its intrenchments and garrisoned stone houses. To the left rose the fortified hill of *Contreras*. Nearer yet loomed *Chapultepec*, also a strongly fortified hill, and at its foot, *Molino del Rey* (the King's Mill), and a fortified stone wall. "These defences covered every practicable road to the city," and, as Scott had foreseen, must be taken before Mexico could be entered. At three o'clock on the morning of the twentieth, decisive action began, and before the sun sank from sight that day, all these formidable works had been brilliantly stormed and taken—three battles being in progress at once! Scott *might* have crowned these results by marching victoriously into the city itself on the same day: but wishing to "conquer a peace" as he expressed it, and avoid any unnecessary shedding of blood, he halted his army at its gates; and on the twenty-second, commissioners to treat of peace were appointed on both sides. But Santa Anna violated the armistice, and on the seventh of September it was terminated and the victorious army resumed its triumphant advance.

On the eighth, the immediate defences of the city were taken; and on the fourteenth, after surmounting almost interminable difficulties, the army marched into the Grand Plaza of Mexico. The stars and stripes were given to the breeze, and, just at this moment, Scott, in full uniform, rode through the column to the Plaza. "A tremendous *hurrah*" broke from the ranks. The old chieftain, waving his cap, while tears ran down his cheeks, exclaimed: "My heart is with you!" It was nine o'clock in the morning, and the Second Dragoons played "Yankee Doodle," as he made his way to the National Palace.

"Wherever Scott moved among the soldiers he greeted them with warm affection. . . . These short but emphatic addresses had a profound effect on the men. As he passed a portion of the Rifle Regiment, he returned their salute, saying with emphasis: 'Brave Rifles! Veterans! You have been baptized in fire and blood and have come out steel!'"

History will place its greenest chaplet on the brow of this war-worn hero when "it will be remembered that he was not only made illustrious by battles, but was also graced by humanity to a fallen foe, and a generous gratitude to his companions-in-arms."

This wonderful Mexican campaign, which terminated on the seventeenth of September, speaks for itself in the "eight battles gloriously won; two cities besieged and taken; two castles and numerous strongholds, with thousands of prisoners and an immense quantity of all the munitions of war." The ultimate results were more than a "conquered peace." Mexico was restored to order. California, Utah and New Mexico were added to our possessions for the peaceful entry of freedom and thrift. New enterprises awoke. The gold mines of Sierra Nevada gave us their wealth, and the Pacific coast was ours, whence commercial intercourse with Eastern nations could be maintained.

In this campaign, Scott demonstrated the splendor of his military genius, his energy, his executive power. He made sure aim at the high mark of success and achieved it. His victories were brilliant and—to his eternal credit be it spoken—their harsher features were softened by his humanitarian conduct.

What need we say more of the war-begrimed and splendid old soldier? His magnificent reception in the city of New York, on his return to the United States, the steady course of subsequent events—these require no mention here. Civic wreath and song are his, and "Hail to the Chief," his most appropriate requiem. We see his tall figure looming for the instant athwart the horizon of public affairs, as the thunders of civil strife first break over Charleston Harbor in 1861, and then it disappears forever. We prefer rather to remember him as he reined his warhorse on the Grand Plaza of the City of Mexico, surrounded by the tried ranks of veteran soldiery, and framed in by the ancient halls of the Montezumas. The fruits of victory which there culminated, are his best eulogy, and appropriately transmit to posterity his honored name and fame.

CHAPTER XIV.

ZACHARY TAYLOR.

His Characteristics.—Duty, his Constant Watchword.—Lineage.—Early Plantation Life.—Indian Foes.—Lieutenant in the United States Army.—At Fort Harrison.—Battle with Tecumseh.—Brevet Major.—The Florida War.—Okeechobee.—Ordered to Corpus Christi.—Palo Alto.—Resaca de la Palma.—Promoted to Major-General.—At *Montery.—Bloody Buena Vista.—Colonel Marshall's Opinion.—General Taylor's Dislike for a Uniform.—Ovations on his Return.—Elected President.—Stern Death.—Last Scenes.—Universal Sorrow.

THE blaze of glory which is concentrated upon the name and life of Zachary Taylor, reveals a hero as true in metal, as sterling in virtue, as intrepid in action and tender of heart, as ever lifted sword in the cause of honor or country. On him has fallen that most sacred mantle of renown woven from the fabric of a people's confidence, and lovingly bestowed—not as upon a being of superior race to be worshipped, but because he was a leader from among themselves—truly *of* the people.

He was honored with their fullest trust in his integrity, and with their largest faith in his uprightness as a man. As Mr. Webster truly said, the best days of the Roman republic afforded no brighter example of a man, who, receiving the plaudits of a grateful nation and clothed in the highest authority of State, reached that pinnacle by more honest means; who could not be accused of the smallest intrigue or of pursuing any devious ways to political emolument in order to gratify personal ambition. All the circumstances of his rise and popularity, from the beginning of his career, when, amid blood and smoke, he made the heroic defence of Fort Harrison, to the wonderful battles of Palo Alto, Resaca, and Buena Vista, and at last the attainment of the President's chair—all repel the slightest suspicion of sinister motive or a wish for individual aggrandizement. The unwavering rule of his life—his guide in every action, was the simple watchword, "duty."

As to his qualities of leadership, they shone out in high relief, from first to last. In the war of 1812, he was only a captain, yet at Fort Harrison he inspired the scanty garrison with a belief in his power and they gave him their devoted support. In the Florida campaign he commanded only a brigade, yet he seemed to infuse into every soldier the most courageous bravery. In the beginning of the war with Mexico he marched into action at the head of a single division. And when this force afterwards swelled into an army, it did not prove too much for the resources of its commanding general. The frowning heights and barricaded streets of Monterey, bristling with ten thousand Mexicans, did not daunt him. What though he had only six thousand men with which to hold them in siege? The assault was fearlessly made, the streets were stormed, the heights were carried, the city was won—and kept.

The brilliant victory of Buena Vista, where five thousand Americans hurled back and repulsed a tumultuous Mexican horde of twenty thousand, only reiterates the same marvellous story of superior leadership. "Every rank was steadied, every eye kindled to enthusiasm by the presence of this man, beloved of his soldiers, whose resolution never faltered, whose spirit rose highest where perils swarmed thickest."

Fresh from these splendid achievements, he received the nomination for president over the names of Henry Clay, Daniel Webster, and General Scott. It was a spontaneous expression of the people's confidence, unheralded and unsought. And when he was triumphantly elected over the democratic and free-soil candidates—General Cass, Martin Van Buren and Charles Francis Adams—he accepted the high office in a spirit of humility and simple compliance with duty.

Descended from a distinguished English family which emigrated to Virginia in 1692, his family name is closely interwoven with the history and growth of that State. His father, Colonel Richard Taylor, was a companion-in-arms of Washington, and served throughout the Revolution, an active participant in its principal battles. Zachary was his third son, and a year after his birth he removed to a large Kentucky plantation near Louisville. Here, amid farm life and labor, passed the boyhood of Zachary, and in attendance at such a school as the times and country afforded. But even this life was not altogether tranquil: for Indian depredations and massacres in the neighborhood were of frequent occurrence, and the road between his father's plantation and the school-house was a journey full of hazard. But the ever-watchful and over-guarding Fates preserved the life of the noble boy for his future high destiny, and thus, in hardy sports, in hunting through the trackless forest and in marshalling mimic soldiery, the first eighteen years of his life fled swiftly by. Then occurred the death of his brother Hancock, who was a lieutenant in the United States army. Zachary applied to Mr. Jefferson for the vacant commission and received it. He was therefore only eighteen years old when, on May third, 1808, he was appointed first lieutenant in the Seventh Regiment. At this time the war excitement preceding the outbreak of 1812 had risen to great height on account of the seizure of the United States frigate "Chesapeake" on the high seas, by the British frigate "Leopard." Young Lieutenant Taylor partook of the prevailing excitement; but from this period until war was openly declared in 1812, there is little to record in his history. A few weeks previous to this date he had been placed in command of Fort Harrison, a block-house and stockade on the Wabash, about fifty miles above Vincennes, which had been built by General Harrison, Governor of the Northwest Territory, for frontier defence. A captain's commission from President Madison accompanied his appointment as commander of the fort, and as this was one of the most advanced posts on the outskirts of the Indian territory, the young captain was thus thrown into the front of hostilities.

Tecumseh had selected this as a point of attack, and on September fifth, 1812, after making an ineffectual attempt to get possession of the fort by strategy, he led a furious assault on the works at the head of four hundred Indians. That night, at about eleven o'clock, the sharp report of a sentry's rifle cut the air, and a moment after, an alarm of fire was given. The lower block-house was in flames, and for a few despairing moments the little garrison of fifty men, two-thirds of whom were disabled from sickness, were thrown into the wildest confusion. Between the terror of fire and the tomahawk, they thought death certain.

But the young commander had grasped the situation and saw that by throwing off part of the roof where the buildings joined, the fire could be stopped and breastworks thrown up in the breach. Orders to this end were instantly given, and "never," said Captain Taylor, in his official report, "did men act with more firmness or desperation." For seven hours the conflict raged with undiminished fury, but the defence was conducted with such skill and determined resistance that at six o'clock the savage foe retired from the fort repulsed, having suffered severely from the well-directed fire of the brave little band.

The fame of this noble conduct at Fort Harrison spread throughout the west, and did not pass unnoticed by government. The young commander received official thanks for his services, and President Madison conferred on him the rank of major by brevet—the first instance of the kind given in this country.

His services between this period and the Florida war furnished no opportunity for the display of his special talents. In 1814, he commanded an expedition against the British and Indians on Rock River. In 1815, when peace was declared and the army reduced, he was returned to his former rank of captain; whereupon he immediately resigned and retired to his Louisville plantation. In 1816, his former rank of major having been restored, he was ordered to Green Bay, Wisconsin.

Three years later he went to New Orleans on military duty, and in 1819 was commissioned lieutenant-colonel. In 1832, he was promoted to the rank of colonel. Then followed an expedition against Black Hawk, which took him to Fort Crawford at Prairie du Chien. In 1837, he was ordered to the seat of the Seminole war in Florida and placed in command of the United States forces operating against Osceola, their principal chief. Marching from Fort Gardner for the everglades, with a force of eleven hundred men, he encountered all the obstacles presented by cypress swamps, marshy thickets, and a wet, yielding soil. On the twenty-fifth of December, they came upon the edge of a dense swamp near Lake Okeechobee, where the Indians were gathered in force, and after halting, to form line of battle, charged their unseen foe across the sedgy morass, into which they sank knee-deep at every step. When half way across the slough, the Indians opened fire upon them and the brave troops were mowed down by scores. Yet, undismayed, they struggled on. Against their solid ranks the Seminoles broke in disorder, rallied, were broken again, and again gathered themselves together for a last vain resistance. Nothing could stand before the advance of that unflinching column. The Indians were driven from their position, and the renowned victory of Okeechobee had become history.

After this battle, Taylor was promoted to the rank of brevet brigadier-general and given the chief command in Florida. In 1840, he was placed over the first military department of the southwest, and remained at Forts Jessup and Gibson until the beginning of the Mexican war.

On March first, 1845, Congress passed the resolution admitting Texas into the Union, claiming the Rio Grande as her southwestern boundary. Mexico disputed the claim beyond the Neuces, and prepared to defend the disputed territory or perhaps re-conquer the entire lost province of Texas.

General Taylor was ordered to Corpus Christi in November, occupying that place with an army of four thousand men. On March eighth, 1846, he advanced in the direction of the Rio Grande and built Fort Brown, opposite the port of Metamoras. The Mexican General Ampudia demanded that he should retire across the Neuces while negotiations were pending; but General Taylor replied that his instructions did not permit his compliance with the demand. Whereupon, General Arista, who succeeded Ampudia, crossed the Rio Grande with a force of six thousand. General Taylor had twenty-three hundred men with which to meet them.

On the evening of May seventh, General Taylor and his little army set out on their return march from Point Isabel to Metamoras, and the next morning, when within a few miles of that place, on reaching a level plateau bordered with trees, called Palo Alto, they encountered the Mexicans under General Arista, drawn up in battle array across the road.

When within sight of the enemy, General Taylor halted his men, gave them an hour's rest and then formed them in order of battle. When within a few hundred yards of the Mexicans, a heavy artillery fire was opened upon them, which was returned. The opposing columns began to waver, when General Arista ordered a cavalry charge. But a steady fire of artillery from Major Ringgold and Ridgeley's batteries continued to pour destruction into their ranks, opening great gaps in the advancing line of horsemen, until they staggered and reeled and at last fled in precipitate haste.

For a short time after this the battle raged furiously,

until one of Captain Duncan's pieces ignited the prairie grass. Clouds of smoke rolled up from the ground, obscuring friend and foe. Both armies reformed their battle-line, and when the smoke dispersed, the Mexican infantry made a second advance. But their ranks were mowed down as before, and soon both infantry and cavalry were flying in disorder. Kind night, which often puts an end to strife, interposed between vanquished and victor, and forbade pursuit. Six hundred dead and wounded Mexicans left on the field, emphasized this victory. But the next day, May ninth, at three o'clock in the afternoon, the contest was continued at Resaca de la Palma, a deep ravine in an open strip of land crossed by the road leading to Metamoras.

The Mexicans had entrenched themselves in this ditch, which gave them a position of great natural strength. The battle was again opened by the artillery. The American batteries were pushed close to the enemy's line, and the havoc was awful—the ground being literally heaped with dead and wounded.

The Mexicans were forced across the ravine, but their artillery was so well posted in the gullies, that Captain May was ordered to charge the guns with his dragoons. With resistless bravery, May and his men swept down upon the gunners, and after a fearful struggle, at last carried the batteries.

The Tampico battalion were the last to yield. Their standard-bearer tore the flag from its staff, and was flying with the precious possession, when he and his trophy were both captured.

The rout was complete. Arista's head-quarters, his plate and private property, arms, ammunition, pack saddles—all fell into the hands of the Americans. Seventeen hundred men under General Taylor had on this field repulsed and put to flight six thousand Mexicans. The enemy's loss was one thousand, the American one hundred and ten.

In June, Congress promoted General Taylor to the full rank of major-general, and throughout the Union he was voted testimonials of gratitude for his heroic services.

In September, he marched against Monterey with six thousand six hundred and twenty-five men, and after ten days' siege and three days' desperate fighting, Ampudia capitulated, and the fortressed town was entered and occupied by American troops.

General Taylor now established his head-quarters at Monterey, but on the twentieth of December, took up his march for Victoria. General Quitman entered that place without opposition on the twenty-ninth, and on January fourth, General Taylor arrived with Twiggs' division. News was received that Santa Anna, who had been placed in command of the Mexican forces, designed making an advance in force, and it was at this inopportune time that General Scott withdrew the greater portion of the troops under General Taylor, to aid in his operations on the Gulf.

On learning of the approach of Santa Anna, he advanced to Agua Nueva from Monterey, where he had again taken up his head-quarters. He remained at Agua Nueva, twenty miles south of Saltillo, until the twenty-first of February. On that day intelligence was received of Santa Anna's approach at the head of his entire army. Believing that the mountain pass of Buena Vista, eleven miles to the rear, would be a much more desirable point from which to confront the overwhelming numbers of the enemy, he fell back to that place, took a strong position, and calmly awaited the onset of Santa Anna's hosts. The road here narrows into a defile, with a deep ravine on the right, and on the left, the mountain ranges of the Sierra Madre, towering two thousand feet high. The American troops were disposed along a spur of foot hills, running from the mountain nearly to the ravine, the space of ground between the hills and ravine being occupied by five pieces of light artillery under Captain Washington. Wide ravines were between the two armies. The nature of the ground was such as to render almost useless the artillery and cavalry of the enemy.

In the choice of this position, General Taylor exhibited the same masterly forethought which had distinguished his previous military operations. Some hours elapsed after these dispositions had been made, before the battle commenced. It was about four o'clock in the afternoon of the twenty-second of February, when the clouds of dust rolling up from the direction of Agua Nueva, announced the approach of the enemy. Two thousand lancers, with weopons glinting in the sunlight, composed the leading division. And what seemed an immense host, followed.

The Kentucky cavalry and Arkansas troops, posted near the mountain as skirmishers, brought on the action, engaging fifteen hundred of the enemy's light troops, deployed on the mountain top. Then followed the brilliant but deadly conflict, in which skill and generalship proved their superiority to numbers. The battle raged until night, and on the morning of the twenty-third, was renewed with added desperation. The history of that day was a succession of advances and retreats. The enemy moved in three heavy columns upon the American lines, turning their left. But the centre and right stood like rocks, repelled the battle-wave, and at length, drove the enemy back. The Mexican infantry on the right were driven from the field and two cavalry charges were gallantly repulsed. At this stage in the action, Santa Anna massed his entire army into one column and threw them with almost irresistible force upon the American front. It felt the shock severely, wavered and fell back for a short distance, when the artillery came gallantly to the rescue and saved the day. On the evening of the twenty-third, the opposing armies occupied nearly the same relative position as in the morning. But the Americans had won a splendid victory, and during the night the Mexicans retreated. They had lost two thousand men in this desperate conflict. The American loss was placed at seven hundred and forty-six.

General Taylor, during this battle, seemed to be "everywhere at the same time, animating, ordering and persuading his men to remember the day and their country and strike home for both!" When the breast of his coat was pierced by a canister-shot, he coolly remarked, "These balls are growing excited." "Throughout the action, he was where the shot fell hottest and thickest, and constantly evinced the greatest quickness of conception, fertility of resource, and a cool, unerring judgment not to be baffled."

Deprived of the greater portion of his troops

previous to the action, surrounded by an army four times larger than his own, and in the heart of the enemy's country, he was probably the only man, says the Baltimore *American*, who would have fought the battle of Buena Vista; the only man probably who could have won it.

His humanity and kindness of heart were as pronounced as his military genius. Perhaps one of the best sketches extant of this hero's character was given by Colonel Humphrey Marshall, of Kentucky, in a speech at a barbecue, tendered to the Kentucky volunteers. "If I tried to express," he said, "in the fewest words, what manner of man General Taylor is, I should say that in his manners and appearance, he is one of the common people of this country. He might be transferred from his tent at Monterey to this assembly and he would not be remarked among this crowd of respectable old farmers, as a man at all distinguished from those around him. Perfectly temperate in his habits; perfectly plain in his dress; entirely unassuming in his manners, he appears to be an old gentleman in fine health, whose thoughts are not turned upon personal appearance and who has no point about him to attract particular attention. In his intercourse with men he is free, frank and manly. He plays off none of the airs of some great men whom I have met, who try to preserve their reputation by studied gravity; as who should say:

"'I am Sir Oracle:
When I ope my mouth let no dog bark!'

. . . . . He is an honest man. I do not mean by that merely that he does not cheat nor lie. I mean that he is a man who never dissembles and who scorns all disguises. He neither acts a part among his friends nor assumes to be what he is not. . . . He is a man of rare good judgment. . . . He is a firm man and possessed of great energy of character. . . . He is a benevolent man. . . . No one who had seen him after the battle of Buena Vista, as he ordered the wagons to bring in the wounded from the battle-field, and heard him as he cautioned his own men that the wounded of the enemy were to be treated with mercy, could doubt that he was alive to all the kinder impulses of our nature. . . . He was about five feet six inches high, very thick-set and slightly stoop-shouldered; . . . had remarkably short legs in proportion to the length of his body, . . . a fine head, high forehead, keen penetrating eye and firm, compressed lips; . . . his face was almost always lit up by a benevolent smile; . . . was extremely fond of a joke and ever ready with a witty repartee, or a kind word for all who addressed him. . . . He had an unconquerable dislike for a uniform, and was generally seen in warm weather with a linen round-about, cotton pantaloons, straw hat, and the celebrated brown overcoat that protected him during his Florida campaigns in cold or rainy seasons. . . . The most remarkable traits of General Taylor's character were the wisdom and foresight with which he laid his plans, the energy and promptness with which he executed them, and his firmness, decision and self-possession in the hour of trial. No emergency, however sudden, no danger, however threatening, and no contingency of whatever nature, were ever able to throw him off his guard."

And thus is faintly drawn the portrait of the brave and simple general whom his soldiers loved as few commanders have been loved, and who was lifted on a vast tidal wave of popular enthusiasm into the nation's chair of State.

After Buena Vista, he retired to Monterey, where he remained until November, 1847, when, growing tired of a forced inactivity, he asked permission of the government to return to the United States. He reached his home in Baton Rouge towards the last of that month. His arrival in the United States was the occasion of the wildest demonstrations of joy and enthusiasm from the people. Assembled multitudes greeted him everywhere with warm welcome. Invitations poured in upon him from town, city and State, and New Orleans honored him with bonfires and a public procession.

Before his return from Mexico, after the battles of Palo Alto and Resaca, his name had been proposed as a presidential nominee; and after the added renown gained by Monterey and Buena Vista, he became at once the most popular candidate. Newark, New Jersey, first set the example of a formal nomination at a meeting which convened irrespective of party preferences. These meetings soon became general through the United States, and the nominations tendered were without discrimination from Whigs, Democrats and Independents alike. "There seemed, indeed, to be almost one universal voice from one end of the Union to the other, in favor of his nomination." With this state of sentiment, so widespread, his triumphant election was a matter of course. He was inaugurated President on Monday, March fifth, 1849, and his opening address was in keeping with the man; full of strength, simplicity and manly avowal of principle. But his reign, though full of honor, was brief. On July ninth, 1850, it was ended by the stern arbitrament of death, just as political entanglements of a serious nature began to manifest themselves. The deep grief of the heart-stricken group which gathered around the dying hero's bed, was only less poignant than that which communicated itself to the nation at large: for never, between the days of Washington and Lincoln, has there passed one so universally and sincerely mourned.

Just before dissolution he was asked if he was comfortable. "Very," he replied; "but the storm, in passing, has swept away the trunk."

His last words were, "I have endeavored to do my duty: I am prepared to die. My only regret is in leaving behind me the friends I love." This utterance, sublime in its simplicity, the outspoken consciousness of a pure and upright life, gave token of his devotion to principle to the last, and was worthy the closing moments of this patriot chief.

A people's mourning lamentations swept after him as his brave spirit parted company with earth.

> "Thus, clothed with many scars,
> Bursting these prison bars,
> Up to his native stars
> His soul ascended!"

He sleeps on the immortal couch of the hero, draped in the beloved flag of country, beneath whose starry folds he fought so gloriously. In imitation of another, let us reverently pronounce the parting words, Glorious leader! intrepid soul! great heart! hail and farewell!

CHAPTER XV.
WILLIAM JENKINS WORTH.

Early Life.—The War of 1812.—At West Point.—The Seminole War.—With Taylor in Mexico.—At Monterey.—Given an Independent Command.—Description of the Assault.—His Generalship.—Storming of Federacion Hill.—Conducting the Capitulation.—At Vera Cruz.—Perote and Puebla.—Capture of El Molino del Rey.—Storming of Chapultepec.—Brevetted Major-General.—Sword Presentations.—Monument in Madison Square.

THE famous battles of Chippewa and Niagara in the war of 1812, first gave to the outside world a hint of the fine military qualities of William Jenkins Worth. He was born in Hudson, on the Hudson River, of an old English family, and though only eighteen when the war broke out, decided without hesitation, to enter the army. He became private secretary to Major-General Lewis, who recommended him to General Scott, and he was thereupon immediately appointed *aide* on that officer's staff.

In the official report of Niagara, he received honorable mention for his bravery, and in August, 1814, became a captain. When the war, at length, ended, he was stationed at West Point for several years, as instructor of tactics. He afterwards received the appointment of colonel of the Eighth Regiment, and on the outbreak of the Seminole war, was ordered to Florida. His operations in connection with the red warriors of Osceola were so satisfactory and terminated so successfully, that at the close of the war, government conferred on him the rank of brevet brigadier-general.

When, in 1846, Taylor was ordered to Mexico, with his "Army of Occupation," General Worth joined him as second in command. While opposite Metamoras on the Rio Grande, a dispute, regarding military etiquette, arose between Worth and Colonel Twiggs, in consequence of which Worth resigned his commission and went to Washington. On arriving there and learning that Taylor's army was in great danger on the Rio Grande, he immediately asked permission to withdraw his resignation and return to his troops. His request being complied with, he retraced his steps and reported at General Taylor's headquarters, reaching the Rio Grande just previous to the taking of Metamoras.

At the siege and storming of Monterey, he was assigned an independent command. The difficult task was given him of storming the chain of batteries on Federacion and Independencia Hills, which he did under a terrific fire—it being impossible, as he said, to mask the movements of the storming party. An eye-witness of the scene thus speaks of it: "The position General Worth then occupied might have been considered as critical as it was dangerous. Separated from the main body of the army, his communication cut off and no possible route less than eight miles to retain it, with scanty supplies of provisions for four days, surrounded by gorges and passes of the mountains, from whose summits belched forth shot, shell and grape, he was liable at any moment to be attacked by an overwhelming force in the direction of Saltillo, which had been reported to be daily expected. . . . .

It was feared, too, from his impetuous nature, that he would rush his command into unnecessary danger by some rash and desperate attempt. But it was not so. He was collected, calm and cool, and bore himself with that proud, resolute and commanding mien which inspired men and officers alike with confidence. He never appeared better than on that day; and all felt that with Worth, they were sure of victory. He knew that General Taylor had staked the issue of the battle on him, and he felt the responsibility that rested on the course he should pursue.

"As he surveyed with his glass the enemy's works, he seemed to feel that not a moment was to be lost. He saw, at once, that it would be necessary to carry by storm the battery on Federacion Hill, as well as the fort called Soldada—as these two batteries commanded the approaches from the Saltillo road. . . . It was now about twelve o'clock, and the meridian sun poured down its hottest rays. Before us stood the steep and rugged hill about three hundred and eighty feet high, whose slopes were covered with thick and thorny chapparal. A swarm of Mexicans crowned the height, while its cannon looked down at us in defiance; . . . the men looked forward to meet death calmly in the face. . . . General Worth rode up as the command moved off, and, pointing to the height, said: 'Men, you are to take that hill and I know you will do it!' With one response they replied, '*We will.*' . . . The words of Worth had nerved every arm, and hearts swelled with that proud feeling of enthusiasm which makes men indomitable before the foe."

The streets of Monterey were heavily barricaded

with masonry, and the Mexican troops fought from the tops of houses, sheltered behind parapets, piled with sand-bags.

During a cessation of hostilities previous to the surrender, Ampudia met General Taylor at Worth's head-quarters, and Worth was appointed principal of the delegation to negotiate the capitulation. It is said he contributed more than any other man to a final settlement of the pending issues. General Taylor, in his report of the victory, expresses his obligation for the efficient aid rendered by Worth at this momentous siege.

General Worth subsequently took possession of Saltillo, where he remained until the middle of January, when he was ordered to join Scott at Vera Cruz. An eye-witness of the brilliant landing of our army on the Mexican coast says: "General Worth, certainly the most useful man in command here, had a smart brush with a body of Mexicans last night (March twelfth) and this morning, in which they were beaten. A cemetery, about one mile from the city, was taken possession of and fortified by General Worth." He "received the commendations of General Scott and was appointed to negotiate the terms of surrender of Vera Cruz." He was also appointed military governor of the city, but shortly afterwarbs led his army on its march to the capital.

At Cerro Gordo, he supported General Twiggs in his attack, and in conjunction with him, captured the redoubt. On April twenty-second he marched upon and captured the town of Perote, and after chasing Santa Anna with fifteen hundred lancers across the plains of Amasoca, entered and took possession of Puebla.

On the seventeenth of August, General Worth left Puebla and renewed his march to the capital. He established himself at the hacienda of Buvera, where the enemy's batteries opened upon him with a hot fire. On the twentieth he was ordered to aid in the attack on Valencia, and subsequently he captured San Antonia.

Following close on these victories came the brilliant capture of El Molino del Rey, an apparently impregnable position, directly under the guns and castle of Chapultepec. It was composed of a group of strong stone buildings adjoining the grove at the foot of the hill, on whose summit Chapultepec stood.

This battle was fought and won on the eighth of September, 1847, under the immediate command of Major-General Worth. The enemy was driven from these strong works by five hundred picked men and officers, constituting an assaulting party. The slaughter was terrible. But no higher exhibition of courage could be presented, than was furnished at this desperate assault, by both men and their commanders. A participator in the action says: "General Worth commenced the attack at early daylight, and in less than two hours every point was carried, all the cannon of the enemy were in our possession, an immense quantity of ammunition captured, and nearly one thousand men, among them fifty-three officers, taken prisoners.

"For more than an hour the battle raged with a violence not surpassed since the Mexican war commenced, and so great was the odds opposed, that for some time the result was doubtful. The force of the enemy has been estimated at from twelve to fifteen thousand, strongly posted behind breastworks, and to attack them our small force of scarcely eight thousand was obliged to approach on an open plain and without the least cover; but their dauntless courage carried them over every obstacle, and notwithstanding the Mexicans fought with a valor rare for them, they were finally routed from one point after another until all were driven and dispersed. The defeat was total."

On the thirteenth Chapultepec was stormed and taken with equal bravery, General Worth and his command rendering distinguished service in its reduction; thereby contributing largely to the victorious result which placed in our hands the ancient city of the Montezumas. For his services in the Mexican war, Worth was brevetted major-general and received swords from Congress, from the State of New York, and from his native county. After the war he was placed in command of the "department of the southwest," which he retained until his death in 1849. A monument was erected to his memory by the city of New York, in Madison Square, where it yet proclaims the esteem in which he was held by the great metropolis.

CHAPTER XVI.

JOHN E. WOOL.

War of 1812.—Wool's Volunteer Corps.—Captaincy in the Thirteenth.—Bravery at Queenstown.—Death of General Brock.—Battle of Plattsburg.—Promoted for Gallantry.—Letter from President Madison.—Another Promotion.—Mexican War.—The March to Monclova.—Capture of Parras.—The Mission of Mercy.—Buena Vista.—Wool Entrusted with the Details.—Birthplace.—Where he Died.—Fortress Monroe.—*Hic Jacet.*—The Chief's War Horse.—Military Funeral.

WHEN the first wave of the war of 1812 surged over the land, John E. Wool was found in the patriot ranks, assisting in raising and organizing a volunteer corps. Soon afterwards, his efforts were rewarded by a captaincy in the Thirteenth Infantry. At Queenstown, in the face of a terrible fire, he charged and took a battery that was playing havoc among our ranks, and when the British General Brock attempted to retake it, Captain Wool tore down a white flag raised by one of his men, and a second time charged and defeated their advancing ranks with conspicuous success. In this charge, General Brock fell a sacrifice to the fortunes of war.

During the campaign of 1813, Wool's gallantry was so marked as to win for him the rank of major. At the battle of Plattsburg, Major Wool so stubbornly contested the enemy's advance on the Beekmantown road, and won such encomiums for his behavior on the field, that he was brevetted lieutenant-colonel. A very complimentary letter from President Madison accompanied the announcement, stating that the rank was conferred on account of bravery at Plattsburg.

After the close of the war, he continued in the military profession, doing service in a variety of ways, and in June, 1841, was commissioned brigadier-general. In the war with Mexico, he was entrusted with the command of an expedition against the provinces, and marched his army over the country to the city of Monclova. Here he was met by the governor, who surrendered the place without parley. Soon afterwards General Taylor ordered him to move upon the city of Parras, which he reached on the sixth of December, 1846. The people of this place became so much attached to him, that on his march to Saltillo, the ladies offered their services if he would leave his sick in their care—an offer which they afterwards made good.

At Buena Vista, General Wool was placed in immediate command of the troops, the details of action having been committed to him by General Taylor. During the progress of the battle, when Santa Anna sent a message to Taylor desiring to know what he wanted, General Wool was despatched to the Mexican chief with the reply, and afterwards when the army encamped at Walnut Springs, three miles from Monterey, Taylor gave the command over to General Wool, while he made a visit to his family in the United States. The greatest confidence seems to have been reposed in him, and he was always spoken of by his chief in complimentary terms.

Wool was born in Orange county, New York, and resided in the city of Troy, in that State, from 1812, or earlier, until his death, which took place at the close of the last war. At its outbreak he was placed in command of Fortress Monroe, soon after Major Anderson retired from Sumter. In the subsequent rush of greater events, his star was eclipsed in the splendor of other names which loomed above the horizon of war, and left behind a path of glory. The zenith of his day had past and little more was heard of him in public life until the "*hic jacet*" was placed above the mound of earth beneath which he now sleeps.

A story is told of the war horse which General Wool brought home from his Mexican campaigning, and which died in Troy. The beating of drums or firing of cannon always filled the animal with excitement. He would prance and snort as if he snuffed afar the tide of coming battle, and was anxious to meet it. At his death the Trojans gave this modern Bucephalus a military funeral with all the pomp of procession, and the last mournful volleys fired above his grave. In the busy rush and whirl of to-day, with new generations constantly pressing upon and obliterating old scenes, both horse and rider are fast becoming only a shadowy remembrance of the past.

CHAPTER XVII.

SAM HOUSTON.

Early History.—Scotch Ancestry.—Birthplace.—School Days in the Forest.—Hard Work on the Farm.—Homer's Iliad.—Off to the Woods.—Among the Cherokees.—Military Service.—The Soldier under Jackson.—Battle of the Horse-Shoe.—Desperate Bravery.—Wounded.—Promotion.—Role as a Lawyer.—Rises Rapidly to Distinction.—The Domestic Cloud.—Return to the Forest.—Emigration to Texas.—Houston as General.—Massacre of the Alamo.—Battle of San Jacinto.—The Young Republic and her President.—Annexation.—In the United States Senate.—Houston as Governor.—Last Days.

DURING the troublous transition times when Mexican perfidy, trampling upon every sacred and sworn obligation, had steeped the Texan plains in blood, Sam Houston, stalwart and strong, stood by the side of the young Texan Republic, her shield of defence. His sword flashed vengeance on her oppressors, and through her he struck brave blows for liberty everywhere. His name became her rallying cry. He was her hero, whom she followed with an enthusiasm truly French—her ruler whom she elected by acclamation.

His early history was as striking and romantic as his after life. It is the history of the mountain stream which begins alone among isolated peaks, and gathering strength as it rushes onward to the vast ocean-basin, at last becomes the mighty and resistless river.

The mountain current of Houston's blood began in a Scotch ancestry among the followers of John Knox. Driven from the Scottish Highlands to the north of

Ireland this congregation of families emigrated to Pennsylvania during the siege of Derry, and afterwards the parents of Houston settled and married in Virginia.

Timber Ridge Church, seven miles east of Lexington in Rockbridge county, was the birthplace of the future hero, and time marked the calendar of the auspicious event at March second, 1793. His father fought in the Revolution and held the post of inspector of General Moore's Brigade until he died—an event which took place in 1807. The death of the father changed the fortunes of the family, and the brave and bereaved mother—herself noble in her intellectual and moral strength—emigrated with her growing family of boys and girls to the frontier, on the banks of the Tennessee River, then the boundary line between aggressive whites and the Cherokee race of Indians.

The location of this forest home, the nursery of the future hero, was not far from Marysville.

As for the wisdom of the schools—beyond the rudiments of reading, writing and ciphering—young Houston acquired very little of it before he left Virginia, and in his new and wild home the facilities for an education were about as meagre. It was said he never entered a school-house before he was eight years old, and afterwards, if he evinced any literary taste, it showed itself only in peculiar directions, and his efforts to obtain the instruction he craved suffered total defeat.

During the most of those young years he was kept hard at work, and after the death of the father his portion of labor became still heavier, in breaking and tilling the virgin land of his pioneer home.

About this time an academy was established in East Tennessee near his mother's farm, which for a while he attended. In some way he obtained possession of two or three books—Homer's Iliad among the number—which he read constantly, with a keen thirst for knowledge born of long abstinence. Indeed, it was said he could repeat the entire translation of the Iliad from beginning to end. A desire to obtain some knowledge of the primitive languages in which these were written led him to ask the master's permission to study Latin and Greek. He was refused—for what reason we know not. The refusal so incensed him that he declared he would never recite another lesson while he lived, and for ought that can be gleaned of his history, it seems very probable he kept his word.

During these boyish years, his elder brothers tyrannized over him to the extent of at last compelling him to enter a country dry-goods store, and take his place behind the counter as clerk. But this was the feather which broke the camel's back, and the young and high-blooded boy was suddenly missing from his place. For several weeks he was nowhere to be found. The truth was he had crossed the Tennessee and gone to live among the Indians, and when at last they found him and asked him the reason of his sudden and strange departure, he replied that he "preferred measuring deer-tracks to tape, that the wild liberty of the red man was more to his liking than the tyranny of his brothers, and that if he could not study Latin in the Academy, he at least could read a translation from Greek in the woods," and with this message he sent them back. When at length, after a prolonged absence, he appeared before his mother's door, she received him kindly, and his worn-out clothes were replaced by new ones. For a time everything went smoothly, but the first act of tyranny on the part of his brothers drove him again to his wild life in the woods, from whence he returned after that, only once or twice a year to be re-fitted with the needed new clothes. This wild life went on until he was eighteen years old, when by dint of perseverance he obtained a school among his pale brethren which he taught for the purpose of paying some odds and ends of debt. These had been contracted by purchasing presents for the Indians during his semi-occasional visits to the white settlements. After the debt was paid he shut up his school and went back to his old master with Euclid in his hands. But the war on the high seas with Great Britain came on apace, and in 1813, a United States recruiting-party came to Maryville. Of course, as might be supposed, this young son of the forest and of freedom enlisted. His mother did not withhold her consent. "There, my son, take this musket," said she, as she gave him the weapon, "and never disgrace it; for remember I had rather all my sons should fill one honorable grave, than that one of them should turn his back to save his life."

Perhaps it is not a matter of wonder that such a woman should be mother to such a son. Thus he entered on his career as soldier, and marched to Fort Hampton, in Alabama. He was soon promoted to sergeant, and after that to ensign, and shortly became the best drill in the regiment.

Returning to Knoxville, he assisted in drilling and organizing the Eastern Battalion of the Thirty-ninth

Regiment of Infantry, and taking up his line of march for the Ten Islands, remained at that encampment some time. The regiment then went to Fort Williams, and descended the river Coosa to To-ho-pe-ka, where General Jackson fought the celebrated battle of the Horse-Shoe, and where young Houston so covered himself with glory and with wounds. The Horse-Shoe or Tohopeka, was formed by a bend of the Tallapoosa River, and here, on the twenty-seventh of March, a thousand Creek Indian warriors had assembled, determined to stake all on this last desperate struggle for existence. General Jackson's army of two thousand men confronted them, and the battle was stubbornly fought. Here young Houston found his first opportunity, and from that bloody conflict he emerged a hero. He scaled the breastworks unmindful of the storm of barbed arrows falling about him or the rattling musketry. Right and left he cut his way among the savages, leading in the terrible onset. An arrow pierced his thigh which was pulled out after several unsuccessful efforts, and a stream of blood followed. When the wound was dressed, General Jackson ordered him not to re-cross the breastworks to the front. But this was an order which the impetuous young ensign could not obey, and when his general called for a body of men to lead a forlorn hope and make a last desperate charge on a concealed party of red warriors, Houston, waiting a moment for some captain to lead forth his company and waiting in vain, rushed forward, calling on his platoon to follow him, though he had to charge the very port-holes bristling with a deadly array of rifles and arrows! When rallying his men within five yards of the port-holes, two rifle-balls received in his right shoulder struck his arm powerless to his side and he sank to the earth. He could do no more. The Indians were at last dislodged and the battle was won. The sun of the Creek Nation had set in ruin and above it gleamed the rising star of young Houston. The army rang with his praises. He had been tried in the hour of peril and had not been found wanting.

It was a long time before he recovered from his dangerous wounds, and when at last peace was proclaimed, he was retained in the army as first lieutenant, being detailed on duty in the adjutant's office stationed at Nashville, from January first, 1817. Here he remained until the following November, when he was sent by Jackson as Indian agent among the Cherokees. During the winter he conducted a delegation of Indians to Washington, and found that attempts had been made to injure him with the government, for having prevented the smuggling of negroes into the Western States. He vindicated himself, but thought the government gave a cold recognition of his services. He returned from Washington, resigned his commission and went to Nashville to study law. This role as civilian and lawyer was begun in June, 1818, in the office of Hon. James Trimble. He advanced rapidly, completed his studies and was admitted to the bar in a third of the time usually prescribed. Establishing himself in Lebanon, thirty miles from Nashville, soon afterwards, he was appointed adjutant-general of the State with the rank of colonel. His genius conquered everything, and with such giant strides did he go forward that in October he was elected district-attorney of the Davidson District.

A second time he took up his residence in Nashville. In the practice of his profession he rose to great and sudden distinction. In 1821, he was elected major-general by the field officers of the State, and in 1823, was a candidate for Congress, being elected without opposition. In the National Legislature he was returned by his constituency the second time by an almost unanimous vote. In 1827 he was elected governor of the State of Tennessee by a majority of over twelve thousand. Honors fell thick upon him, and his personal popularity was almost unlimited. In January, 1829, he married a young lady of respectable family and gentle character, and in less than three months afterwards society was thrown into a tumult of excitement by the announcement of their separation. Concerning the causes of this unhappy affair, Houston maintained the strictest silence. To the questioning of friends and enemies alike, he had but one reply: "'This is a painful but it is a *private* affair," he said. "I do not recognize the right of the public to interfere in it, and I shall treat the public as though it had never happened. . . . If my character cannot stand the shock, let me lose it." But the public would not let the matter rest, and taking up arms for and against Governor Houston, party spirit ran high and no calumny too vile could be heaped upon his name by the pseudo-friends of the lady. Through it all, Houston remained firm in his silence, ignoring all aspersions on himself and never permitting a breath of reproach in his presence against the character of her, whom he had once called wife. But at last he sought escape from the arrows of slander, and resigning his office of governor, went into voluntary exile among his old friends, the children of the forest. The King of the Cherokees had long ago adopted Houston as his son, and now the man who had been elected to his high office by acclamation—who had received a people's applause, laid down the sceptre and sought the wigwam of his adopted Indian sire. His friends parted from him in sorrow, but they felt that this was only an eclipse of name and fame from which he would emerge brighter than ever. The journey of the self-exiled governor was a long one. Four hundred miles to the northwest where the Falls of the Arkansas resound, near the mouth of the Illinois, the old chief's ample wigwam awaited the return of his wandering son, and the welcome given him was said to have been touching in the extreme. Eleven winters had passed since last they met.

For three years was the future hero of San Jacinto lost to the world, living his wild forest life. Three years! But he was learning the wrongs suffered by his red brethren, the frauds of Indian agents who cheated them, and he was preparing to be their future champion.

We must hurry over the intervening period between this life and the life of his future fame as the great liberator of Texas — the staunch champion around whom her well-nigh despairing sons rallied on a last, desperate issue. For a year he came forth from his seclusion and boldly advocated the rights of the cheated red men, at the Nation's gates—achieved much, suffered the slings and arrows of slander aimed at his lion heart, and when at last his foes retired from the contest covered with defeat, he again sought the seclusion of the forest. Proffered places of honor, even though held out by General Jackson, no longer allured him. The returning current of praise which followed the ebb-tide of abuse, could not keep him from his firm purpose to pursue a quiet life on the free prairies. He went to Texas with the intention of becoming a herdsman. But the people among whom he came urged him at once to become their leader in the councils of State, and a strange fate made this gateway the road to Texas free. His emigration to the Lone Star State took place in 1832.

We pass in rapid review the rights of Texas trodden down—the iron heel of Santa Anna determined on establishing a military despotism—the uprising of the people—their unanimous election of Houston as commander-in-chief of their armies—their declaration of independence, March second, 1836—and then the opening career of the general on his great mission—infusing strength and courage into the handful of men gathered around him—into the convention held at the seat of government, trembling lest they should be swept out of existence by Santa Anna sweeping towards them on his dire purpose of extermination. Then follows the woeful slaughter of the Alamo, and the horrible massacre of Colonel Fannin's regiment of seven hundred men at Goliad, who, had he obeyed the orders of his general, would have been saved. After this the thrilling tragedy of San Jacinto opens, in which Houston achieved by one mighty stroke the independence of Texas, and hurled forever to its eternal doom Mexican oppression and Mexican rule. It was miraculous that Houston's men, numbering less than half as many as Santa Anna's, should not only overwhelm them with one of the most crushing defeats

HOUSTON CATCHING THE SOUND OF BATTLE.

in the history of battles, but that bringing such havoc and slaughter to the ranks of the foe, themselves escaped with the loss of only seven men killed and thirty wounded. It seems incredible, yet it was true. Eight hundred prisoners had been taken—over six hundred of the enemy had been left dead on the field— the river of San Jacinto was choked with the fleeing and drowning ranks of the enemy, and multitudes had met their fate in the morass and bayous. Besides two hundred and eighty of the enemy's wounded, only seven are known to have escaped from the field! But the Texans rushed to their work with a desperation which brooked no resistance. They fought for their homes, their liberties, and to avenge the murder of their dead companions. Before the battle came on, Houston had addressed them eloquently, and had given them a war cry which fired them to the highest pitch of desperation. He had charged them to remember the Alamo, and with that cry on their lips they rushed to battle. A victory scarcely without parallel in history followed. Santa Anna was captured, and thus almost at one stroke the chains were stricken from bleeding Texas—her freedom was achieved and Houston was the man who had done it. It passed into a proverb that "Houston was the only man that could have kept the army in subjection, or achieved the independence of Texas, or preserved it after it was won."

He had come out of the battle of San Jacinto with a shattered ankle, and the wounded limb took him to death's door. Not able to obtain the necessary medical assistance in Texas, he was obliged to be taken to New Orleans before help could be given him. He was received there with crowds and music, though they carried him on a litter from the pier. After his recovery, he returned once more to his wilderness home and found the infant Republic turbulent as a wild sea, with party faction. It was universally conceded that Houston was the only man in all Texas who could quell it. He allowed his name to be placed before the people as a candidate for the Presidency only twelve days before the elections, and he was accorded that high place by acclamation. The turbulence of party everywhere yielded to national enthusiasm, and the hero of San Jacinto was placed at the helm on the Ship of State. He was inaugurated October twenty-second, 1836, and his administration was a marvel of success. Out of chaos he brought order, and the majesty of law took the place of misrule. He conciliated the Indians and by his wise forecast prevented another Mexican invasion.

In no portion of the world had civil government ever been established in so short a space of time. His term closed December twelfth, 1838, and by the provisions of the constitution he could not be elected for a second consecutive term. The law and order and credit which he had established, and the peaceful relations which he was fast bringing about, were all ruthlessly trampled upon by his successor. Anarchy and confusion took the place of firm rule, and the work of Houston's administration was well-nigh undone. But in December, 1841, he again took the Presidential chair and once more the people had a government One of his first measures was to despatch a minister to Washington to open negotiations for the annexation of Texas, and it was almost entirely through his wise policy that the young Republic was at length welcomed among the band of sister States and invited to take her seat in the councils of the Nation.

England and France were looking towards a foothold on this continent, and it is believed that had a man less patriotic or less noble than Houston been at the head of government, Texas would never have held the place she now does in our constellation of free States. After the event of annexation, Houston was sent to the Senate at Washington to represent his State, and held that honorable position with such marked ability as to reflect honor on the nation and add glory to his own noble fame. He proved himself the statesman as well as the general. His speeches were noted for an earnest force—a clear logic and pointedness which ever won the rapt attention of the auditor. He remained in the Senate from 1846 to 1859, and was Governor of Texas from that time until 1861. He opposed the secession movement and resisted the clamor for an extra session of the Legislature. At last, he retired from office rather than take the oath required by the State convention. He went to his home at Independence, Texas, full of honors and surrounded by a halo of victory.

His private character as husband and father is quite as captivating as his public career. He *might* have grown rich, had he gathered into his hands the vast domains which fell into the possession of others less honest than himself. He might have amassed wealth through Texas liabilities, as did many others—but he would not. Thomas H. Benton spoke of him in the Senate as "frank, generous, brave; ready to do or to suffer whatever the obligations of civil or military duty imposed, and always prompt to answer the call of honor, patriotism or friendship." He was the founder of a Republic and twice its President. He defeated the trained armies of an ancient empire, captured its leader and paralyzed his power. He was the champion of temperance—the hero whose blood was spilled in the cause of two Republics—a truly *great* man of the nation, who rose above party faction and saw only country and the liberties of a people.

CHAPTER XVIII.
JAMES SHIELDS.

The Land of his Nativity.—First Army Experience.—The Mexican War-cloud.—Promotion.—The March through Mexico.—At Cerro Gordo.—Brilliant Achievement.—Wounded unto Death.—The Storming of Contreras.—Aid to Smith.—A Generous Piece of Conduct.—Chapultepec.—Under a Galling Fire.—Refuses to Leave the Field though Wounded.—His Return to the United States.—The War of Rebellion.—The Spring of '62.—Defeat of "Stonewall" Jackson.—Leaving the Army.

GENERAL JAMES SHIELDS was a son of Erin's green island—the land of the harp and the sword, of oppression and martyrdom, the land that has given to the world so many noble patriots and illustrious men. After making this country the home of his adoption in early life, we first hear of him in a military capacity during the last war with Great Britain. He entered the American army as second lieutenant of the Eleventh Infantry and served with credit throughout the contest. After the war he seems to have dropped out of sight, but suddenly merged into view again when the Mexican difficulty obscured our national horizon and operations had commenced on the Rio Grande. Here he received the appointment of brigadier-general. He joined the division of General Wool and made the march through the country to Monclova, where he was detached to reinforce the army of General Scott. His bravery at Vera Cruz, exposed to the heaviest belching of the cannons' thunder, was only surpassed by the skill he displayed at Cerro Gordo, which won praises from General Scott and his associate officers. On the enemy's left, on the Jalapa road, he succeeded in cutting off their retreat and engaging them in such a way as to contribute largely to the victory of that day. In this engagement, while attacking a battery of five pieces, supported by a heavy force of cavalry and infantry, Shields fell dangerously wounded, with a ball through his lungs. He was borne from the field, and Colonel Baker, of Illinois, succeeded to the command, and led his troops forward in the successful attack.

At Contreras, Shields was sent to a village near by to support Smith's brigade. In the night and the darkness he was obliged to conduct his troops through a rugged ravine, difficult of passage. Posting a strong picket guard he ordered his main force to lie upon their arms until midnight. The pickets encountered and drove back a body of Mexican infantry who were approaching the city, and Shields reached the encampment of Smith without accident. Smith had previously matured his plans for the capture of the position, which afterwards proved so brilliant. Shields, however, as superior officer, arriving on the ground, could have assumed command and reaped the fame of the subsequent victory. But with a rare magnanimity he refused to do so. He intercepted and cut off the retreat of the enemy on the main road, and so effectively disposed his forces in the stubborn fight, charged the Mexican ranks with such intrepidity and success as to put them to utter rout. The flying foe was pursued to the very gates of the city.

On the tenth of September, Shields was ordered to the vicinity of Chapultepec, where a heavy cannonading was kept up for several days until he advanced to the assault. Although severely wounded in the arm he refused to leave the field, and fought valiantly on in the face of the most galling fire. The Mexican fortifications, one after another, fell into our hands, until at length the stars and stripes waved from the gateways of Chapultepec in triumph. General Shields was carried from the field exhausted, and suffering severely from his wound. But owing to a good constitution his recovery was speedy. When his Mexican campaign terminated, he returned to the United States, and did not again appear on the stage of public life until called forth by the war of Rebellion.

In the spring of 1862 he distinguished himself by defeating the famous Confederate general, Stonewall Jackson, at the little village of Kernstown near Winchester. Shields marched his soldiers up from the Shenandoah to Fredericksburg, where General Augur was at that time stationed, and, hearing that Jackson was in the valley, he faced about and marched back again to meet the veteran rebel hero. It was Jackson's first defeat, and notwithstanding the fact that his force was double that of Shields, he was for once handsomely whipped, and went flying before our pursuing troops. But Shields followed Jackson too far and rashly placed his army in jeopardy. For this he received severe censure, and after that memorable day seems to have disappeared almost mysteriously from the public gaze and the army.

CHAPTER XIX.

CHARLES MAY.

Colonel May a Native of Washington.—Commissioned a Lieutenant by President Jackson.—Ordered to Florida.—Participates in the Capture of the Indian Chief Philip.—Opening of the Mexican War.—Joins General Taylor.—Co-operates with Captain Walker.—Famous Charge at Resaca de la Palma.—Gallant Conduct at Buena Vista.—Returns to the United States.

THE name of Colonel Charles May will ever be associated with the gallant heroes who under the leadership of Scott and Taylor won undying laurels on the plains of Mexico. For courage, intrepidity and impetuosity in battle no man in the American army was superior to Colonel May. His dragoon fights along the Rio Grande, his charge at Resaca de la Palma, and his heroic conduct at Buena Vista have rarely been surpassed, and have won for him a reputation as brilliant as any that adorn the pages of Spartan warfare.

But little is known of May's early life except that he was a native of the city of Washington, and son of Dr. May. He was commissioned second lieutenant in the Second Regiment of Dragoons by President Jackson, and ordered to Florida. His duties were most arduous in these campaigns against the red men of the everglades, and it is recorded that he was foremost among those who captured the famous Indian chief Philip.

When General Taylor marched into Texas with his army of observation, and matters were wearing a hostile appearance, Captain May joined him with a company of dragoons and aided in the defence of Point Isabel. Co-operating with the gallant Captain Walker, he was stationed between that place and Taylor's advance camp with instructions to keep the communication open if possible. This service was perilous; but May's bravery and rapid movements overcame all obstacles.

On the twenty-eighth of April, 1846, he ascertained that a large force of Mexicans intended to surround General Taylor's camp, and at once set out with his dragoons to communicate with the general. After proceeding twelve miles, he encountered fifteen hundred of the enemy under the immediate command of Santa Anna. Most of his men being inexperienced, fell back at the appearance of such an overwhelming opposition. The few that remained around their bold commander firmly received the attack of the Mexicans, and gave them battle for upwards of half an hour. They then retreated, and were pursued to within a mile of Point Isabel. It was reported that May was slain, but at night he came into the fort, and with that indomitable spirit for which he was distinguished, at once offered to communicate with General Taylor, provided he could have four men as his companions. This proposition, under such circumstances, with the enemy in force, and lurking in every path and thicket, was considered rash. But six Texans volunteered, and after several bold adventures, in one of which they charged through a large body of Mexican lancers, they reached the camp of General Taylor on the thirtieth.

In consequence of the information thus received, General Taylor marched from camp on the first of

May, and reached Point Isabel the day after. On the third, the Mexicans commenced a bombardment of the river fort. Anxious to know how Major Brown sustained this attack, the general despatched Captain May, with one hundred dragoons, assisted by Captain Walker and six rangers, for the purpose of opening communications. At two o'clock in the afternoon, May started, and just after night-fall came in sight of Arista's camp-fires. Though the whole Mexican army was before him he manœuvred so skilfully as to escape observation, pass around its front, and find ambush in some thick chaparral a few miles from the fort. Captain Walker was then sent forward to the fort, with instructions to note particularly any force he might observe along the road. He reached his destination without accident, while May and his troops remained waiting in their saddles. Owing to several unforeseen causes, Walker was unable to rejoin May that night, and daylight approaching, the latter returned to Point Isabel.

The victory achieved by General Taylor at Resaca de la Palma, was perhaps more largely due to the part performed by Captain May than that of any other officer. The battle had continued for some time without any decided advantage to the Americans, and General Taylor perceived that the enemy could not be driven from his position until his artillery was silenced. He therefore ordered Captain May, who was stationed in the rear, to report himself for duty. May soon appeared with his dragoons, and was directed to charge and capture the Mexican batteries at whatever sacrifice. After exhorting his men to remember their regiment, the captain pointed towards the bat-

MAY'S CHARGE AT RESACA DE LA PALMA.

teries and bade them follow. Striking spurs into his horse, he dashed forward, followed by his command in column of fours.

On arriving at the post occupied by Ridgely and his brave cannoneers, May halted to learn the position of the Mexican batteries. Knowing the danger attending a charge upon their pieces when loaded, Ridgely desired him to wait until he drew the fire of their batteries. He suddenly applied the match, and before the reverberation of his pieces had died away, the enemy replied, their shot sweeping like hail through his ranks.

Instantly the squadron of dragoons sprung forward, May in the advance, with his long hair streaming behind like the rays of a comet. The earth shook beneath the iron hoofs of their chargers, and the rays of the tropical sun flashed back in flame from their burnished sabres as they swept along, cheered by a shout of exultation from the artillerists and infantry. "Still foremost, May reached at length the batteries in the road, and upon the right of it; and as his steed rose upon the Mexican breastworks, he turned to wave on his men to the charge. Closely pressing upon him was Lieutenant Inge, who answered to the challenge with a shout, and turned in like manner to encourage his platoon, when a terrible discharge of grape and canister from the upper battery swept down upon them, and dashed to the earth, in mangled and bloody masses, eighteen horses and seven men; among them the gallant Inge and his charger. May's steed at a bound cleared the batteries, followed by Lieutenant Stevens, and the survivors of the First and Second platoons. Their impetus carried them through and beyond the batteries, when charging back, they drove the enemy from the guns and silenced their fire. Captain Graham, and Lieutenants Winship and Pleasanton, with the Third and Fourth platoons, in the meantime swept to the left of the road, and at the point of the sword carried the battery situated there.

"Perceiving the small force by which they were assailed, the Mexicans recovered from their panic, and rushing back to the batteries, prepared to fire them. Gathering around him a few followers, May charged upon them with irresistible force, while the terror-stricken enemy shrunk back from the blows of his sword, which descended with a flash and force like that of lightning. An intrepid officer, however, kept his place, and endeavored to rally his men. With his own hands he seized a match and was about to apply it, when he was ordered by Captain May to surrender. Finding himself without support, he acknowledged himself a prisoner, and handed his sword to his gallant captor. It was General Vega, a brave and accomplished officer.

"The fire of the enemy's batteries was silenced, but a terrible struggle now commenced for their possession. The Fifth Infantry, under the brave Lieutenant-Colonel McIntosh, though separated into detachments by the chaparral, rushed on through a sweeping fire of musketry, and at length crossed bayonets with the enemy over the cannon-muzzles."

At Buena Vista, Colonel May was associated with Captain Pike's squadron of Arkansas cavalry, and rendered good service in holding the enemy in check, and covering batteries at several points. Extracts from his report will show the nature of these duties.

"Before the squadron of the First Dragoons could be recalled, it had gone so far up the ravine as to be in close range of the enemy's artillery. It was thus, for a short time, exposed to a severe fire, which resulted in the loss of a few men. The other two squadrons and the section of artillery were in the meantime placed in motion for Buena Vista, where a portion of our supplies were stored, and against which the enemy was directing his movements. Lieutenant Rucker joined me near the rancho, and in time to assist me in checking the heavy cavalry force, which was then very near and immediately in our front. A portion of the enemy's cavalry, amounting, perhaps, to two hundred men, not perceiving my command, crossed the main road near to the rancho, and received a destructive fire from a number of volunteers assembled there. The remaining heavy column was immediately checked, and retired in great disorder towards the mountains on our left, before, however, I could place my command in position to charge. Being unable, from the heavy clouds of dust, to observe immediately the movements of the body of cavalry which had passed the rancho, I followed it up, and found it had crossed the deep and marshy ravine on the right of the road, and was attempting to gain the mountains on the right. I immediately ordered Lieutenant Reynolds to bring his section into battery, which he did promptly, and by a few well-directed shots, dispersed and drove the enemy in confusion over the mountains. I next directed my attention to the annoying column which had occupied so strong a position on our left flank and rear during the whole day, and immediately moved my command to a position whence I could use my artillery on the masses crowded in the ravines and gorges of the mountains. As I was leaving the rancho, I was joined by about two hundred foot volunteers, under Major Gorman, and a detachment of Arkansas mounted volunteers, under Lieutenant-Colonel Roane. Believing my command now sufficiently strong for any contingency which might arise, I advanced it steadily towards the foot of the mountains, and to within a few hundred yards of the position occupied by the enemy. I then directed Lieutenant Reynolds to bring his section again into battery; and in the course of half an hour, by the steady and destructive fire of his artillery, the enemy was forced to fall back. This advantage I followed up; in doing which I was joined by a section of artillery under Captain Bragg. My command still continued to advance, and the enemy to retire. We soon gained a position where we were able to deliver a destructive fire, which caused the enemy to retreat in confusion. While the artillery was thus engaged, by order of General Wool, I steadily advanced the cavalry; but owing to the deep ravines which separated my command from the enemy, I was unable to gain ground on him. The enemy having been thus forced to abandon his position on our left and rear, I was again directed to assume a position in supporting distance of Captain Sherman's battery, which occupied its former position, and against which the enemy seemed to be concentrating his forces. After having occupied this position some time, the general-in-chief directed me to move my command up the ravine towards the enemy's batteries, and to prevent any further advance on that flank. This position was occupied until the close of the battle, the enemy never again daring to attempt any movement towards our rear. The cavalry, except Captain Pike's squadron, which was detached for picket service on the right of the road, occupied, during the night of the twenty-third, the ground near where I was directed last to take my position before the close of the battle. Finding on the morning of the twenty-fourth, that the enemy had retreated, I was joined by Captain Pike's squadron, and ordered in pursuit."

Colonel May returned to the United States soon after the battle of Buena Vista, where he remained several weeks. The fame of his daring achievements had preceded him, and he was everywhere welcomed as a representative of the gallant ones with whom he had battled in Mexico. .

PART THIRD.

The War for the Union.

SUBJECTS:

Chapter	Page
XX. ULYSSES S. GRANT	245
XXI. WILLIAM TECUMSEH SHERMAN	263
XXII. PHILIP HENRY SHERIDAN	278
XXIII. GEORGE BRINTON McCLELLAN	287
XXIV. AMBROSE EVERETT BURNSIDE	298
XXV. GEORGE HENRY THOMAS	304
XXVI. JOSEPH HOOKER	314
XXVII. GEORGE GORDON MEADE	326
XXVIII. HENRY WARNER SLOCUM	332
XXIX. JAMES BIRDSEYE McPHERSON	337
XXX. WINFIELD SCOTT HANCOCK	347
XXXI. JOHN CHARLES FREMONT	352
XXXII. OLIVER OTIS HOWARD	357
XXXIII. DAVID GLASCOE FARRAGUT	361
XXXIV. FRANZ SIGEL	368
XXXV. HUGH JUDSON KILPATRICK	375
XXXVI. PHILIP KEARNY	387
XXXVII. NATHANIEL LYON	391
XXXVIII. ELMER EPHRAIM ELLSWORTH	396
XXXIX. EDWARD DICKINSON BAKER	407
XL. GEORGE ARMSTRONG CUSTER	417

CHAPTER XX.
ULYSSES SIMPSON GRANT.

The Grants of the Early Scotch Monarchy.—Family Crests.—Direct Ancestry.—Boyhood.—Feats of Horsemanship.—Loading Wood.—Old "Dave" and Young Ulysses.—At West Point.—Experience in Mexican War.—Marriage.—Resigns His Commission.—In the Leather Business.—Beginning of Last War.—Recruiting a Company.—Battle of Belmont.—Cairo Expedition.—Fort Donelson. — Shiloh.— Vicksburg.— Chattanooga.— Missionary Ridge and Lookout Mountain.—Opinions of a Sachem.—The Last Campaign.— Lee's Surrender. — Elected and Re-elected President.

THE occasion often creates the man, but the man who *masters* the occasion is born, not made. Many are pushed to the surface momentarily, by the pressure of events, and then subside into common levels; but he is the true commander during a crisis, who can wield the waves of difficulty to advantage and be a sure pilot amid the on-rush of events, when they thicken and deepen into a prolonged struggle.

When, during the late war, our country needed a leader to face and quell the threatened danger of disunion and conduct her armies to successful issues, and when government intrusted those momentous issues to Ulysses S. Grant, "the man and the moment had met"—the occasion had found its master.

Napoleon said that the most desirable quality of a good general was that his judgment should be in equilibrium with his courage. To no commander of modern times could this rule apply with more force than to Grant. A man of no outward clamor of character—no hint of bluster or dash—quiet-voiced, self-controlled, but not self-asserting, he yet displayed vast power as an organizer, as a tactician, and in masterly combinations of large forces so as to produce the most telling effects. It has been truly said of him that no general ever stamped his own peculiar character upon an army more emphatically than did Grant upon the Army of the Tennessee. It was the only large organization which, as a whole, never suffered a defeat during the war. It was noted for its marvellous persistence—its determined fighting qualities—and had the reputation of being sure to win any battle that lasted over a day, no matter what the odds against it. It was at Grant's recommendation that a united command was concentrated in the Mississippi Valley—which concentration has since been acknowledged to be the basis of all our subsequent victories.

Generosity, mildness, and kind-heartedness shone as conspicuously in Grant's character as his firmness and great generalship. Simplicity of manner and kindness of heart are always characteristic of the true hero.

> "The bravest are the tenderest,
> The loving are the daring."

The rapid and bold descent upon Fort Donelson, the unconquerable determination exhibited at Shiloh, the brilliant capture of Vicksburg and the high military science displayed at Chattanooga Valley, Lookout Mountain, and Missionary Ridge—these have never been surpassed in military history, in splendor of execution, or judiciousness of combination.

It is not known with certainty whether the family of Grants originated in Scotland, Denmark, or France. The balance of evidence, however, goes to show that they were Norman and came over with William the Conqueror in 1066. In the early days of the Scotch monarchy, they became noted as a powerful clan. Gregory Grant was "Sheriff Principal" of Inverness, between 1214 and 1249. At "Halidoun Hill," 1333, John Grant commanded the right wing of the Scotch army. They came, originally, from the Strathspey country, noted for its forests of fir and lovely scenery. A certain Lieutenant-General Francis Grant was buried in Hampshire, England, December second, 1781. On his monument was carved the family crest, representing a mountain peak burning. It bore the motto, "Steadfast." Another crest of the Grants had four burning peaks and the mottos, "Stand sure; stand fast; Craig Ellachie." On yet another one, an oak was sprouting under the full blaze of the sun. Its accompanying motto was, "Wise and harmless." The crest of Grant of Leith was a rock: motto, "Immobile." Grant of Grant had the burning mount and the motto "Stand sure." During the Sepoy rebellion in India, there was a Highland regiment composed almost entirely of Grants, whose colors bore the ancient motto, "Stand fast, Craig Ellachie." These legends are supposed to express a leading characteristic of the clan, and their resemblance to some of the traits of our latter day Ulysses is somewhat striking when looked at in the light of heredity.

The great-grandfather of Ulysses was Captain Noah Grant, who was killed at the battle of White Plains, during the French and Indian wars, in 1776. His grandfather, Noah Grant, Jr., fought at Lexington as lieutenant of militia, and afterwards, during the Revolution. His father, Jesse, emigrated from Pennsylvania to Ohio, and was married at Point Pleasant, Ohio, June, 1821, to Hannah Simpson, whose father was also from the Keystone State. Ulysses was born the following year, April twenty-seventh, 1822.

There was something of a contest over his baptismal name; one suggested Theodore; his young mother preferred Albert; his grandfather thought Hiram would be the proper cognomen, but his step-grandmother—a great reader and admirer of the Homeric Ulysses—triumphed with the name of the Grecian hero, little dreaming that it would one day also become the name of an American hero, scarcely less illustrious. His earliest feats were connected with horsemanship. At six years of age he was a good rider, at ten a skilful driver, doing full work in hauling wood, carrying loads of leather to Cincinnati from his father's tannery and bringing passengers back to Georgetown, where the family then lived. At twelve, he rode horses at full speed, standing upon their backs and balancing himself by the bridle reins. An incident is related of these early years in connection with a trained circus pony, which the young Ulysses was invited to ride by the facetious clown, in the full expectation that he would be thrown. But in spite of every effort to dismount him, by both pony and clown, the boy rode on; as a last resort, a trained monkey was let loose upon his shoulders, but without effect: the boy continued to ride, quietly victorious, wearing the same undisturbed expression for which he was afterwards noted in battle. He was always of a peaceable and even disposition, evinced great calmness and presence of mind, and was full of quiet resolution and persistence.

From childhood, he developed rare judgment and was decidedly a boy of resources. In illustration of this, a story is told of his loading a wagon with logs, any one of which would have been a heavy lift for twenty men. He accomplished the unusual feat by the aid of a big horse called "Dave," and a tree which had fallen across a stump, with one end resting on the ground. Ulysses had hitched his horse to the logs, pulled the ends over the fallen tree, and after backing the wagon under them, used "Dave," on the lever principle, to haul them one at a time, on the wagon. Here was a hint of the engineering brain which afterwards compassed such well-laid plans for the direction and movements of a vast army. And here, also, we find another illustration of the rule that "the boy is father to the man." At eighteen, Ulysses obtained an appointment as cadet at the West Point Military Academy through Mr. Hamer, who, knowing that his mother's name was Simpson, sent in his application as Ulysses S. Grant. This accounts for the superfluous middle letter which his fellow-students construed into "Sam," making, with his first initial letter, the nick-name, "Uncle Sam," by which he was familiarly known.

He graduated in 1843, ranking twenty-first in a class of thirty-nine. He could easily have taken a higher grade, had he thought it worth the extra trouble. He excelled in mathematics and all military exercises, and surpassed nearly all his classmates in horsemanship and cavalry drill. He never violated rules, submitted readily to discipline, never was induced to taste liquor of any sort, was noted for his gentleness of disposition united to great firmness, and was reputed to be "tender-hearted" to a rare degree. In 1845, when Taylor was sent to Mexico, Grant, as second lieutenant in the Fourth Regular Infantry, accompanied the "army of occupation." He fought in the battles of Resaca, Palo Alto and Monterey: was transferred to Scott's army, and participated in the brilliant campaign beginning with Vera Cruz and ending with the City of Mexico. At the storming of Chapultepec he took command of a mountain howitzer with such decided skill, and otherwise so distinguished himself that he was brevetted captain. In 1848, he married Julia T. Dent, of St. Louis, Missouri, sister of one of his classmates. He was soon after stationed at Detroit, from whence he was transferred to Sackett's Harbor, and in 1852, accompanied an expedition to Oregon, where he received his full captain's commission. In 1853, he resigned and took up his residence on a small farm near St. Louis. About this time he received a proposition from his father to become a partner in his leather business, and went at once to Galena, Illinois, where the firm of "Grant and Son, Leather Dealers," was established. This was in 1859. Two years later, when the guns of Fort Sumter echoed over the nation, he dropped everything, at once recruited a company, and tendered it to the governor. He assisted in organizing the State quota, but when Governor Yates proposed to send his name to Washington for a brigadier-generalship, Grant declined the doubtful honor, saying he "did not *ask* promotion—he wanted to *earn* it." In June he received the appointment of colonel to the Twenty-first regiment, and was ordered to Missouri. In August, being made brigadier-general, he was assigned to the Cairo district. Taking possession of Paducah, which he regarded as a strong strategic point for future movements, he issued a proclamation to the citizens in which he said: "I have nothing to do with opinions, and shall deal only with armed rebellion and its aiders and abettors." Determined to break up the enemy's camp opposite Columbus, he projected an expedition down the river, and, as a result, on the seventh of November the battle of Belmont was fought. In a congratulatory order to his troops after the battle, he said it "had been his fortune to have been in all the battles fought in Mexico by Generals Scott and Taylor except Buena Vista, and he never saw one more hotly contested, or where troops behaved with more gallantry."

Following Belmont was the "Cairo expedition"—a venture comparatively barren of results. An order issued about this time to the troops composing the expedition, throws a strong ray of light on the character of its commanding general, in which his high moral ground and firm stand against vandalism shine out in prominent relief. The order commands "that the severest punishment be inflicted upon every soldier who is guilty of taking or destroying private property, and any commissioned officer guilty of like conduct, or of countenancing it, shall be deprived of his sword and expelled from the army, not to be permitted to return."

On the sixth of February the brilliant reduction of Fort Henry, on the Tennessee, was accomplished by Foote, and Fort Donelson, twelve miles distant, was next in line. Grant and Foote were co-operating by land and water; but Foote did not meet here with the same success that attended him at Fort Henry. It was the fifteenth of February, and Grant had spent two or three days in making an investment of the high and wooded bluff from which frowned the guns of Donelson. Before daybreak, on the fifteenth, he had gone on board the flagship of Foote, in consultation as to the time and manner of attack, when the enemy swept from their works and fell upon the Union lines with tremendous force. The fighting became furious at once, and for some time the battle-line swayed to and fro, between victory and defeat. It was desperate work; brigades and regiments were repulsed and by turns advanced—the brave commands disputing every inch of the rocky and difficult battle-field. When Grant reached the scene it was "to find his right thrown far back, ammunition exhausted and the ranks in confusion." With quick inspiration he took in the situation at a glance, comprehended that the enemy had exhausted his greatest strength, and ordered an immediate attack by the left on the Confederate works in front. General Smith was in command of this portion of the army, and had not actively participated in the conflict. He therefore brought fresh troops to the assault. McClernand was also ordered to reform his shattered ranks and advance. The combined forces charged with splendid valor up the rocky steeps, in the blaze of a withering fire poured down upon them from the fort. They did not falter for a single instant, but reaching the summit, swept over and into the Confederate works with ringing cheers. On the next morning a white flag was seen flying from the fort, and under its protection proposals for an armistice were sent in. Grant replied that unconditional surrender, and that immediately, must be made or he would move on their works at once. Thereupon, Buckner, who was in command, surrendered the fort with its thirteen thousand men.

This splendid victory blazoned the name of Grant all over the country, and he immediately became the people's hero. But at this stage of his ascending career, envy hurled its poisoned shaft of slander against him and willing believers petitioned for his removal. But Lincoln stood firm, the slanders fell short of their mark, Grant was created major-general, and his district enlarged into that of the West Tennessee. His second campaign was under Halleck. A concerted attack on the Confederate forces under Beauregard and Johnston, at Corinth, was planned for Buell and Grant. They were to meet at Pittsburgh Landing, one going down the Tennessee, the other across the country from Nashville. The Confederate general had become aware of the plan, and before Buell's army could arrive, Johnston swept down upon the unprepared Union forces with terrible power. Our troops were thrown into disorder at the very commencement of battle, and though they fought gallantly, there was a lack of concerted strength or well-ordered cohesiveness which lost the first day of Shiloh, and piled the field with dead. The next morning Buell arrived and the fighting continued. The enemy was forced back over the ground he had conquered the previous day, our artillery was recovered and the lost field won. But the human sacrifice on this altar of blood was appalling, and the news of victory carried with it an exceedingly heavy ground-swell of grief. The adverse criticism of Grant which followed

Shiloh, did not weaken either his prospects or his position.

His next achievement, the capture of Vicksburg, was wonderful indeed. Its natural strength of position on a high bluff, one hundred feet above the water-level, added to the formidable array of defences which bristled defiance to all foes, made Vicksburg a very citadel of power, and the fifty thousand men stationed there under Pemberton and Price, did not lessen the difficulties to be overcome. A fort, mounting eight guns, sentineled the approach to the city from beneath, while the heights above were guarded by a three-banked battery. Eight miles of batteries lined the shore above and below Vicksburg. Grant made several fruitless attempts to get to the rear of the city by digging canals across the strip of land on which it stood, and making an inland route; but each one, after Herculean labor, had been abandoned. He now decided on the bold enterprise of running the gauntlet of these batteries with his transports. This desperate feat was successfully accomplished; but before he could land his troops at Grand Gulf, which he had selected as his starting point, it was necessary to run its batteries as he had those of Vicksburg, land his troops farther down the river, and capture the place by hard fighting. He waited for nothing. Hurrying forward the moment he touched land, his object was to take Grand Gulf before the enemy could reinforce it. "He saw that it must be swift marching, quick fighting, sudden and constant victories, or the storm would gather so heavily about him that his advance would be stopped. He ordered as little baggage to be taken as possible and set the example himself. Congressman

SCENE AT THE BATTLE OF VICKSBURG.

Washburn accompanied the expedition, and says that Grant took with him 'neither a horse nor an orderly, nor a camp-chest, nor an overcoat, nor a blanket, nor even a clean shirt. His entire baggage for six days was a tooth-brush. He fared like the commonest soldier in his command, partaking of his rations and sleeping upon the ground, with no covering but the canopy of heaven.'"

After conquering Grand Gulf, where he expected Banks to join him, he was confronted with the refusal of that general to co-operate with him. In this dilemma nothing but a master-stroke of genius could wring success from the materials of defeat. He saw what was before him, and with true inspiration became the master of circumstances. At the head of his brave command he pushed inland, aiming to crush the enemy "in detail before he could concentrate his forces." By a rapid series of brilliant marches, battles, victories, Grant had, at last, on the nineteenth of May, succeeded in completely investing Vicksburg. The whole plan from its outset was brilliant to an extraordinary degree, and the tireless persistence and energy shown in its accomplishment, stamped this man as a very Gibraltar of military genius.

An assault on the enemy's works at first, had proven a failure, and now the wonderful siege began. For forty-six days the digging and mining went patiently forward, while screaming shells and booming shot produced a reign of terror in the city, until at last, Pemberton could hold out no longer and surrendered his starving garrison to the superior prowess and strategy of Grant. It was the morning of the fourth of July, when our troops took possession of Vicksburg and run up the stars and stripes from the top of the Court House. The soldiers, standing beneath it, sang "Rally round the Flag," and Grant became more than ever the popular hero. On the thirteenth of July, Lincoln wrote him a letter of "grateful acknowledgment for the almost inestimable service" he had rendered the country. In September, he was placed in command of the "Departments of the Ohio, of the Cumberland and of the Tennessee, constituting the military division of the Mississippi."

Grant was now ordered to Chattanooga, where Rosecrans had been penned up, to unravel the desperate state of affairs drawn around our army at that point. Bragg's lines extended along Missionary Ridge to Lookout Mountain south, and to the river north of Chattanooga, cutting of communications so nearly that "all supplies had to be dragged for sixty miles across the country over abominable roads." There was momentary danger of losing this strong strategic point, and the troops shut up there with it. The clear-headed, prophetic planning, the far-reaching judgment, the unremitting effort, the persistent fighting which Grant applied to this problem, demonstrated his vast resources as a general, and placed him where none can stand above him in military genius. The concerted action between Hooker sweeping down from Lookout Mountain, Sherman on the left, and Thomas and Grant in the centre, was grand in the extreme. As the brave divisions cleared the rifle pits at the base of Missionary Ridge, and mounted the "rocky hill four hundred feet high," in an awful blaze of artillery and musketry fire, it seemed impossible that they could ever reach the top But at sunset the herculean feat was accomplished, the

Union banners fluttered from the heights, and a tremendous shout of victory came down the mountain sides to the anxious watchers below. Bragg was in full retreat, and over seven thousand prisoners had been taken. Immediately President Lincoln issued a proclamation for a day of thanksgiving over these great successes, and sent Grant the following letter:

"MAJOR-GENERAL GRANT:

"Understanding that your lodgment at Chattanooga and Knoxville is now secure, I wish to tender you and all your command, my more than thanks—my profoundest gratitude for the skill, courage and perseverance with which you and they over so great difficulties have effected that important object. God bless you all.

"A. LINCOLN."

In the congratulatory order which Grant issued to his army, he said:

"The general commanding thanks you individually and collectively. The loyal people of the United States thank and bless you. Their hopes and prayers for your success against this unholy rebellion are with you daily. Their faith in you will not be in vain. Their hopes will not be blasted. Their prayers to Almighty God will be answered. You will yet go to other fields of strife, and with the invincible bravery and unflinching loyalty to justice and right which have characterized you in the past, you will prove that no enemy can withstand you, and that no defence, however formidable, can check your onward march."

Congress created the rank of lieutenant-general, and bestowed it on Grant in answer to a unanimous demand from the entire people that he should be chief of our armies.

An Indian sachem who was on Grant's staff at the

battle of Chattanooga says: "It has been a matter of universal wonder that General Grant was not killed, for he was always in front, and perfectly heedless of the storm of hissing bullets and screaming shells flying around him. . . . . Roads are almost useless to him, for he takes short cuts through fields and woods, and will swim his horse through almost any stream that obstructs his way. Nor does it make any difference to him whether he has daylight for his movements, for he will ride from breakfast until two o'clock next morning, and that too without eating. The next day he will repeat the same until he has finished the work."

Grant assumed the duties of his high office without flourish of any sort, and proceeded to inaugurate the successive steps of his last great campaign. Sherman was placed in command of the vast Western army "with Atlanta as his objective point," while "six hundred vessels of war hung like full charged thunderclouds around the Confederate fortifications." The military resources which centered in the hands of Grant were stupendous, but had they fallen under the control of a man less great than he, their very immensity would have rendered them powerless.

The splendid army of the Potomac was on the move by May third, and the last march to Richmond had begun. Then came the three-days' battle of the Wilderness on the south bank of the Rapidan, bloody and terrible and strange, during which some of our troops were fighting continuously for forty-eight hours; and following close after came also Spottsylvania, which was the result of an endeavor to cut off Lee's retreat. This, too, was a desperate conflict, where precious blood flowed in rivers. Then followed the race between the two opposing armies, for the North Anna. After crossing this river, and finding the Confederates occupying a fortified position on the South Anna, Grant "swung his army around to the Pamunky, and pitched his headquarters at Hanover Court House." These masterly flank movements, in which he manœuvred his vast army with such ease, exhibited his marvellous genius, in stronger light than ever before.

From the Pamunky he advanced to the Chickahominy, and, after the battle of Cold Harbor, made a rapid but quiet change of front on the night of the twelfth of June, and two days afterwards crossed the James and advanced against Petersburg. The attack, at first a success, failed through a blunder, not Grant's; and then began the long siege which ended at last in the evacuation of Petersburg and Richmond. Nowhere was the joy more heartfelt over these results than among the released captives of Libby Prison.

Lee made a desperate endeavor to escape the "manifest destiny" that pursued him, and led his army a "race for life." But Grant, close on his track, environed him on all sides, and the surrender at Appomattox became inevitable. When, at the final scene, Lee presented his sword to Grant, the great General handed it back to him, saying, "it could not be worn by a braver man."

Grant now became universally beloved, universally lionized—everywhere an object of hero-worship. He was looked upon in a sense as the savior of the nation. It is not strange that, at the next election, he was placed in the Presidential chair, almost by popular acclaim. At the close of his term, the further compliment of a re-election was paid him, and after eight years of public service as President of the United States, he went abroad. The splendid ovations and public demonstrations which have greeted him all over England and Europe—the greatest ever accorded any public person from America—evince the respect and admiration in which he is held by foreign nations. Nothing, however, seems to disturb the calm equipoise of his temperament. He preserves always the same impassive exterior, the same simplicity of manner for which he has been noted from early youth. It is said by those who know, that he was never heard to utter a rude word or vulgar jest: that no unfeeling speech, no ill-natured criticism, nor oaths, nor imprecations ever escaped him; that though slow to anger, he cannot tolerate injustice, inhumanity or brutality. And though so taciturn in public, yet with his intimate friends he talks fluently and with charming ease, upon all subjects. His memory is retentive, he is a deep student of human nature, is full of personal reminiscence concerning men and manners in all parts of the country—is a true friend, a magnanimous enemy, and in personal habits and tastes, is extremely simple. In brief, under all the strange variety of circumstances through which he has passed, he exhibits the unostentatious bearing, the gentleness, self-poise and kindness of heart belonging to true manhood.

CHAPTER XXI.

WILLIAM TECUMSEH SHERMAN.

Distinguishing Characteristic of Political Revolutions.—Birth of General Sherman.—Suddenly Left an Orphan.—Adopted by Hon. Thomas Ewing.—Sent to West Point.—Ordered to California.—Becomes a Banker.—Is Made President of the Louisiana Military Academy.—Opposed to Secession.—Tenders his Resignation.—Assists in Organizing Troops for the Suppression of the Rebellion.—At Bull Run.—At Shiloh, Pittsburgh Landing, Chattanooga and Missionary Ridge.—Defeats Hood.—From Atlanta to the Sea.—Campaign of the Carolinas.—Receives the Surrender of Johnston.—Enthusiastic Reception at Washington.

GREAT revolutions are distinguished by the appearance of new men emerging from obscurity. Opportunity invites the development of talents, and the field of strife and danger is soon crowded with aspirants to fame and fortune who were before unknown. The English Revolution in the seventeenth century and the French Revolution in the succeeding century each furnished a brilliant array of statesmen and soldiers, who then first became historical—arbiters of peace and war, and architects of empire.

The American Revolution, by which the independence of the United States was established, was not less fertile in the production of distinguished characters. A host of statesmen and soldiers, whose names were previously known only in limited circles, soon became illustrious throughout the civilized world.

Our recent civil war, and the social and constitutional changes which it produced, may well be said to constitute a second American Revolution. In its progress, as in other revolutions, there suddenly sprang from comparative obscurity many, both in civil and military life, whose names will be remembered in history.

Lieutenants, captains and colonels at the beginning of the struggle became on one side and the other, brigadier, major and lieutenant-generals. Some of these sudden elevations only developed incapacity, while others revealed abilities of the highest order. Among the most conspicuous of those who achieved an enviable distinction on the battle-fields of the Rebellion, and who deserve well of their country, is the illustrious soldier whose life forms the subject of this sketch.

William Tecumseh Sherman was born in Lancaster, Fairfield County, Ohio, on the eighth day of February, 1820. At the age of nine years he was suddenly thrown upon the world through the death of his father, who died of cholera while away from home in the discharge of his duty as Judge of the Superior Court. Soon after Judge Sherman's death, one of his most intimate friends, the Hon. Thomas Ewing, adopted William as his son, and placed him in the academy at Lancaster. He kept him in this school until his sixteenth year, when he sent him to the West Point Military Academy. He graduated four years later, the sixth of his class, and entered the service as second lieutenant of the Third Artillery. For services rendered in the Florida war he was promoted to a first lieutenancy, and afterward stationed at Fort Moultrie, South Carolina. At the opening of the Mexican war in 1846, Lieutenant Sherman was ordered to California, where he shared the fortunes and glories of those remarkable campaigns. Returning from the shores of the Pacific with the rank of captain, which had been given him for meritorious services, he was married in 1850, to the eldest daughter of his benefactor, Thomas Ewing. The old attachment of his school-boy days was rekindled on meeting the estimable young lady who had first awakened in his bosom emotions of love. Three years after his marriage in 1853, becoming tired of the monotony of a profession which consisted chiefly of the stereotyped round of camp and garrison duties, he resigned his commission, and was made president of a banking-house in San Francisco. Captain Sherman continued in the role of banker until 1860, when he was tendered and accepted the presidency of the Louisiana State Military Academy at Alexandria, which position he promptly resigned when he saw that the champions of slavery were determined upon Secession, and that war was inevitable. The closing sentence of the letter, tendering his resignation, was the key-note of his subsequent career, and nobler words were never committed to paper. They are worthy of being inscribed in gold on the front of the National Capitol. He says to the board of supervisors: "I beg you to take immediate steps to relieve me as superintendent the moment the State determines to secede; for on no earthly account will I do any act or think any thought hostile to or in defiance of the old Government of the United States."

His resignation being accepted, Sherman went to St. Louis, and from thence to Washington just prior to the attack on Fort Sumter. He laid before the President and Secretary of War his views concerning the attitude of the South in the impending crisis. President Lincoln was unwilling to believe that the people of the South were really determined to inaugurate a civil war; he still clung to the delusive idea to which he gave utterance while on his way to Washington to be inaugurated, that it was an artificial excitement, and said, jocularly, in response to Sherman's earnest representations: "We shan't need many men like you: the whole affair will soon blow over."

With a penetration which is allotted to but few mortals, he discerned the approach of a conflict the like of which the world had never seen, and was astonished at the apparent ignorance and incredulity of the Government as to the true condition of affairs. Entertaining such views and alarmed at the apathy around him, he wrote Secretary Cameron, saying that as he was educated at the expense of the United States and owed everything to his country, he had come on to tender his military services, and declared in emphatic terms that a conflict was inevitable, and that the administration was unprepared for it.

The bombardment of Fort Sumter ultimately convinced the authorities at Washington that the South not only talked war, but actually meant it, and a call for seventy-five thousand men was immediately issued. Sherman was now urged to go home to Ohio and superintend the organization of troops there enlisting under the call of the President. He rejected the proposition with scorn. When interrogated as to what steps should be taken to suppress the Rebellion, he replied: "Organize for a gigantic war at once; call out the whole military power of the country, and with an overwhelming, irresistible force strangle secession in its very birth."

When it was decided to attack the enemy at Manassas, McDowell was desirous of giving him an important command, and he was immediately commissioned colonel and assigned to the Thirteenth Infantry. At the battle of Bull Run, which soon followed, Colonel Sherman commanded the Third Brigade of Tyler's division, and gallantly performed the part assigned him in that disastrous struggle. Taking position in front of the Stone Bridge, he co-operated for a time with Hunter and Heintzleman. When those generals came down the further bank of Bull Run Creek opposite his brigade, he crossed over and united with the division under Hunter. His timely arrival at this juncture of the battle prevented the rout, if not the annihilation, of Hunter's command, for as his four regiments came upon the scene, he saw that Burnside's brigade was nearly overpowered by the Confederates. Pressing swiftly forward he poured in upon the exultant foe a withering, destructive fire, and then, pushing on at double-quick with the bayonet, checked, routed and won a victory over the Confederates on this part of the field at least. How Sherman and his brave men fought in this first great battle of the Rebellion, may be inferred from the fact that two-thirds of the casualties in the division fell on his single brigade, the loss being over a fifth of that sustained by the entire army.

Leaving the field of Bull Run, we pass hurriedly to Fort Donelson, and from thence to the bloody battle of Pittsburgh Landing, where under Grant he commanded the Fifth Division. It is said of him by another, that in this action "he rose at once to the peril of the occasion, and all day long moved like a fabled god over that disastrous field. Clinging to his position till the last moment, fighting as he retired, his orders flying like lightning in every direction, and he himself galloping incessantly through the hottest fire; now rallying his men, now planting a battery, he seemed omnipresent and to bear a charmed life. Horse after horse sunk under him; he himself was struck again and again; and yet he not only kept the field, but blazed like a meteor over it. At noon of that Sabbath day, he was dismounted, his hand in a sling and bleeding, giving directions to his chief of artillery, while it was one incessant crash and roar all around him. Suddenly he saw to the right his men giving way before a cloud of rebels. 'I was looking for that,' he exclaimed. The next moment the battery he had been placing in position opened, sending death and destruction into the close-packed ranks. The rebel commander glancing at the battery, ordered the cavalry to charge it. Seeing them coming down, Sherman quickly ordered up two companies of infantry, which, pouring in a deadly volley, sent them to the right about with empty saddles. The onset was arrested, and our troops rallied with renewed courage." Thus he acted all that fearful Sabbath day.

As Sheridan was the rock that saved Rosecrans at Stone River, and Thomas the one that saved him at Chickamauga, so Sherman was the rock that saved Grant at Shiloh. At its close his old legion met him, and sent up three cheers at the sight of his well-remembered form. Rousseau in speaking of his conduct in this battle said: "No man living could surpass him." General Nelson a few days before his death remarked: "During eight hours the fate of the army on the field of Shiloh depended on the life of one man: if General Sherman had fallen, the army would have been captured or destroyed." Grant said: "To his individual efforts I am indebted for the success of this battle;" and Halleck in his despatch bore this unqualified testimony: " It is the unanimous opinion here, that Brigadier-General W. T. Sherman saved the fortunes of the day on the sixth of April." " He was a strong man in the high places of the field, and hope shone in him like a pillar of fire when it had gone out in all other men."

The next day, when Buell's fresh battalions took the field, Sherman again led his battered regiments into the fight, and enacted over again the heroic deeds of the day before; for as Rousseau said, he "fights by the week." Untiring to the last, he pushed out the third day after the victory and whipped the enemy's cavalry, taking a large supply of ammunition.

In the subsequent advance to Corinth, his division bore the most conspicuous part, and was the first to enter the deserted works of the enemy. In the meantime he had been promoted to major-general of volunteers.

The limits of this chapter will not allow us to follow General Sherman in the details of his grand movements; but, glancing at the siege of Vicksburg, the operations around Chattanooga and Missionary Ridge, the masterly manœuvering that led to the defeat of Hood, and the capture of Atlanta, we come to the crowning glory of his military career—the march to the sea.

This magnificent campaign from Chattanooga to Atlanta, and from Atlanta to the sea, was so unlike anything that preceded it in war history that it is called "the great march," to distinguish it from all other marches ancient or modern. He could never have accomplished the wide results obtained by it, had he undertaken to do so by direct assault against fortressed cities, well-chosen positions, and an opposing army of sixty thousand infantry, and ten thousand horse. Strategy by flanking movements constituted the key-note to his operations, and thenceforward he became known as "the great flanker."

Predictions were not wanting on all sides that such a march through an enemy's country could not be performed and yet preserve the lines of communication and supply with so far distant a base. It never *had* been done, and that fact to the minds of many, seemed a potent reason why it could not be successfully undertaken by Sherman. But the possibilities which would have appalled a smaller genius, only served, with the invincible Sherman, as a tonic influence by which hitherto undreamed-of achievements became splendid realities.

The first battle and victory of the great march took place at Resaca, where Johnston, having been compelled to abandon a position of great strength near Dalton, met the troops of McPherson, which had come up eighteen miles in his rear. The fighting continued several days, and about one thousand prisoners were captured.

At Marietta, an important railroad junction was seized by Hooker; and the great game of move, and counter-move, and feints, by which the enemy's force was focussed in directions away from the point of march, began. Threatenings in front, flank and rear first mystified, and then maddened the foe. The only mis-

SHERMAN'S MARCH BY TORCHLIGHT THROUGH THE SWAMPS OF GEORGIA.

take of the great campaign, apparently, was the murderous battle of Kenesaw Mountain. The fruitlessness of direct attack on so impregnable a height was demonstrated at the cost of immense slaughter. After this experience, Sherman again resorted to his old mode of flanking, and, crossing the Chattahoochie, forced Johnston back into Atlanta. The road from Chattanooga to this point had been one long battle-field, and now the Gate City saw the conquering hosts of Sherman at her very portals. A fight and siege followed. But neither siege nor battle availed to unlock the situation. The bold design was then formed of cutting Atlanta from her base of supplies, by occupying the Macon road. This difficult task was given to Kilpatrick and his gallant cavalry, and brought to successful issue. The march of the several infantry chiefs proceeded with perfect concert of action, with Howard on the right, Thomas in the centre and Schofield on the left. On the first of September, the three wings were close on Atlanta and compelled a battle, in which the enemy were assaulted and defeated. Hood then evacuated Atlanta, burning the stores he was obliged to leave behind. The skies at night became lurid with the red glare of blazing cotton bales, a hundred cars, six engines and other supplies.

Lighted by this funeral pyre of lost hopes, Hood conducted his depleted ranks towards Macon.

The marvellous foresight and genius exhibited in this campaign can hardly be over-rated. Every difficulty—and their name was legion—was overcome, and every contingency provided for. A new departure from military science had been taken, and old rules laughed down the wind.

The great victory was thundered in salute from hundreds of guns at the North, and the magic word "Atlanta" inscribed on the banners of the conquering host. But greater things were to follow. From Atlanta, Sherman beheld Savannah by the sea, and, to the surprise of North and South and the astonishment of England, reached forth and grasped that prize. By the aid of his secondary base at the mountain pass of Allatoona (made efficient in its moment of peril by the heroism of Corse, who "held the fort" against awful odds till Sherman came), with the co-operation of the great Thomas, the intrepid McPherson, and Slocum, and Schofield, and the invaluable services rendered by Kilpatrick and his fiery dragoons, concealing from the enemy the real objects of Sherman—with these superb supports, the grand journey from Atlanta to the sea was accomplished. And while every one else looked on in doubt, mystified and not knowing how it would all end or where he would strike, Sherman himself, with the sublime confidence born of genius, never for a moment doubted his success.

On the fifteenth of November, the army swept seaward. The goal in the distance faintly loomed, nearly three hundred miles away. Village, town and plantation were rapidly passed *en route*.

A halt of a few days was made at Milledgeville for rest, and at Macon, the capital, the soldiers took possession of the legislative halls, from whence the Confederates had fled in confusion, and held mock sessions of State. Sherman also had the honor of sleeping on the floor of the deserted executive mansion.

At Millen, another halt was made. On the second of December, the several columns marched out of this place and on six different roads continued the advance to the sea. Vast tracks of pine forest lay in their line of march, and the scenery grew poetic and picturesque. Cities and villages, the open country and the Georgian pines were rapidly left behind. At last they reached Fort McAllister, at the mouth of the Ogeechee River, a few miles south of Savannah.

Here the gallant and desperate assault by Hazen's division carried the works against well-nigh overwhelming odds. Sherman watched the proceedings from the roof of a rice mill on the other side of the Ogeechee. His excitement, intense but controlled, found vent in half exclamations.

Howard stood beside him, and their respective staffs were grouped around. Sherman gazed on the assault, through his glass, with breathless interest.

"See that flag in the advance, Howard!" he says. "How steadily it moves!—not a man falters! There they go still! Grand! Grand!" Then a momentary pause falls between the sentences. "That flag still goes forward! There is no flinching there! Look! it has halted! They waver—no, it's the parapet! There they go again—now they reach it—some are over! Look there! a flag on the works! Another! Another! It's ours—the fort is ours!" He turns to his aid with face aglow. "Captain, have a boat ready. I am going down to the fleet." Then a hurried despatch is written to Washington, telling of victory.

In a few days from the fall of Fort McAllister, Savannah surrendered, and the grand and triumphant march to the sea was accomplished. In the casualties of march and battle, it had not cost over a thousand men. Sherman telegraphed the President as follows:

"I beg to present you as a Christmas gift the city of Savannah, with one hundred and fifty guns and plenty of ammunition, and about twenty-five thousand bales of cotton."

The joy which Sherman's invasion of Georgia carried to thousands of hearts waiting for their prison doors to open, is fully appreciated by the author, then an escaped prisoner, lying in cypress swamps by day and travelling through an unknown country by night. Coming, as we did one day, unexpectedly upon the trail of the great army, with its scattered debris, was like signalling liberty from the gloomy gulfs of despair; and no music ever sounded sweeter than the booming of Sherman's guns in distant battle.

After reaching Savannah the army rested, gaining strength for its next equally bold campaign through the Carolinas to Goldsboro' and Raleigh. The distance to be traversed was five hundred miles; the difficulties, as before, innumerable. Rivers and swamps must be bridged, railroads rebuilt, highways cleared. The swift magic with which these obstacles were overcome was due to the perfect working of the Construction Corps. It seemed as magical as the work of the Cinderella fairy, who turned pumpkins into carriages and "rats to horses fine." Sherman had the most absolute faith in his plans, and never for a moment hesitated in their execution. He completely baffled the enemy as to his designs, and went straight through, without a break in the connection of his work, from Savannah to Columbia, from Columbia to Waynesboro', then to Fayetteville, Goldsboro' and Raleigh. At Goldsboro' he heard of the fall of Petersburg and Richmond, and as he entered Raleigh the news of Lee's surrender reached him. Here, of course, ended his war career. At Washington and at the North he was received with acclamations and enthusiasm wherever he went.

As a military man, Sherman showed himself to be a tremendous power. The boldness and originality of his achievements put old maxims and previous standards to the blush. He became a "law unto himself" in matters of war, and was successful in the face of all adverse prediction.

If he who peruses these pages is a friend of the Union, his heart will beat with admiration and pride for the invincible Sherman who pushed forward day by day, bearing grandly at the head of his resistless columns the Stars and Stripes, until over hill and plain, through the smoke of victorious battles, the national standard waved in triumph over the rebel cities of the sea, over beautiful Savannah and the long-vaunted "impregnable" Charleston.

CHAPTER XXII.

PHILIP HENRY SHERIDAN.

Impetuosity of Character.—A Poor Irish Boy.—At West Point.—Wild Conduct.—Graduation.—Service in Western Territories.—Captain of the Thirteenth Infantry.—Quartermaster under Halleck.—As a Cavalry Officer.—Battle of Booneville.—Promotion to Brigadier-General.—Murfreesboro'.—At Chickamauga and Missionary Ridge.—In Pursuit of Early.—Cedar Creek.—Sheridan's Ride.—The Victory.—At Five Forks and Appomattox.—After the War.

SHERIDAN is probably the most intense type of "soldiership" brought to light by the last war. Nor can any other war furnish an individual example that will surpass him in fiery concentration. In battle, he is the very soul of vehement action—the incarnate wrath of the storm. No historian can ever portray the man so truly as did the remarkable victory of Cedar Creek—a result solely of his extraordinary power. The marvellous will-force with which he could hurl himself in the front of battle, and infuse his own spirit of unconquerable daring into the ranks, is phenomenal, to say the least.

An Irish lad, and poor, he was born at Somerset, Perry county, Ohio, March sixth, 1831. No especial account is given of him until he went to West Point in 1848. He was then seventeen, and had managed to attract the notice of the Congressman from his district, who secured him the appointment. He proved an apt and energetic student, but in other respects his life at West Point was a continual succession of quarrels and fights in which he became involved through his quick temper. He graduated, however, in 1853, escaping failure only by five points.

After leaving West Point, he served in Texas and on the Pacific coast until May fourteenth, 1861, when he was made captain of the Thirteenth Infantry. While in those far western territories he had become inured to hardship and perils, and on one or two occasions had so far distinguished himself that he was complimented by General Scott and honorably mentioned in general orders.

After his appointment to a captaincy, he joined his command at Jefferson Barracks, Mo., and was made chief quartermaster of the army at that point.

In March, 1862, after Halleck had taken command in the west, he was made chief quarter-master of the Western Department, ranking as major. But Halleck seems to have discovered his special value as a cavalry officer, and in May, 1862, made him colonel of the Second Michigan Cavalry. The battle of Booneville, conducted by Sheridan on July first, was such a brilliant piece of strategy, where wit outgeneralled numbers, that he was recommended by Grant for promotion and received the appointment of brigadier-general of volunteers, dating from that battle.

In the fight at Murfreesboro', Sheridan's splendid qualities of generalship shone pre-eminently. On that field, he was in command of the left division of the right wing of our army, and by the firm stand he made after the other two divisions were surprised into rout, saved the day to Rosecrans. That general, in his report of the battle, said of Sheridan: "The constancy and steadfastness of his troops enabled the reserve to reach the right of our army in time to turn the tide of battle, and changed a threatened rout into a victory. He has fairly won promotion." This praise was fully deserved, and "Little Phil." was consequently given a major-generalship.

He fought with characteristic bravery at the bloody battle of Chickamauga, though without avail; and at Missionary Ridge, he was in the thickest of the fray. His dauntless leadership contributed not a little to the successful results of that day.

When Grant became lieutenant-general, Sheridan was given the command of the cavalry of the Army of the Potomac, and all his subsequent movements evinced wonderful daring, skill and energy. No trust committed to his charge was ever misplaced, no matter what its magnitude or importance.

When the Confederate Generals Ewell and Early were sent into the Shenandoah Valley, and went so far north as to threaten Washington, Grant consolidated the four military divisions of the Susquehanna, Washington, Monongahela and West Virginia into the "Army of the Shenandoah," and placed Sheridan in command. He defeated Early at Opequan, September nineteenth—for which he was made brigadier-general of the United States army; defeated him again at Fisher's Hill, on the twenty-second, and on October nineteenth occurred the battle of Cedar Creek.

The position of Sheridan's army at this time was along the crest of three hills, "each one a little back of the other." The Army of West Virginia, under Crook, held the first hill; the second was occupied by the Nineteenth Corps under Emory, and the Sixth

Corps, with Torbet's cavalry covering its right flank, held the third elevation. Early, marching his army in five columns, crossed the mountains and forded the north branch of the Shenandoah River, at midnight, on the eighteenth. He knew that Sheridan had gone up to Washington, and wanted to take advantage of his absence to surprise the unsuspecting camp. The march was conducted so noiselessly that though he skirted the borders of our position for miles, nothing came to the ears of our pickets, save in a few instances, where a heavy, muffled tramp was heard, but disregarded as of no consequence.

The gray gloom of early morning hovered over the camp, when a reconnoitring force from Crook's army was preparing to go out. Suddenly a wild yell burst through the fog, which hid from view the Confederate army. A withering musketry fire and the clash of arms quickly followed. Before our surprised and panic-stricken troops could be formed in battle-array, the enemy were upon them, and after a short and sharp encounter, the Army of Western Virginia was thrown into utter rout—a mass of fugitives flying before the pursuing foe back towards the second hill where the Nineteenth Corps was encamped.

The few regiments of Crook's force which endeavored to make a stand were swept back before the swelling tide of fugitives in full and disordered retreat.

The Nineteenth Corps attempted to arrest the Confederate advance, but the enemy getting in our rear and enfilading us with our captured batteries, the troops broke rank and fell back in confusion towards the encampment of the Sixth Corps on the third hill in the rear.

A new line of battle was formed by Wright, who was making desperate attempts to stay the onward tide of fugitives which steadily poured to the rear. Early's hungry troops now began to leave their ranks in large numbers to plunder the two deserted camps of their rich booty. Had Wright been aware of this fact, perhaps he could have successfully resisted the Confederate advance. As it was, after having hurled back a fierce onset of the enemy and covered the retreat of the disordered crowd in his rear, he began to fear that his communications might be endangered and therefore fell back towards Middletown. Wright had thus heroically interposed himself and his command between our army and its threatened destruction.

Merritt and Custer, with two divisions of cavalry, were ordered to our left, to check the murderous fire assailing it, and a severe fight ensued in the fields of Middletown. A concentrated fire from the heights, where Early had planted his batteries, was poured upon the Union left, compelling it to retreat.

Sheridan, meantime, was at Winchester, where he had arrived the night before, intending to go on to Cedar Creek the next morning. As he sipped his coffee at breakfast, he did not, for an instant, dream of the terrible rout and disaster hovering, at that moment, over his army. When he rode out of Winchester, the vibrations of the ground under the heavy discharges of artillery in the distance, gave the first intimations of danger. But he was not yet alarmed, knowing the security of his position. As he went onward, however, the thunder of the cannon deepened, and then the terrible truth flashed upon him. He dashed spurs into his horse and was soon tearing madly along the road, far ahead of his escort.

For five anxious hours the desperate struggle had gone on when Sheridan arrived on the field, encountering first, the stream of fugitives surging northward. They turned about as they saw their invincible leader flying towards the front, and even the wounded along the roadside cheered him as he passed. Swinging his cap over his head, he shouted: "Face the other way, boys!—face the other way! We are going back to our camps! We are going to lick them out of their boots!"

It was about ten o'clock when, with his horse covered with foam, he galloped up to the front. Immediately, under his quick commands, the broken ranks were reformed and when the Confederates made their next grand charge across the fields, the terrific repulse that met and hurled them back, showed the turn of the tide and compelled them to relinquish the offensive. For two hours Sheridan rode back and forth along the line, seeming to be everywhere at once, infusing into the men his own daring courage and enthusiasm. Shouts and cheers followed him; and though the tired soldiers had been fighting for five long hours and had eaten nothing since the night before, his presence was both food and inspiration, and everything seemed to be forgotten in an all-controlling impulse to follow their glorious leader to victory.

Early retired his troops a short distance after their repulse, and began throwing up breastworks. But the intrepid Sheridan had no notion of allowing him to retain that position. He meant to regain Cedar Creek and rout the enemy. At half-past three a bold charge was made. An awful musketry and artillery fire was poured into the advancing Union columns, and, at first, the lines broke and fell back; but Sheridan rose at once to the needs of the crisis, and with superhuman efforts restored order and resumed the advance. Then came "the long-drawn yell of our charge," and "everything on the first line, the stone walls, the tangled wood, the advanced crest and half-finished breastworks, had been carried."

The panic-stricken enemy was sent flying in utter rout on through Middletown, through Strasburg, through Fisher's Hill, and to Woodstock, sixteen miles beyond. Early was thus effectually driven out of the Shenandoah Valley, and permanently crippled.

This wonderful victory, due to Sheridan's personal presence alone, put a crown on his head which few warriors could pluck from the heights of Fame.

The story, as set to verse by Mr. Read, has all the spirited ardor of the headlong and impatient rider.

"Up from the South at break of day,
Bringing to Winchester fresh dismay,
The affrighted air with a shudder bore,
Like a herald in haste, to the chieftain's door,
The terrible grumble, and rumble, and roar,
Telling the battle was on once more,
And Sheridan twenty miles away.

"And wider still those billows of war
Thundered along the horizon's bar;
And louder yet into Winchester rolled
The roar of that red sea uncontrolled,
Making the blood of the listener cold,
As he thought of the stake in that fiery fray,
And Sheridan twenty miles away.

"But there is a road from Winchester town,
A good, broad highway leading down;
And there through the flush of the morning light
A steed as black as the steeds of night
Was seen to pass as with eagle flight;

SHERIDAN BACK FROM WINCHESTER.

As if he knew the terrible need
He stretched away with his utmost speed.
Hills rose and fell; but his heart was gay,
With Sheridan fifteen miles away.

"Still sprung from those swift hoofs thundering south,
The dust, like smoke from the cannon's mouth,
Or the trail of a comet sweeping faster and faster,
Foreboding to traitors the doom of disaster.
The heart of the steed and the heart of the master
Were beating like prisoners assaulting their walls,
Impatient to be where the battle-field calls;
Every nerve of the charger was strained to full play.
With Sheridan only ten miles away.

"Under his spurning feet, the road
Like an arrowy Alpine river flowed,
And the landscape sped away behind,
Like an ocean flying before the wind;
And the steed like a bark fed with furnace ire,
Swept on with his wild eye full of fire.
But lo! he is nearing his heart's desire,
He is snuffing the smoke of the roaring fray
With Sheridan only five miles away.

"The first that the general saw, were the groups
Of stragglers, and then the retreating troops;
What was done? what to do? a glance told him both,
Then, striking his spurs, with a terrible oath,
He dashed down the line 'mid a storm of huzzas,
And the wave of retreat checked its course there, because
The sight of the master compelled it to pause.

"With foam and with dust the black charger was gray;
By the flash of his eye, and the red nostril's play,
He seemed to the whole great army to say,
'I have brought you Sheridan all the way
From Winchester down, to save the day.'

"'Hurrah! hurrah for Sheridan!
Hurrah! hurrah for horse and man!
And when their statues are placed on high,
Under the dome of the Union sky,

> The American soldier's Temple of Fame,
> There, with the glorious General's name,
> Be it said in letters both bold and bright:
> 'Here is the steed that saved the day
> By carrying Sheridan into the fight
> From Winchester—twenty miles away.'"

Sheridan's next promotion to major-general in the regular army occurred soon after the battle of Cedar Creek; and on April first, 1865, he gained the battle of Five Forks, thus insuring the abandonment of Petersburg and Richmond. He also aided materially in the environment of Lee's army which brought about the surrender at Appomattox Court House.

After the war, July seventeenth, 1866, he was appointed to the command of the Gulf military division, and in March, 1867, of the fifth military district, including Louisiana and Texas. On September twelfth, he was placed over the department of the Missouri, with head-quarters at Fort Leavenworth, and on March fourth, 1869, received the promotion of lieutenant-general, and was appointed to the command of the division of the Missouri, of the Platte, and of Texas, with head-quarters at Chicago, where he still remains.

CHAPTER XXIII.
GEORGE BRINTON McCLELLAN.

Birth and Education.—In the Mexican War.—Services in Surveys of Railroad Routes.—A Model Report.—Sent to the Crimea.—Superintendent of the Illinois Central.—Response to Governor Dennison.—Over the Department of the Ohio.—Virginia Campaigns.—In Command of the Army of the Potomac.—Movement to the Peninsula.—Siege of Yorktown.—Army Withdrawn.—McClellan's Letter.—Again in Command of the Potomac Army.—South Mountain and Antietam.—Relieved of his Command at Warrenton.—Nominated for the Presidency.—In Europe.—Governor of New Jersey.

THE third day of December, 1826, is duly vouched for as the birth-date of McClellan. His father was a physician of Philadelphia, and in that city of brotherly love, the subject of this chapter was born. His youthful life ran in peaceful channels and sheltered nooks, under the guiding rays of kindly home influences and the protecting ægis of his father's roof. In 1846, he graduated at West Point, second in his class, and was ordered at once to Mexico, after having received the brevet of second lieutenant. He went to Mexico full of enthùsiasm for the cause, and, once among his soldiers, soon became the object of their devoted love. That strong personal magnetism which afterwards so won his followers on the Peninsula, here first indicated itself. He distinguished himself in the Mexican war at Vera Cruz, Monterey, Molino del Rey and Cerro Gordo, being especially noted for coolness under fire. At Cerro Gordo it was he who had charge of the difficult task of dragging those heavy howitzers up the rocky steep on the night preceding that wonderful battle, where from the summit they blazed victorious thunder into the astonished Mexican ranks. At Chapultepec he was commended for "gallant and meritorious conduct," and received promotion in consequence.

Between the Mexican war and 1861, there is a long hiatus in the military experience of McClellan. But during that period he was appointed by the Secretary of War to the joint command of an expedition having for its principal object "the discovery and survey of a railroad route from the Pacific ocean to the Mississippi river across the Cascade Range." The successful execution of this mission was especially commended.

In 1851, he had been ordered to Fort Delaware to superintend its construction, and the next year accompanied Captain Randolph B. Marcy in an exploration of Red River. Afterwards he went with General P. F. Smith to Texas, to survey the rivers and harbors of that State.

On his return from Oregon he was ordered by government to investigate the entire railroad system of the United States, "with a view to obtain all necessary data on construction, equipment and management for the successful operation of the Pacific railroad." This report, which was considered a model of clearness and strength, became the leading authority on that subject and was the means afterwards of making him Superintendent of the Illinois Central line.

In 1854-5 McClellan was sent on a secret mission to the West Indies, and subsequently he was one of a commission of three army officers despatched to the Crimea to study the organization of European armies. The results of these labors were published by order of Congress, March second, 1861. The use of earth fortifications, rifled arms, railroads as utilized for purposes of war, the adaptation of iron-plated vessels, the employment of steam transports, the balloon telegraph, the floating ram, the sanitary commission, the improved hospital and other improvements in the art of war, we owe, it is said, to the labors of this commission.

In 1857, McClellan became general superintendent of the Illinois Central Railroad, and subsequently, also, its vice-president.

Then came the troubled wave of civil war, and on the twenty-third of April, 1861, he was appointed by Governor Dennison, of Ohio, to organize the mass of unarmed men collected in that State, in response to the first call of the President. On the thirteenth of May, he was assigned to the command of the Department of the Ohio. Then followed the two campaigns in Western Virginia, with the battles of Grafton, Rich Mountain and Laurel Hill, whose results gave us entire control of all that part of the State north of the Great Kanawha, including the contiguous eastern passes. For these brilliant operations McClellan received the thanks of Congress.

On the twenty-second of July, 1861, while at Beverly, conducting affairs for the relief of the Upper Kanawha Valley, he was telegraphed from Washington to turn over his command to Brigadier-General Rosecrans and go at once to the capital. Here he was assigned to the command of the Army of the Potomac, and immediately began the organization of that incoherent congregation of volunteers which soon assumed shape under the effects of his superior discipline, and gained a reputation as a magnificent body of soldiery.

The North Carolina expedition was begun, and operations south and west were now set in motion. He had been placed in command of the army six days after the battle of Bull Run, and some correspondence ensued between President Lincoln and himself relative to proposed plans for the capture of Richmond, and offensive movements in general.

It is freely accorded by all that in McClellan's defensive operations about Washington—in the wonderful transformation which he wrought with the disordered mass of raw recruits constituting the Army of the Potomac—in his work on Maryland soil and the restoration of West Virginia to the Union, he displayed rare genius and great qualities as a general. It is the Peninsular campaign which now followed that set in motion such contrary currents of opinions.

When the movement to the Peninsula began, a large force from the Army of the Potomac was retained in Washington for its defence, and the day after McClellan reached his base of operations, ten thousand men under General Wool were also detached from his command. The naval armament, too, was withdrawn, and when he was about "turning Yorktown by West Point," the First Corps of sixty thousand men, under McDowell, was suddenly sent to Harper's Ferry by order of the President, instead of being allowed to join him as he expected.

In his report McClellan says: "It was now, of

course, out of my power to turn Yorktown by West Point. I had, therefore, no choice left but to attack it directly in front as I best could with the force at my command."

Then followed the siege of that place, which lasted until May fifth, and finally resulted in the disastrous retreat to the James, at Harrison's Landing—July fourth and fifth, 1862—famous at the time as the great " change of base."

In the following month the army was withdrawn to the relief of Pope in Eastern Virginia, and McClellan was left for a brief time without any separate command. While in this anomalous condition he wrote the following letter to Washington:

"ALEXANDRIA, VA., *August 30th*, 1862.

* * * * * * * * * * * * *

" I cannot express to you the pain and mortification I have experienced to-day in listening to the distant sound of the firing of my men. As I can be of no further use here, I respectfully ask that if there is a probability of the conflict being renewed to-morrow, I may be permitted to go to the scene of battle with my staff, merely to be with my own men, if nothing more; they will fight none the worse for my being with them. If it is not deemed best to intrust me with the command even of my own army, I simply ask to be permitted to share their fate on the field of battle. * * *

"I have been engaged for the last few hours, in doing what I can to make arrangements for the wounded. I have started out all the ambulances now landed.

"As I have sent my escort to the front, I would be

glad to take some of Gregg's cavalry with me, if allowed to go."

But this was not permitted. In September, after Pope's disasters, he was once more placed over the forces defending Washington, and from thence followed Lee into Maryland, where the battles of South Mountain and Antietam were fought—September fourteenth and seventeenth.

But the delay which followed these movements created intense dissatisfaction at Washington. On the seventh of November, therefore, while at Warrenton, Virginia, with a plan of advance about to be put in operation which augured the fairest results, he was relieved of his command, Burnside was substituted in his place, and the military career of McClellan, with reference to the civil war, ended.

He immediately retired to New Jersey, and on August thirty-first, 1864, received the Democratic nomination for the presidency. Lincoln, however, was re-elected by an overwhelming majority, and the only States which gave their votes to McClellan were Kentucky, New Jersey, and Delaware.

He resigned his commission as major-general on election day, and in the spring of 1865, embarked for Europe. On his return to this country, in 1868, he was appointed superintendent of the construction of Stevens' battery and also of the railroad bridge across the Hudson. In 1870, he was made chief engineer of the department of docks in New York city, a position which he resigned in 1872.

He is the author of several military reports, text-books, and manuals, which take high rank in their school. He was elected governor of New Jersey in 1877, a station which he occupies at the present time.

Partisan opinions are, of course, rife regarding the conduct of what is known as the Peninsular campaign; those who sustain McClellan, believing with him, that all that was needed to strike the final blow and secure Richmond after the seven-days' battles, was to form a junction with McDowell and his sixty thousand men; and that the suspension of this movement by order of the President, precipitated the disaster of continued war and doomed McClellan.

There seems, however, to be abundant evidence which goes to show that inefficiency of management was the dominant cause of failure and disaster in the miasmatic swamps of the Chickahominy, and afterwards.

No satisfactory reason has ever been given for the five months of inaction succeeding December, 1861, under which our army of one hundred thousand finely disciplined troops was obscured, while the Potomac was blockaded, and an enemy, inferior in numbers, equipment, and organization, was within twenty miles of the Union lines.

No satisfactory reason has ever been given, why the advance upon Richmond, when it at last began, was so exceedingly slow, allowing the enemy plenty of time to make effective preparations for their reception. Four weeks were occupied in the siege of Yorktown, when, in the opinion of able military authority, it might have been taken by assault at once. The battle of Williamsburg was said to have been fought without any concert of action, and won by the heroism of division commanders and the bravery of their soldiers. Fourteen days were occupied in marching between

Williamsburg and Bottom's Bridge, on the Chickahominy, a distance of forty miles, and an average of three miles a day.

The battle of Williamsburg was fought on the fifth of May: had the approach to James River been seized upon at once, and the co-operation of the navy thus secured, those historic seven days of subsequent battle might have been avoided. But the brave army was doomed. According to some statements, sixty thousand of them found graves in the Peninsula.

Once having decided on the retreat from the Chickahominy to the James, as a "change of base," that most difficult of all military operations, a flank march in the presence of a flushed and exultant foe of largely superior numbers, was undertaken. There is no doubt that this retreat was conducted with great skill and consummate generalship. The dissatisfaction did not rest there, but with previous movements which rendered it necessary.

The tragedies of Gaines' Mill, Savage Station, White Oak Swamp, Seven Pines, Chickahominy, Charles' City, and Malvern Hill, were heroically enacted, and the devoted army at length reached rest and safety on the banks of the James. Those days were, indeed, as the general, who conducted the seven battles, says, "classical in American history; in which the noble soldiers fought an overwhelming enemy by day and retreated from successive victories by night, through a week of battle, closing the terrible scenes of conflict with the ever memorable victory at Malvern, where they drove back, beaten and shattered, the entire eastern army of the Confederacy." On the fourth of July, after they had reached Harrison's Landing, McClellan reviewed the troops, and was received with irrepressible enthusiasm, storms of cheers following him from line to line.

The Peninsular campaign, like other campaigns that succeeded it, is freighted with individual instances of heroism and of dramatic situations of peril and pathos.

After the battle of Savage Station, Dr. Marks, chaplain of the Sixty-third Pennsylvania Regiment, rode to that place to see what could be done towards removing the thousands of sick and wounded men collected there. General Heintzleman said nothing could be done— that the ambulances must depart empty. It was deemed a necessity to leave the wounded in the enemy's hands. A colonel rode into the hospital grounds to withdraw the pickets, announcing that the rebels would be there in a half hour. Every patient who could leave his cot, now endeavored to escape. "I beheld," says Dr. Marks, "a long, staggering line of the patients, some carrying their guns and supporting a companion on an arm, others tottering feebly over a staff which they appeared scarcely to have strength to lift. One was borne on the shoulders of two of his companions, in the hope that when he had gone a little distance he might be able to walk. One had already sat down, fainting. Some had risen from the first rest and fell in the road, but after a few moments in the open air and stimulated by the fear of the enemy, they could walk more strongly. Never have I beheld a spectacle more touching and more sad."

The battle of Gaines' Mill is described as especially picturesque. The plain was broken into heavily-wooded crests. The sunlight of a June day reflected the weapons of over a hundred thousand combatants.

The infantry were defiling in the open spaces or climbing the hills or charging with headlong fury on the foe. Cavalry squadrons swept in swift curves around the crests, and flying artillery dashed from ridge to ridge, while batteries thundered, and mounted lancers with "fluttering pennons" waited, in reserve, along the edge of the ravine, the order to rush to battle.

> "By Heaven! it was a splendid sight to see,
> For one who had no friend or brother there!"

Rev. William Dickson, chaplain of the Twelfth Pennsylvania Reserves, was in a hospital in this ravine when an alarm came that the enemy were upon them. He ran up the side of the ravine and saw the foe at hand. At the same moment some one shouted from a patriot battery in rear of him: "Lie down! You are right in our way!"

He fell on his face while a screaming shell went over his head. Knowing that the guns were fired in line and that his only retreat lay along that line, he sprang up, ran a few steps and again threw himself—thus running the gauntlet of two batteries in full play. The men at the guns shouted: "Out of the way, or you'll be shot!"

He shouted back: "Fire away! I'll take care of myself!" And he did.

Skilful retreats from peril have contributed as much to military renown as campaigns conducted by direct assault; they afford an opportunity for even greater generalship; and probably no portion of the record of our civil war is brighter with splendid achievement and valorous daring than that which relates the actions of those seven days on the Peninsula. But McClellan was censured by press and people; everywhere indeed.

except in the army—which seemed to idolize him blindly—he was charged with the defeat of that army and the terrible results of leading it into the Chickahominy trap.

A committee of investigation, ordered by Congress, made a report which was the means of deposing him from his command. The facts of the case, in all their bearings, are before the public, and McClellan's own report is very voluminous. The public can judge whether he was rightly or wrongly condemned for inefficiency. We leave that judgment with them and with posterity.

CHAPTER XXIV.

AMBROSE EVERETT BURNSIDE.

His Scotch Blood.—Graduates at West Point.—In New Mexico.—As an Inventor.—Marching to the Front.—At Bull Run.—Promotion.—In Command of the North Carolina Expedition.—Capture of Newbern, Fort Macon and Beaufort.—At Antietam.—Slaughter at Fredericksburg.—Tenders his Resignation.—Brilliant Capture of East Tennessee. — Before Petersburg. — Elected Governor of Rhode Island.—In Congress.

THE career of Burnside as a military leader during the last war seems to be pretty evenly sandwiched between great disaster and brilliant success. For his victories in East Tennessee he received the thanks of Congress. His utter failure before Petersburg called forth the severest censure. These extremes go far towards illustrating the character of his leadership.

He comes of Scotch ancestry, and was born at Liberty, Indiana, May twenty-third, 1824. He attended the school at West Point and graduated in 1847. He was in New Mexico, in command of a squadron of cavalry, and acted as quarter-master in the boundary commission of 1851. From New Mexico he was sent to Washington as bearer of despatches, and in December, 1852, was made first lieutenant. About this time he invented a breech-loading rifle and made extensive arrangements for its manufacture, resigning his commission on that account. But the contract for selling large quantities to the government fell through and his project proved a failure. Afterwards he became treasurer of the Illinois Central Railroad at the company's office in New York city.

The war spirit which flamed over the land in 1861 found an immediate response in him, and in four days after the President's call for troops, he was marching to Washington as colonel of the First Regiment of Rhode Island Volunteers.

At Bull Run he commanded a brigade, and was complimented by McDowell for the courageous part he took in that battle. He was afterwards promoted to a brigadier-generalship.

In the month of January, 1862, he commanded an expedition to North Carolina for the capture of Newbern and Roanoke. These were important military positions, and the expedition was planned to operate in concert with McClellan and the Potomac army in their advance to Richmond. The fleet consisted of twenty-three gunboats and transports, carrying fifteen thousand men. In his journey from Hampton Roads he encountered storm and misfortune, but at length, after surmounting many difficulties, he had conquered the coast as far as Newbern, against which he prepared to move on the night of March twelfth. Everything being in readiness, the appointed signal was given, and the fleet sailed southward from Hatteras, down Pamlico sound, entered the mouth of the Neuse, and anchored within a few miles of Newbern. A line of water-batteries commanded the river, and field fortifications reached inland, connected with them to prevent the enemy from advancing by shore. Six miles down the river the guns of the lower fort threatened the daring intruder, and from that point back to the city there extended a continuous chain of forts and batteries. Near the city, a fort mounting thirteen heavy guns and bomb-proof, was so arranged as to command both the water and the only land approaches on that side. In fact, the entire area for several miles before the city, was filled with forts, earthworks, ditches, rifle-pits, and all the other mechanical appliances of warfare.

On the morning of the thirteenth the troops were landed at a point called Slocum's Creek, sixteen miles below Newbern. Four hours of battle followed. Then a daring assault was made which swept everything before it. The contest was severe, the fighting desperate, the victory that followed brilliant in the extreme. It blazoned the name of Burnside far and wide, and in four days afterwards he was made major-general. The city was put under military rule at once, and order and quietness prevailed.

The capture of Newbern made the final reduction of Beaufort and Fort Macon sure, and eventually placed Burnside in command of the Army of the Potomac.

Burnside immediately invested Fort Macon and Beaufort, and after much skilful planning and an immense amount of labor, compelled their surrender.

When McClellan retreated from the Chickahominy, he took his army to Newport News, and soon after was ordered to Fredericksburg. He took part in the battle of South Mountain, and also in bloody Antietam, where he commanded the left wing of McClellan's army, and from some unexplained cause failed in the part assigned him. McClellan attributed his own failure to overthrow Lee at this point to Burnside's lack of co-operation.

Soon after the battle of Antietam, McClellan was removed and Burnside put in his place. He accepted his new position with great reluctance, unfeigned self-distrust, and only as a matter of obedience to orders.

The battle of Fredericksburg was fought on the thirteenth of December following—an action precipitated, it has been thought, by the force of public sentiment at the north, which demanded a decisive forward movement, the key-note of which was heard in the newspaper cry of "On to Richmond!" But whatever influence brought on the final catastrophe, it was a battle without apparent results—a grand carnival of slaughter, where the bravest of troops marched to their bloody doom, a useless sacrifice, except in the terrible lesson learned. Burnside's purpose was to get in the rear of Lee's army, but failing in this, he marched boldly up to the lion's mouth, attacking the enemy in his intrenchments. Crossing the Rappahannock, the needless butchery was enacted on its south bank, and the depleted Union ranks re-crossed to the northern shore without result of any kind except the sad record of twenty thousand dead and wounded left on the field.

Another attempt to cross the Rappahannock in January, met with failure on account of heavy rains which transformed the solid land into liquid mud, and rendered the transit of an army next to an impossibility.

Between these failures and the violent criticism which they evoked, Burnside resigned, and Hooker succeeded him as chief in command.

He next figured in the Department of the Ohio, over which he was placed, having his head-quarters at

Cincinnati. Here he succeeded in calling out a storm of opposition, by prohibiting the circulation of the New York *World* and the Chicago *Times*, to suppress, as he said, all open hostility to government. But excitement ran so high in consequence, that the order respecting the Chicago *Times* was revoked.

Then followed the expedition into East Tennessee, co-operating with Rosecrans. He made a brilliant entry into Knoxville, and by skilful movements and rapid marches, surprised and cut off a force of two thousand at Cumberland Gap, captured them and with them fourteen pieces of artillery. The loyal East Tennesseeans received him with the wildest demonstrations of joy. On the line of his march between Kingston and Knoxville, "sixty women and girls stood by the roadside, waving Union flags and shouting, 'Hurrah for the Union!' Old ladies rushed out of their houses who wanted to see General Burnside and shake hands with him, and cried, 'Welcome! welcome, General Burnside, to East Tennessee!'" A public meeting was also called, which he addressed.

Burnside successfully resisted the desperate assault on Knoxville by Longstreet's army, which afterwards besieged the place until Sherman's too near approach alarmed them into retreat.

Burnside's military record between this date and Petersburg is a record of bravery and sound judgment, and for what he did in East Tennessee he received the thanks of Congress.

For a month and more he sat down before one of the principal redoubts at Petersburg, busy with the work of excavation and running a secret mine under the hostile lines. At the proper moment the mine was fired and the assaulting column rushed in. But not at once—nor in time. When they did, it was too late to be victorious. The enemy had had time to recover, closed around the Union troops, and hacked and slew without mercy. The mine proved a success for the Confederates rather than the troops of Burnside.

Of course this failure brought down on his head a storm of censure, and an investigation was ordered, in which "confusion became worse confounded." His resignation was immediately proffered, but the President refused to accept it. He was, however, granted a leave of absence, and finally resigned, April fifteenth, 1865.

In 1866, he was elected Governor of Rhode Island, and re-elected the succeeding two years. In 1870, he went to Europe, and while there endeavored to mediate between the German and French belligerents, though without success. He has since gained an enviable reputation in Congress as a faithful representative, and in private life is a man of fine character and high social standing. Little Rhode Island has repeatedly given him her enthusiastic endorsement as a leader of sterling qualities.

CHAPTER XXV.

GEORGE HENRY THOMAS.

A Second Washington.— Birth and Education.— Promotion for Bravery.— In Mexico.— Prompt Response at the Outbreak of Civil War.—The Battle of Mill Spring.—Declines to Supersede Buell.—At Murfreesboro'.—Chickamauga.—Position of Troops Under Thomas.—Their Firm Stand.—"The Rock of Chickamauga."—At Chattanooga.—The Atlanta Campaign.—Grant's Telegram.—Battle of Nashville.—Thanks of Congress and Gold Medal.—End of the War.—Goes to the Pacific Coast.

THOMAS had so much grandeur of character, both in his military and private life—so much equipoise of temperament, so much ability and so much modesty, that he has been called the Washington of the last war. He was a tower of strength on the battle-field, and a tower of wisdom in council. He had immense reserve power, great repose in action, and great comprehensiveness of mind. He was endowed, also, with pronounced ability to focalize all the energies of battle upon a given point—like many streams converging to make a mighty river, which then sweeps everything before its resistless rush. This was illustrated forcibly at Nashville, and at Chattanooga—if, as is claimed, the plan of action at Missionary Ridge was his.

When given the responsibility of an independent command, he never went into battle until his methods were fully ripened, even though ordered to do so by his superiors in rank. The reply to such an order invariably was, that if dissatisfaction with his course existed, he would cheerfully act as subordinate to whosoever might be put in his place, but that if *he* were held responsible, he could not move until his judgment dictated such a step. This maturity of action was, perhaps, one of the secrets of his great success. His clear foresight and skill in direction won him the reputation of being "the brains of the army."

Thomas was born on July thirty-first, 1816, in Southampton County, Virginia, and through his mother came of French Huguenot blood. Reared in wealth, he was educated for the law; but his decided inclination for a military life led him to seek admittance at West Point. He graduated from that school in 1840, ranking twelfth in a class of forty-five. In a few months afterwards he went to Florida as second lieutenant in the Third Artillery, and while there was brevetted first lieutenant for gallant conduct. "In January, 1842, his regiment was ordered to the New Orleans barracks, but in June was transferred to Fort Moultrie, in Charleston harbor. The next December he was sent to Fort McHenry, Maryland, where, in May, he was promoted to first lieutenant of artillery. The next spring he returned to Fort Moultrie, where he remained until the war with Mexico."

After joining General Taylor, he was among the brave little garrison which defended Fort Brown on the Rio Grande, against such overwhelming odds. At Monterey he was brevetted captain, and at Buena Vista major, for bravery on the field.

The fortunes of a soldier shifted him from Mexico to Texas in August, 1848, from thence to Fort Adams, Rhode Island, in December, then to Florida again, and then, in 1851, to Boston harbor. Three months afterwards he was occupying the post of instructor of artillery and cavalry at West Point. During the four years of his life here, he met and married Miss Kellogg, of Troy, New York.

The outbreak of the last war found him in Texas, but he immediately reported for duty and was ordered to Carlisle Barracks, Pennsylvania, to "remount his old cavalry regiment." In May, he was promoted to the rank of colonel and commanded a brigade in Northern Virginia under Patterson. Created a brigadier-general of volunteers in August, he first distinguished himself at the battle of Mill Spring, on the Cumberland River, in Kentucky, where the Confederate General Zollicoffer met his death. He joined Grant's army just after the battle of Shiloh, and participated in the succeeding campaign, during which he held the rank of major-general of volunteers in the army of the Tennessee. Transferred to the Army of the Ohio in June, on September eighth he was placed in command of the post at Nashville. When he fell back to Louisville at the close of the month, a telegram was received from Washington removing Buell and appointing Thomas to the vacancy. But Thomas sent a despatch in reply, declining the position and urging the claims of Buell to be retained. His earnestness prevailed for the time, with government authorities, and Buell was kept at his post.

When Rosecrans afterwards succeeded Buell in the chief command, his most faithful adviser and the one on whom he most relied, was Thomas.

At Murfreesboro', Thomas at the head of the Fourteenth Corps, held the centre firm and fought on alone when the right had been compelled to give way and the enemy were swarming on all sides of him. Rosecrans might well give him the generous praise bestowed in his official report of the battle.

The next field of distinction where Thomas won immortal laurels was at Chickamauga. The battle of Chickamauga, fought on the nineteenth and twentieth of September, 1863, was the result of an attempt by Bragg, to regain possession of Chattanooga and the roads leading to it, which he had been compelled to abandon in order to prevent his reinforcements from being hopelessly cut off.

In this battle, Thomas held the left, and the slight rise of ground on which his troops were posted, afforded the key to the position. During the night they had built a rude breastwork of logs and rails for their protection. Soon after the opening of battle on the second day, a furious fight was raging around the Union left, between the veteran troops of Thomas and the attacking lines. Again and again the Confederates charged the ranks of Thomas, behind their breastwork of logs and rails, with impetuous fury: but, as often as they charged, they were hurled back, repulsed. At eleven o'clock, Longstreet brought his troops to the attack. The encounter was desperate on both sides, but Longstreet made a steady advance. The Confederate General Walker had ordered forward Buckner's battery of twelve pieces, which caused a fatal break in the battle line where the divisions of Van Cleve and Palmer were forced to give way in confusion, and gave deadly aid to the enemy's onset. The Union army was now cut in two, and the rout of the right and centre complete. This result was, doubtless, due largely to the terrible work of Buckner's battery.

Thomas had formed his line of battle in a semi-circular position, with the right at the Gap, as the arc of the circle, and a hill near its centre forming the key to the position. His left rested on the Lafayette road. At this point the troops which had hurled back the rebel right in the morning, were rallied, together with portions of Sheridan's and other divisions.

Longstreet, sweeping onward with a career unchecked during the day, now hurled his battalions against this position. But Thomas, intrenched behind his earthworks, held the Ridge securely against every assault of the enemy and sent him back with terrible repulse. About mid-afternoon, the Confederate columns began pouring through a break in the Union right flank, but Granger with his reserves reaching the field at this time, succeeded in pushing them back.

The storm of battle now broke over Thomas and his stalwart men on Missionary Ridge with greater fury than before. His troops, formed in two battle-lines, advanced to the crest of the Ridge and delivered their volleys in rotation. As the deadly rifle-blast of one line blazed out on the air with terrible accuracy, the men, falling back a little, dropped on the ground to re-load, while the second line marched to the crest and discharged their fire into the ranks of the enemy. With desperate valor the Confederates came forward again and again to take by assault this strong position; but their efforts were in vain. The division of Preston succeeded in partly ascending the hill, but was swept back as the previous attacking divisions had been, with repulse and loss.

At last, as twilight darkened the bloody field, the enemy retired beyond the range of our artillery, and Thomas was master of the situation.

The grand courage here displayed, the unshaken firmness and dauntless valor, won for the noble commander of the left, the title of the "*Rock of Chickamauga.*"

At Chattanooga, Thomas commanded the centre, on which rested the issue of battle, and occupied Orchard Knob, overlooking the Confederate rifle-pits. Here he waited with suppressed excitement, while the thunder of battle broke on his right and left, until the signal cannon-shots told him he might bid his army move. The three conquering divisions then poured across Chattanooga Creek, swept up the steep face of Missionary Ridge and grasped victory at its top. They dealt the finishing blow in the fight.

Thomas remained at Chattanooga for the winter, and when Sherman made his grand march to the sea, the brave "Army of the Cumberland" and its heroic commander were his main reliance. They were constantly engaged during this campaign, and the battle with Hood on the Macon road, which cut off his supplies and forced him to retreat, settled the fate of Atlanta.

It was previous to the battle of Nashville, December fifteenth and sixteenth, 1864, that Grant, wondering at the delay, telegraphed Thomas to move at once upon the enemy. The answer came quick from Thomas that he was not ready to move; whereupon Grant sent back word that he had more confidence in him than any other man, and requested him to take his time. Thomas *did* take his time, and the result was a splendid victory. The two-days' battle at Nashville was complete, in plan, in execution, in every detail. It revealed the fine generalship possessed by Thomas and gave him a still higher place in the estimation of the people and their government. During these two days of battle he had taken "eight thousand prisoners, between fifty and sixty pieces of artillery, one major-general, three brigadier-generals, and more than two hundred commissioned officers." The grand charge of the second day was spoken of by a captured brigadier-general in the following fashion:

"Why, sir, it was the most wonderful thing I ever witnessed. I saw your men coming and held my fire, a full brigade, too, until they were in close range, could almost see the whites of their eyes, and then poured my volley right into their faces. I supposed, of course, that when the smoke lifted, your line would be broken and your men gone. But it is surprising, sir, it never even staggered them. Why, they did not even come forward on a run. But right along, cool as fate, your line swung up the hill, and your men walked right up to and over my works and around my brigade before we knew that they were upon us. It was astonishing, sir, such fighting."

This battle won Thomas the promotion of major-general in the regular army, and on March third, 1865, he received the thanks of Congress in consequence. On the first anniversary of the victory, the State of Tennessee presented him with a gold medal, in commemoration of that brilliant day.

The stroke here administered, so effectually finished the enemy that little remained to be done. The troops of Thomas participated in the closing scenes of the war, and from June, 1865, to March, 1867, he was in command of the Department of the Tennessee. Afterwards he was assigned to the third military district, comprising Georgia, Alabama, and Florida, and then to the command of the "Cumberland."

In 1868 he was placed over the fourth military division, which included Alaska and the territory on the Pacific slope. He declined accepting the rank of lieutenant-general, on the ground that he had done nothing since the war to entitle him to promotion.

Certainly, such modesty is rare. He died in San Francisco, March twenty-eighth, 1870, leaving behind him a glorious record, a stainless reputation, and the memory of that true nobility of character which confers on its possessor a rank far higher than riches or aught else on earth.

CHAPTER XXVI.

JOSEPH HOOKER.

Lookout Mountain.—The Battle Above the Clouds.—The Splendor of Victory.—The Strange Thanksgiving Day.—Taylor's Description.—The Old Flag at the Top.—General Howard in Lookout Valley.—Hooker at Chattanooga.—The Peninsular Campaign.—"Fighting Joe."—Wounded.—Chief in Command.—Chancellorsville.—The Atlanta Campaign.—Promotion of Howard.—Hooker Resigns in Consequence.—Mustered out of Service.

THE "battle above the clouds," on Lookout Mountain, and the fame of Joseph Hooker are inseparably wedded. They will go down the sounding corridors of the Future together, each reflecting glory on the other. All the surroundings of the action imparted to it the utmost dramatic strength. It is not often that such a battle-field is out-wrought on the map of war. It is infrequent for men to take the honor of leadership from the hands of their officers in such desperate hazards. But so it was at Lookout on that Thanksgiving day. For nobody thought of ordering a charge up the bold and rocky steep, until the enthusiasm of the men overleaped all bounds, and they attempted what seemed the impossible. Then it was that, seeing the spirit of the men, the order rang down the lines, "forward!" It added the last drop of enthusiasm to the souls of the valiant ranks. They rushed up that steep and wild battle-ground, over ravines, felled trees, rough boulders, and the abatis of the foe, in the very teeth of the enemy's batteries planted on its top.

Wrapped round with clouds, so that the straining eyes at Chattanooga could not see them, save through an occasional rift in the mist, these noble sons fought on, climbed the steep, gained the summit, drove the foe before them, and unfurled the old flag on the highest peak of Lookout Mountain, overlooking the Tennessee, fifteen hundred feet below! Poetry and art have breathed their immortal breath upon the picture, and will transmit its living colors to the future.

The ever-to-be-remembered day was November twenty-fourth, 1863. Benjamin F. Taylor has told his experience in that action, and told it so well, that it will bear repetition here.

"Perhaps it was eleven o'clock on Tuesday morning when the rumble of artillery came in gusts from the valley to the west of Lookout. Climbing Signal Hill, I could see the volumes of smoke rolling to and fro, like clouds from a boiling caldron. The mad surges of the tumult lashed the hills till they cried aloud, and roared through the gorges till you might have fancied all the thunders of a long summer tumbled into that valley together, and yet the battle was unseen."

And then is detailed "Hooker's admirable design. His force consisted of two brigades of the Fourth Corps, under the command of General Cruft; the first division of the Twelfth Corps, under General Geary; and Osterhaus' division, Fifteenth Corps, in reserve. It was a formidable business they had in hand; to carry a mountain and scale a precipice two thousand feet high in the teeth of a battery and force of intrenched brigades.

"Hooker thundered and the enemy came down like the Assyrian, while Cruft on the right and Geary's command on the left, having moved out from Wauhatchie, some five miles from the mountain, at five in the morning, pushed up to Lookout Creek, threw over it a bridge, made for Lookout Point, and there formed, the right under the shelf of Lookout Mountain, the left resting on the creek. And then the play began : the enemy's camps were seized, his pickets were surprised and captured, the strong works on the point taken, and the Federal front moved on. And there they stood 'twixt heaven and—Chattanooga. But above them, grand and sullen, lifted the precipice, and they were men and not eagles. The way was strewn with natural fortifications, and from behind rocks and trees they delivered their fire, contesting inch by inch the upward way. The sound of the battle rose and fell; now fiercely renewed, and now dying away. And Hooker thundered on in the valley, and the echo of his howitzers bounded about the mountains like volleys of musketry. That curtain of cloud was hung around the mountain by the God of battles. It was the veil of the temple that could not be rent. A captured colonel declared that had the day been clear, their sharpshooters would have riddled our advance and left the command without a leader; but friend and foe were wrapped in a seamless mantle.

"And now, returning to my point of observation, I was waiting in painful suspense to see what would come out of the roaring caldron in the valley, when something was born out of the mist—I cannot better convey the idea—and appeared on the shorn side of the mountain below, and to the west of the white house.

It was the head of the Federal column! And there it held, as if it were riveted to the rock, and the line of blue swung slowly around from the left like the index of a mighty dial, and swept up the brown face of the mountain. The bugles of this city of camps were sounding high noon, when in two parallel columns the troops moved up the mountain, in the rear of the enemy's rifle-pits, which they swept at every fire. And there in the centre of the column fluttered the blessed flag! 'My God! what flag is that?' men cried. And up steadily it moved. I could think of nothing but a gallant ship-of-the-line grandly lifting upon the billows and riding out the storm. It was a scene never to fade out. Volleys of musketry and crashes of cannon, and then those lulls in a battle even more terrible than the tempest. At four o'clock an aide came straight down the mountain into the city; the first Federal by that route in many a day. Their ammunition ran low—they wanted powder upon the mountain! He had been two hours in descending, and how much longer the return!

"Night was closing rapidly in and the scene was growing sublime. The battery at Moccasin Point was sweeping the road to the mountain. The brave little fort at its left was playing like a heart in a fever. The cannon on the top of Lookout were pounding away at their lowest depression. The flash of the guns fairly *burned* through the clouds; there was an instance of silence here, there, yonder, and the tardy thunder leaped out after the light. For the first time, perhaps, since that mountain began to burn beneath the gold and crimson sandals of the sun, it was in eclipse. The cloud of the summit and the smoke of the battle met half way and mingled. Here was Chattanooga, but Lookout had vanished! Then the storm ceased, and occasional dropping shots tolled off the evening till half-past nine, and then a crashing volley and a rebel yell and a desperate charge. It was their good-night to our boys—good-night to the mountain.

"At ten o'clock a glowing line of lights glittered obliquely across the breast of Lookout. It was the Federal autograph scored along the mountain. They were our camp-fires. Our wounded lay there through all the dreary nights of rain, unrepining and content. Our unharmed heroes lay there upon their arms. Our dead lay there, 'and surely they slept well.'

"One thing more, and all I shall try to give of the stirring story will have been told. Just as the sun was touching up the old Department of the Cumberland, Captain Wilson and fifteen of the Eighth Kentucky, near where the guns had crouched and growled at all the land, waved the regimental flag in sight of Tennessee, Alabama, Georgia, the old North State, and South Carolina, waved it there, and the right of the Federal front, lying far beneath, caught a glimpse of its flutter, and a cheer rose to the top of the mountain and ran from regiment to regiment, through whole brigades and broad divisions, till the boys away around in the face of Mission Ridge passed it along the line of battle. 'What is it? Our flag? Did I help to put it there?' murmured a poor wounded fellow, and died without the sight.

"The Stars and Stripes floated from Lookout on Wednesday at sunrise. At twelve on that day something with the cry of a loon was making its way up the river. Screaming through the mountains it emerged at last into Chattanooga, and its looks were a match for its lungs—an ugly little craft, more like a backwoods cabin adrift than a steamer. It was the sweetest-voiced and prettiest piece of naval architecture that ever floated upon the Tennessee. The flag on the crest and the boat on the stream were part of the same story. . . Never did result crowd more closely on the heels of action."

General O. O. Howard, in his account of the march of the Eleventh and Twelfth Corps to the relief of Chattanooga, says: "I shall never forget General Hooker's first visit to my camp at Bridgeport. It was, perhaps, the fourth or fifth of October. The air was damp, but sharp and penetrating. You could see every breath you exhaled. The Confederates had left behind plenty of camp rubbish and filth of all kinds in every direction. There were no buildings except the old mill and the rough quarter-master shanties for temporary messing and cover. General Hooker looked around and was not a little disgusted at the general appearance of the region, as I also had been; but when we came to the river his whole face lighted, and he exclaimed, 'Grand! grand! Is it not?' So broad, so rapid, so full was its flow at that point, that the sight filled you with those indefinable emotions which strong and active life-power is calculated to inspire."

Speaking of the battle of Lookout Valley, he says: "General Hooker left Geary at Wauhatchie, probably three miles from our position—an important point for securing the valley. . . . Perhaps an hour after midnight, in that country as yet all new to us, we were aroused by heavy artillery firing; soon the noise of musketry, with its unmistakable rattle, was mingling with the roaring cannon. Those ominous sounds seemed to come from the direction of Geary. I was hardly on my feet before Hooker's message came, 'Hurry, or you cannot save Geary. He has been attacked.' Steinwehr was urged to hasten, but Schurz' division being nearest and first under arms, was pushed forward toward the sound, followed by the other division. As soon as the troops were in motion I went forward to General Hooker's position, at a turn of the road a half-mile nearer Geary. Hooker and General Butterfield, who was then his chief-of-staff, were sitting on the slope of a hill with a camp-fire just starting. The night was chilly. Hooker seemed quite anxious, as might be expected. The issues of a night engagement under the best of circumstances are more than ordinarily uncertain, and our ignorance of the situation of the country and of the enemy's position, taken up since nightfall, added to the uncertainty. The general was of opinion that we should secure the ridge of hills that ran along on our side of Lookout Creek as we moved toward Geary's position. To this end orders were given. Then I said to General Hooker, 'With your approval, I will take the two companies of cavalry and push through to Wauhatchie.' He replied, 'All right, Howard; I shall be here to attend to this part of the field.' . . . .

"After leaving General Hooker, with the two companies of horsemen, skirting the Raccoon side of the rough valley, I reached General Geary at Wauhatchie by three or three and a half in the morning. There was then light enough (it may have been only starlight) to see squads of men moving about in the comparatively open space just north of Wauhatchie. This we observed as we emerged from the bushes. The firing was all over and quiet reigned.

"I called out to the strangers so dimly seen, 'Who goes there?' 'We are Steven's men,' was the answer. Perceiving that they belonged to the enemy I said, 'All right: have you whipped the Yankees?' The same voice replied, 'We were on their flank, but our men in front have gone, and we cannot find our way.' My men then gradually approached, revealed themselves and took them prisoners, there being probably as many of them as of us.

"I passed into the thicket and came first upon the tent of General George S. Green, then a brigade commander. He was sadly wounded in the face. After a moment's delay for inquiry and sympathy, his officers conducted me to Geary, who was glad enough to see me. He had repulsed the enemy's attack handsomely, using infantry and artillery. This was the place where the mules broke loose and in terror ran in squads through the enemy's lines, and gave rise to the story told in verse, entitled 'The Charge of the Mule Brigade.' Geary's hand trembled, and his tall, strong frame shook with emotion, as he held me by the hand and spoke of the death of his son, during that fearful night. This son was Lieutenant Edward R. Geary, Battery F, Pennsylvania Light Artillery, killed at his battery during the action. In this way the soldier remembers that the exhilaration of victory was very often softened, or entirely quenched, by real grief over its cost, a cost that cannot be estimated!"

General George H. Thomas, in a complimentary notice directed to General Hooker, congratulated him and the troops under his command, on their brilliant success, and said that the bayonet charge of Howard's troops and the repulse by Geary's division of greatly superior numbers, who attempted to surprise him, would rank among the most distinguished feats of arms of this war.

"Chattanooga sent Northward a cry of distress,
  For the men of the Cumberland, famished and gaunt,
Worn with fighting and vigils and tattered in dress,
  Manned their guns in the trenches in peril and want·
For the foe closely pressed them in hostile array,
  And their guns shrieked and thundered in demon-like glee,·
While Old Lookout's rock front, lined with soldiers in gray,
  Threw its shadows of death o'er the blue Tennessee.

"But on wings of the lightning that cry for help flew,
  To Sherman, to Meade, and from captain to man;
And from Vicksburg marched Sherman's long columns in blue,
  And grim Hooker's tried corps, from the swift Rapidan,
Came with bread for the famished, with lead for the foe,
  Gleamed Wauhatchie's sweet vale with their bayonets bright;
Torn and bleeding, the Ferry guards reeled at their blow,
  And dismayed, up the mountain side fled in affright."

And so, in song and story, "the Lookout Mountain fight is fought again by the ghosts of the fallen," and the "chivalrous figure of fighting Joe Hooker," surrounded by his staff, is the most striking portrait in the imposing spectacle.

Hooker was born in Hadley, Massachusetts, in 1819, and graduated at West Point in 1837. He served in the Florida war, and during the war with Mexico was brevetted captain, for gallant services at Monterey, receiving the promotion successively of major and lieutenant-colonel for similar conduct at the National Bridge and famous Chapultepec. In 1853, he resigned his commission and became a farmer in California, but re-entered the service in 1861, and in May was made a brigadier-general of volunteers. A year later he commanded a division of the Army of the Potomac, and in the following May was promoted to the rank of major-general.

During the Peninsular campaign, he made himself conspicuous for bravery, dash and daring at Williamsburg, Fair Oaks, Frazier's Farm, and Malvern Hill. It was during this campaign that he acquired the appellation of "Fighting Joe." At the battle of Groveton, Hooker's division especially distinguished itself.

During the succeeding Maryland campaign, he was assigned to the First Army Corps and gained a splendid victory at South Mountain. He also participated actively in the actions of Bristoe, the second Bull Run, and Chantilly. At Antietam, his great resources as a commander were exhibited in bold relief. On this field his white horse became too conspicuous a mark for the enemy, and while making a bold reconnoissance he received a wound which compelled him to retire from the field.

On September twentieth he was made brigadier-general in the United States army, and at Fredericksburg commanded a grand division under Burnside. On January twenty-sixth, 1863, he superseded that general as chief in command of the Army of the Potomac, and in May the disastrous and bloody battle of Chancellorsville blocked the wheels of fate in his upward career. It would seem, in this action, as if General Hooker had overlooked the fact that his army had but eight days' supplies at hand; that a treacherous river flowed between him and his depots; that he was surrounded by a labyrinth of forests, traversed in every direction by narrow roads and paths, all well known to the enemy, but unknown even to most of his guides; and that many of his guns of heaviest calibre, and most needed in a deadly strife, were on the other side of the river.

The congratulatory order which he issued afterwards, if not perfectly satisfactory to the country and to the authorities, was generally hailed with applause by the army, which recognized in its sagacious rendering of our difficulties and humiliations the meed of praise awarded where it was due.

It was on this field that the famous Confederate General Stonewall Jackson met his death.

On June twenty-seventh Hooker resigned his command and was superseded by Meade. But in the following September, he was placed over the Eleventh and Twelfth Corps, went down to the relief of Rosecrans at Chattanooga — "that curious place, lying against a concave bend of the Tennessee and walled in by Lookout Mountain below and Missionary Ridge above"—and shortly after occurred the glorious "battle above the clouds," which wreathed his name with fresher laurels and gave him the brevet of major-general in the regular army.

In Sherman's march to the sea, Hooker's Corps became a portion of the Army of the Cumberland, under Thomas, during which his leadership lost none of its pronounced daring. At the terrible assault on Thomas by Hood, near Peach Tree Creek, July twentieth, "Hooker bore the brunt of the shock,"—displaying the utmost heroism. It was the last great conflict in which he participated. In August, 1864, Howard, his inferior in rank, was promoted over him to the command of the Eleventh Corps, and this caused Hooker to resign.

In September he was placed over the Northern Department, in 1865 over the Department of the East, and in 1866 over the Department of the Lakes. He was mustered out of the volunteer service in September of that year, and in October, 1868, brevetted Major-General in the United States army, after which he retired to the seclusion of a private citizen.

CHAPTER XXVII.

GEORGE GORDON MEADE.

Ancestry.—A Fragment of Eventful History.—Birth in Spain.—At West Point.—In the Florida War.—In the Mexican War.—His Part in the Peninsular Campaign.—At Antietam.—In Command of the Army of the Potomac.—A Remarkable Order.—At Gettysburg.—The Desperate Last Effort.—His Report.—Congratulatory Address.—Thanks of Congress.—Advance to the Rappahannock.—Close Friendship between Meade and Grant.—Over the Atlantic Department.—Death in Philadelphia.

GENERAL MEADE came of a family which had an eventful history.

His father, having incurred the ill-will of certain members of the council of war, in Spain, was imprisoned for two years in the castle of Santa Catalina, being released only at the demand of the United States Government. In 1819, he was awarded a certificate of debt amounting to nearly two hundred thousand dollars, for losses incurred at that time; but the fund was distributed before the original vouchers could be procured. Such lawyers as Webster, Clay and Choate afterwards endeavored in vain to obtain it. He was reputed to have possessed the finest private gallery of paintings and statuary in the country, and owned the only bust of Washington taken from life. The grandfather of General Meade was a merchant in Philadelphia and made the continental government a present of ten thousand dollars in gold.

George Gordon was born in Cadiz, Spain, in 1816.

He graduated at West Point in 1839, served in the Florida war, and a year after its termination resigned his lieutenant's commission. In 1842, he re-entered the army as second lieutenant of topographical engineers.

In the Mexican war he was on the staff of both General Taylor and Scott, and distinguished himself at Palo Alto, Resaca and Monterey. He was brevetted first lieutenant for his services, and on his return home, the city of Philadelphia presented him with a sword.

In August, 1851, he was given a full lieutenancy, and ten years later, during the epoch of the civil war, in August, 1861, he was promoted to the rank of brigadier-general of volunteers. This was after the battle of Bull Run. During the Peninsular campaign he fought bravely—was badly wounded at Glendale, and when McClellan went to Maryland, commanded a division in Hooker's Corps. At Antietam, he held the centre and led a desperate charge against the enemy at the beginning of the action. In this engagement he had two horses shot under him, and was himself wounded.

After the battle of Chancellorsville, when Hooker resigned the chief command of the Army of the Potomac, Meade—to the surprise of the country at large—was elevated to the position. His order, on assuming command, was so remarkable for modesty and a certain reserve strength, that to give it, is to illustrate his character as a general.

> By direction of the President of the United States, I hereby assume command of the Army of the Potomac. As a soldier in obeying this order, an order totally unexpected and unsolicited, I have no promises or pledge to make. The country looks to this army to relieve it from the devastation and disgrace of a hostile

invasion. Whatever fatigues and sacrifices we may be called upon to undergo, let us have in view constantly the magnitude of the interests involved, and let each man determine to do his duty, leaving to an all-controlling Providence the decision of the contest. It is with just diffidence that I relieve in command of this army an eminent and accomplished soldier, whose name must ever be conspicuous in the history of its achievements; but I rely upon the hearty support of my companions in arms, to assist me in the discharge of the duties of the important trust which has been confided to me.

The desperate, three-days' battle of Gettysburg soon followed, and here the noble commander won an enduring fame.

The culminating action, on the third day, under the blaze of a hot July sun, was ushered in by one of the most terrific cannonades on record. The Confederates seemed to have gathered up all their strength to hurl it in one last, fierce, desperate effort on our resisting ranks. The flower of Lee's army swept grandly up, like a vast tidal wave, only to be crushed and torn and broken by our enfilading fires "from half a score of crests," and hurled in scattered fragments back. Thus environed by a blazing semi-circle of deadly fire, they could not escape, and especially on the centre and left an immense number of prisoners were captured, during the last half hour. But the Second Corps, under Hancock, bore the brunt of the battle-shock. There it surged most heavily against our lines—became almost resistless and at times threatened to break and dash in pieces the brave front opposed by Hancock and his grand Second Corps.

Our rifle-pits were barricaded with fence rails, and the Confederates under Pickett, Longstreet and A. P. Hill swept up with splendid front, reserving their fire until they reached the Emmitsburg road. Then came a crash from the rifles and a thunder blast from the artillery. Hancock was carried from the field wounded. The command then devolved upon Gibbon, who rose to the fearful crisis. He ordered the men to reserve their fire until the enemy were at short range. Then the guns belched forth in sudden flame and the enemy's advance line withered before it. The second line, undismayed, rushed on, over the bodies of their slain comrades, up to the barricaded pits, and were upon our gunners at their pieces. But at this fatal moment, a storm of grape from the enfilading guns on Cemetery Hill, cut down their advance, and the line "reeled back," crushed into fragments. Our troops behind the guns rushed forward and made captures by the hundreds and thousands. "An entire regiment threw down its arms, and Gibbon's old division took fifteen stand of colors."

What was left of the broken attacking lines now fell back. They gathered themselves together "and slowly marched away. It was not a rout: it was a bitter, crushing defeat."

On the evening of July third, 1863, General Meade penned the following despatch from army headquarters:

"To MAJOR-GENERAL HALLECK, GENERAL-IN-CHIEF:

"The enemy opened at one o'clock in the afternoon, from about one hundred and fifty guns. They concentrated upon my left centre, continuing without intermission for about three hours, at the expiration of which time he assaulted my left centre twice, being, upon both occasions, handsomely repulsed with severe loss to them, leaving in our hands nearly three thousand prisoners. Among the prisoners are Major-General Armistead, and many colonels and officers of lesser note. The enemy left many dead upon the field, and a large number of wounded in our hands. The loss upon our side has been considerable. Major-General Hancock and Brigadier-General Gibbon were wounded.

"After the repelling of the assault, indications leading to the belief that the enemy might be withdrawing, an armed reconnoissance was pushed forward from the left, and the enemy found to be in force. At the present hour all is quiet.

"The New York cavalry have been engaged all day on both flanks of the enemy, harassing and vigorously attacking him with great success, notwithstanding they encountered superior numbers, both of cavalry and artillery. The army is in fine spirits.

"GEORGE G. MEADE, *Major-General Commanding.*"

On the fourth of July morning he also issued a congratulatory address to the army, thanking them for the "glorious result of the recent operations." He says:

"Our enemy, superior in numbers and flushed with the pride of a successful invasion, attempted to overcome or destroy this army. Utterly baffled and defeated, he has now withdrawn from the contest.

"The privations and fatigues the army has endured, and the heroic courage and gallantry it has displayed, will be matters of history to be ever remembered.

"Our task is not yet accomplished, and the commanding general looks to the army for greater efforts to drive from our soil every vestige of the presence of the invader."

President Lincoln made a brief yet comprehensive announcement to the country on the same day, in which he said that the army at Gettysburg had covered itself with the "highest honor," and requested that the day should be remembered with thanksgiving.

The victories of Gettysburg and Vicksburg occurred on the same date, and the destinies of the two generals who led in these actions were afterwards, during the war, strangely mingled.

In January, 1866, General Meade received the thanks of Congress "for the skill and heroic valor with which, at Gettysburg, he repulsed, defeated, and drove back, broken and dispirited, the veteran Army of Rebellion."

Meade's advance to the Rappahannock afterwards was marked by the battles of Bristoe, Brandy Station, New Baltimore, Robertson's River, Kelly's Ford, and Rappahannock Bridge; but no general engagement took place until the next spring. He remained at the head of the Army of the Potomac, but acted in such close conjunction with Grant, who had been made lieutenant-general, that his movements after that period must be attributed to the united counsel of both. Grant exhibited the greatest possible confidence in him, and he always proved equal to the grand military achievements committed to his charge.

At the close of the war he was placed over the entire Atlantic Department.

He died in Philadelphia, on November sixth, 1872, in a house which his countrymen had presented to his wife. A fund of one hundred thousand dollars was afterwards subscribed for his family.

The military as well as private character of General Meade was full of caution, full of reliability, full of goodness and rare modesty. No breath of detraction obscured his fair fame, nor envy marked him for its poisoned arrows. The heroic memories of the field of Gettysburg will enfold his noble dust in a cloud of perpetual incense, and transmit to posterity his best eulogy.

CHAPTER XXVIII.

HENRY WARNER SLOCUM.

Birth and Education.—A Lawyer in Syracuse.—On the War-Path.—In the Chickahominy.—At Antietam, South Mountain and Chancellorsville.—The Field of Gettysburg.—The Repulse of Ewell's Troops.—In Tennessee.—Commanding the Vicksburg District.—The Georgia Campaign.—Marching through the Enemy's Country.—Battle of Bentonville.—A Splendid Fight.—Genius of Slocum.

THIS brave and noble general must have been born under auspicious planetary combinations to have won the reputation of never failing in any enterprise he undertook, and to unite in his individual person so many rare qualifications as a man and a soldier.

He was born in the Empire State, at Delphi, Onondaga County, September twenty-fourth, 1827. Like so many others of our successful war generals, he received his military education at West Point, from whence he graduated in 1852. Then he went to Florida as second lieutenant in the First artillery, and was subsequently sent to Charleston Harbor, and promoted to first lieutenant. At length he grew tired of garrison life, and in 1857 resigned his commission and took up his abode in Syracuse, New York, where he began the practice of law.

But when, in 1861, the tocsin blast of war sounded through our country, and the safety of the Union was menaced, Slocum responded at once to the call and joined the great army of patriots marching to the front. He led the "gallant Twenty-seventh Regiment" at Manassas, and received his first badge of honor in the cause—a wound in the thigh.

In August he was made brigadier-general and placed over a brigade in Franklin's division, and afterwards, on promotion of Franklin, was put in command of the division.

He took part in the seven days' battles of the Chickahominy, and on July fourth of that year, just after the tired army had reached the banks of the James, he was promoted to the rank of major-general. He commanded a division under McClellan at Antietam and South Mountain, and distinguished himself in both those battles.

At Chancellorsville he had charge of the Fifth, Eleventh and Twelfth Corps, and sustained his part in that disaster with more than heroic bravery.

On the field of Gettysburg his conduct shone out with special lustre, even when heroism was the rule, and other leaders won deathless distinction for their leadership. On the second day of that awful fight, Slocum was in command of the right, and had under him the Twelfth Corps and a portion of the Second and Sixth. He held a strong position; but the left wing being heavily pressed, reinforcements from his command were repeatedly sent them, leaving a very much weakened force to defend his own ground. The enemy, having failed to make an impression on the Union left, threw the whole force of his battalions on the thin opposing line of Slocum. Slocum made a splendid stand, but could not be reinforced fast enough to maintain his ground, and at last fell back a short distance. Ewell endeavored to press his advantage, and his troops came on with wild yells—in vain. The dauntless band stood firm. At dawn, on the following morning, Slocum drew his army up for an attack, determined to win back the strong position he had yielded on the previous evening. He was met half way by a reckless charge from Ewell's men. It was indeed "desperation against courage." Slocum's line held their ground without flinching. Volley after volley flashed out from their ranks, and the firing became so rapid that a cloud of smoke enveloped them during the entire action, which raged without cessation for six hours. Ewell hurled his men against this wall of smoke and fire again and again, only to be sent back with awful repulse. The troops in gray fought like demons. "It was hard to believe such desperation voluntary. It was harder to believe that the army which withstood and defeated it was mortal."

After Chickamauga, Slocum was sent to Tennessee to guard the line of communication between Nashville and Chattanooga, and when the Atlanta campaign was organized, and the Eleventh and Twelfth Corps were consolidated into the Twentieth and given to Hooker, Slocum was put in command of the Vicksburg district. From this point he destroyed the railroad bridges at Jackson, over Pearl River, and while returning from this expedition, a heavy force of the enemy concentrated in his rear, with the object of severing him from his base. But the brave commander was equal to this desperate emergency, and after a severe battle, cleared his way to Vicksburg.

In a few days afterwards he took a force to Port Gibson to prevent reinforcements from reaching Hood, and had a battle near Grand Gulf—a night attack by the enemy, whom he signally repulsed.

Slocum took Hooker's place over the old Twentieth Corps when that general was relieved, and guarded the Chattahoochie. In Sherman's Georgia campaign, he had charge of the left wing and marched eastward along the line of the Atlanta and Augusta railroad, which he destroyed as he went. He made a successful march to Milledgeville, the capital of the State. "The mayor and officers of the city met him," as he entered it, " formally tendering its surrender, and begging that private property might be saved from destruction, and the people from violence. Slocum curtly replied that he did not command a band of desperadoes and cutthroats."

At Milledgeville the two wings of the army united and marched into Savannah together. After a month's rest they were again on the march northward. Slocum, with the left wing, was sent up the Savannah River to threaten Augusta. He found the country flooded from the swollen river which had overflowed its banks, owing to a heavy rainfall. But his noble troops bravely breasted the floods, rebridged the streams and cleared the roads, which had been obstructed by felled trees and other debris.

Having drawn the enemy's forces into Augusta from his near approach to that place, he turned about and crossed the upper portion of the State. The two wings then marched towards Columbia, and from Columbia Slocum made a feint in the direction of Charlotte, while his real destination was Fayetteville. When Sherman went from Fayetteville to Goldsboro', Slocum was despatched to threaten Raleigh.

At Bentonville, he came unexpectedly upon the combined forces of Johnston, Hardee, and Hoke; and with half the number to oppose them, he made a perilous but successful fight. The onset was of the most desperate character, for the enemy expected to overpower him by mere weight of numbers, and probably would have done so with a less able general in command than Slocum. One after another the Confederate columns were hurled forward and as often were sent, broken and bleeding, back. Six successive assaults were thus made within an hour, and the last desperate charge caused a momentary break in Slocum's line; but, quickly recovering, his troops repelled as before the shock of onset.

The battle of Bentonville was fought on the nineteenth of March, and proved, as every preceding action had done in which he was engaged, the great generalship of Slocum. His entire career during the war was one of unequivocal success.

Sherman's victorious marches might not have proven so victorious without the disciplined and able concert of action afforded by Thomas and Slocum, commanding the two wings of the conquering host.

The Twentieth Corps, under Slocum's effective discipline, gained a splendid reputation for its invincible qualities, and never failed in an emergency.

General Slocum won the reputation of coolness in danger, of being always able to meet that danger, however unexpected and threatening, and of a comprehensive grasp of mind which could seize upon and master the complications of a battle-field at once. He never failed in anything. His war record, from beginning to end, is one of rare achievement and a glorious adherence to patriotic duty.

After the war, he was placed in command of the Department of the Mississippi.

CHAPTER XXIX.
JAMES BIRDSEYE McPHERSON.

His Ability.—Ancestry and Early Life.—Superior Scholarship at West Point.—In New York Harbor.—On the Pacific Coast.—Sent to Boston Harbor.—Slow Promotion.—On Halleck's Staff.—Services at Forts Henry and Donelson.—Engineering Work at Corinth. — His First Independent Command. — Vicksburg.—Grant's Endorsement.—With Sherman.—In Command of the Army of the Tennessee.—Postponement of Marriage.—March to the Sea.—Battle with Hood.—His Death.—Grant's Letter.

THE military genius of McPherson was of a high order. Comprehensive in his grasp of situations, he seemed always to know just the right combination necessary to achieve success. He never lost a battle.

His character as a soldier and man was both noble and knightly. Perhaps no officer in the last war better exemplified the definition of a hero. He could command not only the respect but the love of those around him. In order to do this a general must be endowed with something more than soldierly qualities—he must have essential goodness of heart.

Grant and Sherman both cherished for McPherson a deep and warm regard, and when the news of his death reached the commander-in-chief of our armies, he burst into tears. Sherman, too, gave way to deep grief when the body of McPherson, pallid in death, was brought to his head-quarters.

It was at the cost of such precious lives as these that the country struggled through its four years' baptism of war.

McPherson was born in Sandusky County, Ohio, on November fourteenth, 1828, and as his name indicates, was of Scotch extraction. He entered West Point when twenty-one years old and at once gained recognition for superior scholarship and ability. He graduated at the head of his class in 1853, was made second lieutenant of engineers by brevet, and appointed to the post of Assistant Instructor of Practical Engineering at the Academy—"a compliment never before or since awarded to so young an officer."

A year afterwards he was made Assistant Engineer on the defences of New York Harbor, and in the Hudson River improvements below Albany. From the Hudson he went to Fort Delaware, and from there to California, where he had charge of the works on Alcatras Island, in San Francisco bay. While on the Pacific coast, in 1858, he was promoted to the rank of first lieutenant, and his pronounced engineering skill received some recognition. When the war broke out he was sent to take charge of the Boston Harbor fortifications, being created, meantime, junior captain of his company.

The fairy of good luck or the presiding spirit of inscrutable fate now touched the current of affairs in his life, and gave him what all must have who win the silver stars of fame—opportunity. For, on the accession of Halleck over the Western Department, McPherson became his *aide*, with the rank of lieutenant-colonel. Busy with engineering duty in Missouri, no hint of his greatness appeared until he was made chief engineer in Grant's movements against Forts Henry and Donelson. For these services he received the rank of brevet-major of engineers, and after Pittsburgh Landing the promotion of brevet lieutenant-colonel was conferred on him. He did not become colonel until the following May.

After his splendid engineering work against Corinth, under Halleck, he was made brigadier-general of volunteers, and his promotion thenceforward went on more in accord with his deserts than it had previously done. When Grant became commander in the West, McPherson was appointed superintendent of all United States military railroads in the Department of Western Tennessee; and after the repulse of the enemy at Corinth by Rosecrans, he was placed in charge of the pursuit and received the rank of major-general of volunteers, dating from October eighth.

The first battle in which he held undisturbed command was fought within a mile of Lamar, about eight miles from Lagrange, where his head-quarters had been established. Grant, under whose direction he acted, considered this reconnoissance one of especial importance.

At the point named, McPherson confronted a force greatly outnumbering his own, and by sending his cavalry in a wide detour to the enemy's left, made a simultaneous attack in the rear and flank. The ruse was eminently successful and the Confederate forces under Price fled panic-stricken to Holly Springs, spreading the report that Grant's entire army was in pursuit. The manner in which this fight was conducted gave evidence of marked genius in leadership, and won for its general, proper recognition.

In the operations now inaugurated against Vicksburg, McPherson bore a conspicuous part. He participated in the battle of Port Gibson, and the brilliant victories at Jackson and Champion Hill were gained under his immediate generalship.

During the siege of Vicksburg, his corps, the brave and renowned Seventeenth, held the centre and made itself exceedingly effective. After the occupation of Vicksburg, the endorsement given him by Grant, in recommending him for promotion, was emphatic to an unusual degree. "He has been with me," said that General, "in every battle since the commencement of the rebellion, except Belmont. At Forts Henry and Donelson, Shiloh and the siege of Corinth, as a staff officer and engineer, his services were conspicuous and highly meritorious. At the second battle of Corinth, his skill as a soldier was displayed in successfully carrying reinforcements to the besieged garrison, when the enemy was between him and the point to be reached. In the advance through central Mississippi, General McPherson commanded one wing of the army, with all the ability possible to show, having the lead in the advance and the rear in retiring.

"In the campaign and siege terminating with the fall of Vicksburg, General McPherson has filled a conspicuous part. At the battle of Port Gibson it was under his direction that the enemy was driven late in the afternoon from a position that they had succeeded in holding all day against an obstinate attack. His corps, the advance always under his immediate eye, were the pioneers in the movements from Port Gibson to Hankinson's Ferry. From the north fork of the Bayou Pierre to Black River, it was a constant skirmish, the whole skilfully managed. The enemy was so closely pursued as to be unable to destroy their bridge of boats after them. From Hankinson's Ferry to Jackson, the Seventeenth Corps marched over roads not travelled by other troops, fighting the entire battle of Raymond alone; and the bulk of Johnston's army was fought by this corps, entirely under the management of General McPherson. At Champion's Hill the Seventeenth Corps and General McPherson were conspicuous. All that could be termed a battle there was fought by the divisions of General McPherson's Corps and General Hovey's division of the Thirteenth Corps. In the assault of the twenty-second of May on the fortifications of Vicksburg, and during the entire siege, General McPherson and his command took unfading laurels. He is one of the ablest engineers and most skilful generals. I would respectfully but urgently recommend his promotion to the position of brigadier-general in the regular army."

In February, 1864, McPherson joined Sherman in his raid to Meridian, and when Sherman became commander of the Department of the Mississippi, he was placed over the Army of the Tennessee. The appointment reached him just as he was about taking leave of absence to fulfil a marriage engagement with a young lady in Baltimore. The marriage was deferred in consequence of the approaching Atlanta campaign, and the brave commander turned from the flowery pathway of love, and heroically took up his march to the sea, amid the besetting dangers of an enemy's country.

After the repulse of Hood by Thomas, near Peach Tree Creek, that Confederate general reorganized his shattered ranks and hurled them with terrible fury on McPherson, who was approaching Atlanta from the direction of Decatur. The onset of the enemy was desperate, and at times it seemed as if they would succeed in breaking McPherson's lines. There came, at length, a lull in battle, and the general availed himself of this opportunity to close a gap between the Sixteenth and Seventeenth Corps—anticipating an attack at that point. A strip of forest, with a road running through it, constituted the space which McPherson ordered closed up at once with a brigade. To give the needed direction it was necessary for him to cross this wooded strip. He halted a moment before entering the road, and then, with but one orderly, dashed boldly forward. But his hour of fate had come. All unseen, death and the foe lurked within the shadowy forest. The skirmish line of the enemy had taken possession of this road, and before he was fully aware of his position, the foe surrounded him. He reined his black charger back suddenly, for one surprised instant, lifted his cap in salute, and then with a bound cleared the road. In vain! The volley that blazed after him had fatal aim, and he fell from his saddle, never again to rise. The well-known black horse, emerging from the woods, wounded and riderless, told the sad story to his devoted soldiers who now came up. Private George Reynolds, though wounded severely through the left arm, was among the sorrowful group which searched for the body of their beloved General and conveyed it to Sherman's head-quarters.

Grant's exclamation on hearing the sad news, "The country has lost one of its best soldiers, and I have lost my best friend!" emphasized by his tears, gave evidence of a rare regard.

Among his soldiers there was universal grief, and "McPherson and revenge!" became their war-cry

DEATH OF GENERAL McPHERSON, BEFORE ATLANTA, GA.

during the continuation of that bloody battle. Everywhere lamented, the nation mourned his loss as of a son; but the blow fell with withering stroke on the heart of his affianced bride—widowed ere yet a wife. A guard accompanied his remains to Sandusky County, Ohio, where they " were conducted to the very parlor," wrote his grandmother, "in which he spent a cheerful evening in 1861, with his widowed mother, two brothers, and an only sister and his aged grandmother, who is now trying to write. His funeral services were attended in his mother's orchard, where his youthful feet had often pressed the soil to gather the falling fruit, and his remains are resting in the silent grave, scarce half a mile from the place of his birth."

In his reply to this letter, Grant says:

"Mrs. Lydia Slocum:

"*My Dear Madam:*—Your very welcome letter of the third instant has reached me. I am glad to know that the relatives of the lamented Major-General McPherson are aware of the more than friendship existing between him and myself. A nation grieves at the loss of on so dear to our nation's cause. It is a selfish grief, because the nation had more to expect from him than from almost any one living. I join in this selfish grief, and add the grief of personal love for the departed. He formed, for some time, one of my military family. I knew him well: to know him was to love. It may be some consolation to you, his aged grandmother, to know that every officer and every soldier who served under your grandson felt the highest reverence for his patriotism, his zeal, his great, almost unequalled ability, his amiability, and all the manly virtues that can adorn a commander. Your bereavement is great, but cannot exceed mine."

McPherson distinguished himself, in addition to other services, at Resaca, Dallas, Allatoona, Kulp House and Kenesaw. He always reconnoitred in person, and his bravery was of that extreme type which verged on recklessness. He was of superb physique, and held that personal sway over the minds and hearts of his soldiers which only needed his presence to awaken their enthusiasm. His lofty courage, tireless energy, sublime patriotism and stainless private record shine like jewels in the crown of his fame, and by the strength of this light many a youth will be incited to nobler endeavor and more courageous soldiership in the long battle of life.

CHAPTER XXX.
WINFIELD SCOTT HANCOCK.

The Brilliant Charge at Williamsburg.—Popular Favor.—Birth and Early Training.—In the Mexican War.—The Florida Campaign.—Ordered to Washington.—At Antietam.—Fredericksburg and Chancellorsville. — His Stand at Gettysburg. — Cemetery Hill.—Wounded.—In the Last Grant Campaign.—Battle at Ely's Ford.—Assault of May Twelfth.—Capture of Stuart.—" I Decline to Take Your Hand."—In Charge of the Veteran First Corps.—In the Shenandoah Valley.—Characteristics.

THE brilliant charge of Hancock's brigade at the battle of Williamsburg, first brought the name of this eminent soldier prominently before the country. It was such a charge as had not been previously made during the war, and the mode in which it was conducted reflected great credit on the skill of its commanding officer. Hancock and his "immortal brigade" in that action were on the left of the enemy's line. When he saw that by taking a certain position his guns could command the Confederate rear, he sent for reinforcements. But, on account of a fear of weakening the centre, they were denied him. He therefore met an overwhelming force of the enemy alone, and fought a desperate battle. As he slowly fell back, with unbroken front, the Confederates mistook the movement for a retreat and rushed on with shouts and cheers, in an endeavor to break his lines. Hancock's eagle eye was watching every movement, and when they had reached a point within forty yards of him, near the top of the rising ground over which he was advancing, he halted his brigade, gave the order to "fire!" and poured a withering musketry blaze into their ranks. Then the whole brigade swept down the slope in a grand charge which put the enemy to rout and completely turned their position.

This splendid piece of skill immediately lifted Hancock into national popularity, and his name has ever since been a synonym of valor and success.

He is a native of Pennsylvania, having been born in Montgomery County, on February fourteenth, 1824. He graduated at West Point when only twenty years old, and was sent to the Indian Territory as second lieutenant in the Sixth Infantry. He rendered distinguished services in the Mexican war, and received the brevet of first lieutenant for brave conduct at Churubusco. He was afterwards stationed in Missouri, and during the Florida war served as captain in the quarter-master's department. He joined the Utah expedition under General Harney, and when the last war broke out, was stationed at Los Angeles, California. The War Department ordered him to report at Washington, and in September, 1861, he was made brigadier-general of volunteers.

After Williamsburg, he figured conspicuously at Gaines' Mill, and "fought side by side with Sedgwick" at Glendale, Malvern Hill, Fair Oaks and Savage Station.

He was in the campaign under Pope, and the subsequent one under McClellan. At Antietam, he rode in the front of battle, the very incarnation of bravery, the embodiment of noble valor. The command of Richardson's division devolved on him, and the marvellous skill with which he handled his troops, exposed to a trying enfilading fire, stamped him a general of great qualities.

He was with Burnside when the heights of Fredericksburg were stormed, and like a true soldier, obeying orders unquestioned though he knew the madness of the attempt, bore his part in the useless and bloody slaughter. He also shared in the Chancellorsville disaster, and when Meade was placed in command of the Army of the Potomac, Hancock had charge of the Second Corps.

At Gettysburg, he is given the credit of having chosen the almost impregnable position of the Union troops, which certainly entered largely into the deciding issues of that battle. After the death of Reynolds, General Meade sent Hancock to *"represent him on the field"*—surely no doubtful praise. During the first day of the momentous conflict, he commanded the left centre on Cemetery Hill, firmly holding his position, besides sending relief to the Third Corps.

About one o'clock in the afternoon of the second day, a terrific cannonade was opened upon him which continued, without interruption, for two hours and more. At mid-afternoon a desperate charge was made by the enemy on Hancock's position. They came forward "forty-five thousand strong and three columns deep." It was a tremendous shock, and superhuman efforts were required to break the devouring human wave which threatened their extinction. Hancock opened a heavy artillery fire, and then, as the enemy came up, swept them with his musketry. He rode along his lines, amid the sheeted flame, inspiring the troops to heroic attempts. And not in vain. When, at last, the enemy's advance had been repulsed and the splendid victory gained, Hancock was carried bleeding from the field, with a bullet-wound in his thigh. This hurt disabled him for a long time. But he had proven himself a hero in the best sense of the term, and from all quarters praises and admiration were lavished upon him.

In Grant's last campaign he had the left wing of the army, and at Ely's Ford, on the Rapidan, made a glorious fight. He crossed the Po River near Spottsylvania Court House, and after taking forcible possession of the Block House Road, worked on through the night with pick and spade to complete two lines of breastworks for its defence. "The lanterns of the workmen hanging to the blossoming cherry trees and picturesque groups of soldiers digging and erecting the works, while batteries stood harnessed up, their cannoniers lying on the ground around the carriages in wait for any emergency," added a dash of pleasant picturing to the dark front of war.

On May twelfth, Hancock made a desperate assault on the intrenchments of the enemy on the southern bank of Po River. The battle lasted for fourteen hours, and the place became "a perfect Golgotha." He captured "an entire division, four thousand strong, and thirty guns."

Stuart was one of the Confederate generals taken prisoner, and in the spirit of kindness which belongs to true chivalry, Hancock offered him his hand. Stuart drew himself up with hauteur, as he said, "I am General Stuart of the Confederate army, and under present circumstances I decline to take your hand!" Hancock's reply is worthy of record: "And under any other circumstances, General, I should have declined it!"

In the subsequent operations of the army, Hancock played a conspicuous part, and at Petersburg, in conjunction with Baldy Smith, "he carried the outer works." At Hatcher's Run, the Second Corps was saved from more than a partial reverse by the skill of its commander.

It now became apparent that Hancock must retire from active fighting on account of his old wound which had not entirely healed when he took the field in the Grant campaign. He was consequently relieved from the command of the Second Corps at his own request, being afterwards placed in charge of the Veteran First Corps, with head-quarters at Washington. He established recruiting-stations, and soldiers flocked around his standard. After Sheridan had made his raid to the James River and joined Grant, Hancock was placed in command of the Shenandoah Valley, "where he remained until the close of the war." He was afterwards appointed to take charge of the Middle Department of the Military Division of the Atlantic.

The people of New York testified their love for him by presenting him with an elegant barouche, just previous to his last campaign, to ride at the head of his corps; but he preferred an army ambulance.

Hancock always displayed the characteristics of a true and chivalrous manhood. Gracious to a conquered enemy, generous in all his instincts, incapable of pettiness, never revengeful, splendid in military qualities, he was such a general as would fitly adorn the annals of any age, however glorious. The student of human nature takes courage in contemplating such a character, and believes afresh in the possibility of the loftiest types of manhood.

CHAPTER XXXI.

JOHN CHARLES FREMONT.

The Hundred Days in Missouri.—Birth and Early Life.—On Board the "Natchez."—Beginning to be an Explorer.—Marriage with Jessie Benton.—Westward Ho!—Discoveries.—Conquest of California.—Across the Continent.—Senator from California.—In Command of the Western Department.—Causes of Removal.—Presidential Candidate.—An Extraordinary Ride.—What He Achieved.

IT is impossible to base any just estimate of Fremont's generalship on the one hundred days of his war career during the last civil conflict. He had but just begun his campaigning when Hunter superseded him in command, and the advantages gained by Fremont were allowed to slip back without further result. But as having compassed heroic achievement in the field of exploration and being closely identified with the political and war history of the Union, he is entitled to the vantage ground of prominence.

Fremont was born in Savannah, Georgia, January twenty-first, 1813. He is of French ancestry, having descended from one of the same name who came to the United States at the time of the French Revolution. His mother was Anne Beverly, daughter of Colonel Thomas Whiting, of Virginia—reputed to be at that time one of the most beautiful women in the State.

For several years the parents of Fremont travelled with their own carriage and servants, in the Southern States, and it was during one of their temporary halts that John Charles was born. He received his education in South Carolina, and became proficient in mathematics and engineering—his genius for these studies being very pronounced.

In 1833, when the sloop-of-war "Natchez" entered Charleston Harbor to enforce General Jackson's proclamation against Nullification, Fremont obtained through the Secretary of the Navy the appointment of teacher of mathematics on board that vessel, and made a cruise of between two and three years, first going to South America. He was afterwards appointed Professor of Mathematics on board the frigate "Independence."

Subsequently, he was made assistant engineer and sent to explore the mountain pass between South Carolina and Tennessee. He then went with Captain Williams on a military survey of Georgia, North Carolina and Tennessee, and from thence to the Upper Mississippi under command of the Frenchman, J. N. Nicollet. The years of 1838 and 1839 were occupied with exploring the region lying between the British line and the Missouri and northern rivers. About this time he became acquainted with the family of Mr. Benton, senator from Missouri, and a strong attachment was formed between Jessie, the second daughter, then fifteen years old, and the young explorer. In the summer of 1841, he was ordered to make an examination of the Des Moines River—Iowa at that time being a frontier region. After finishing the duty he returned to Washington, and on October nineteenth, consummated his marriage with Jessie Benton.

In 1842, he made a tour of exploration to the Rocky Mountain region and penetrated the South Pass. Following this, he planned another expedition to Oregon and went by a new route—joining the Wilkes Exploration party. Subsequently, he became guide to a third expedition westward, during which he discovered the Fremont Basin, the Sierra Nevada, the San Joaquin and Sacramento Valleys, and determined much of the geography of that country. In 1845, Fremont was again on the trail towards the Pacific Slope, and the work he then performed gave California to the United States. In the conquest of Upper California he bore a conspicuous part, but owing to a quarrel with some officers, he was deprived of his command. He declined the President's offer—which was afterwards made—to reinstate him.

His next work was the survey of a route from the Mississippi to San Francisco, during which he penetrated to the Apache country. In one hundred days after leaving Santa Fé, this bold land navigator of trackless wilds stood by the waters of the Sacramento.

In 1849–51, Fremont was sent as one of the first United States Senators from California, and in 1856 was the first Republican candidate for President—running in opposition to Buchanan. It was a very close contest, and Fremont might be said to have been as much the choice of the people as the elected candidate.

In 1846, Fremont had commanded a battalion in the Mexican war, and when the last war broke out, although he was in Paris at the time, he immediately purchased a large quantity of arms for government, and in June landed on his native shores. In July he received the commission of major-general, and took command of the Western Department a short time previous to the battle of Wilson's Creek.

After the death of Lyon, the weight of responsibility as well as of active duty in the field, rested on Fremont.

A proclamation which he issued about this time created some excitement. He declared Missouri under martial law, and ordered every one found with arms to be tried by court-martial. This step was certainly justified by the exigencies of the times.

Fremont arrived in Springfield on the twenty-seventh of October, and the succeeding hundred days embraced his last military record. Just after the Lexington affair, when he was about to put in operation some well-laid plans, orders for his removal arrived and he was superseded by Hunter, who let slip the sheaves of victorious work harvested by his predecessor. Fremont was afterwards exonerated from all blame for not keeping Price out of Lexington. It was shown that as soon as he fitted his men for the field, they were ordered to the Army of the Potomac. "Five thousand men ready to support Mulligan in his defence of Lexington were, at the very moment of their departure, counter-ordered to the East." Fremont's removal from command just at that crisis was afterwards conceded to have been a great military blunder. It broke up his famous "Body Guard," under command of Major Zagonyi—an organization whose personal attachment to their leader was so strong, that when he was suspended and after their brilliant and wonderful charge into Springfield through the enemy's lines, they resolved they would not come together again until they could fight under their old commander.

Notwithstanding the Lexington defeat and Fremont's consequent removal, he had set in motion a current of enthusiasm in the west which would not subside. In 1864 his name was again placed in nomination for the presidency, but he withdrew from the contest.

Since the war he has been associated with a transcontinental railroad.

Fremont's fourth expedition in 1848 was undertaken at his own expense, in quest of a home in the "new State which he had emancipated." It was during the month of March in the previous year that he made his extraordinary ride of nine hundred and sixty miles in seven days, through a rough and dangerous country, from Los Angeles to Monterey and back. He undertook this desperate mission to carry the news to General Kearney of an impending insurrection in Lower California.

The name of Fremont is imperishably written in the "historical, geographical, scientific and political history" of this country. What greater fame need any ambition crave? That he "missed world's honors and world's plaudits" when his voice was ever quick with its "Oh, list!" when the angel of duty spake, is far better than to have won those honors at the sacrifice of an untarnished conscience. Though he missed the presidential chair, his name crowns the loftiest peak of the longest chain of mountains in North America, as its first explorer. He is canonized as the savior of California from Mexican misrule, and as a geographer his fine genius received recognition from Humboldt and the scientific world at large. The court-martial which he underwent in 1848, was so palpably the result of rivalry between Commodore Stockton and General Kearney, that the testimony only served to reveal Fremont in a higher light than ever, as the fearless server of duty in preference to any lesser bidding. The verdict given was one of pure technique. It did not pluck one laurel from his well-earned chaplet, nor take from him the loving esteem of his fellow-citizens.

CHAPTER XXXII.
OLIVER OTIS HOWARD.

The Christian Soldier.—Early Life.—Off to the Wars.—Bravery in Battle.—Loss of an Arm.—Antietam.—Fredericksburg.—Chancellorsville.—Gettysburg.—The Atlanta Campaign.—Chief of the Army of the Tennessee.—Convalescence.—His Religious Convictions.—Story of a Wagon-Master.—In Charge of the Freedman's Bureau.—Sherman's Letter.

OLIVER OTIS HOWARD—distinguished as the "Christian Soldier"—was born on November eighth, 1830, in Leeds, Maine. When he was ten years old his father died, and he was taken in charge by an uncle who sent him to Bowdoin College. After graduating at that school he went to West Point, and completed the military course in 1854.

In 1856, he acted as chief-of-ordnance officer in the Florida campaign. The opening of the last war found him installed as professor of mathematics at West Point. In May, 1861, he was appointed colonel of the Third Maine Volunteers, by the governor of that State. On the field of Bull Run he led a brigade into the thick battle action with so much bravery and good generalship, that, in September, he was promoted to brigadier-general of volunteers. In December, he occupied a place in General Sumner's command. In September, 1863, in charge of the Eleventh Army Corps, he went with Slocum to reinforce the army at Chattanooga.

At Fair Oaks, he lost his right arm, and in the battles of Antietam, Fredericksburg and Chancellorsville his gallant conduct and well-directed fighting won golden opinions.

In the Gettysburg conflict, his position was on Cemetery Hill—the key to the battle-field. Here he displayed such coolness under fire and exposed himself to the hurtling shot and shell so freely, that it might be taken for rashness if one did not know it sprang from the highest kind of bravery.

During the Atlanta campaign, Howard commanded the Fourth Army Corps, and succeeded to McPherson's position as commander of the Army of the Tennessee, after that heroic general's death. In the "great march" from Atlanta to the sea, he held the right wing; and Sherman's confidence in him was absolute.

After the loss of his arm, he went back to his native State, and, during convalescence, the pale and wounded soldier became a recruiting officer and addressed crowds of his fellow-citizens in various parts of the State, appealing to their patriotism in sustaining the war power at Washington. As a result of these efforts, recruits by the hundred responded to his earnest appeals. "Modesty, sincerity and earnestness characterized his addresses," and gave evidence of his strong devotion to duty.

Howard's religious convictions were well known and universally respected by brother officers from highest to lowest; and whoever shared his mess; or partook of the hospitality of his table, always waited for a blessing to be invoked. General Grant said of him: "In General Howard throughout, I found a polished and Christian gentleman, exhibiting the highest and most chivalrous traits of the soldier."

The kind way in which he administered rebuke is

well illustrated in the following story: "On one occasion, a wagon-master, whose teams were floundering through the bottomless mud of a Georgia swamp, became exasperated at the unavoidable delay, and indulged in such a torrent of profanity as can only be heard in the army or among men of his class. General Howard quietly approached, unperceived by the offender, and was an unwilling listener to the blasphemous words. The wagon-master, on turning around, saw his general in close proximity and made haste to apologize for his profane outburst by saying, 'Excuse me, General, I did not know you were here.' The General, looking a reprimand, replied, 'I would prefer that you abstain from swearing from a higher and better motive than because of my presence.'"

After the war, in 1865, General Howard was placed at the head of the Freedman's Bureau—a position which abounded in difficulties, but which he filled most acceptably. There was not, probably, another man in the entire country whose nature and noble purposes and aims were so much in harmony with the peculiar and benevolent work of the Freedman's Bureau as Howard's. On his acceptance of this new post of honor, General Sherman wrote him as follows: "I hardly know whether to congratulate you or not, but of one thing you may rest assured, that you possess my entire confidence, and I cannot imagine that matters that may involve the future of four millions of souls could be put in more charitable and more conscientious hands. So far as man can do, I believe you will, but I fear you have a Herculean task; . . . though in the kindness of your heart you would alleviate all the ills of humanity, it is not in your power. . . . Yet you can and will do all the good one man may, and that is all you are called on as a man and a Christian to do; and to that extent count on me as a friend and fellow-soldier for counsel and assistance."

The traits of General Howard's character always shone conspicuous in the loftiest range of human motive. As a general, he was not great, like Grant, nor brilliant, like Sherman. But, without being a colossus in military genius, he performed his duty as a soldier and citizen faithfully, won golden approval from President, press and people, and deserves an especial niche in the temple of Memory as one who endeavored to soften the rigors of war with the balm of a gentle nature and the outstretched hand of humanitarian kindness.

CHAPTER XXXIII.
DAVID GLASCOE FARRAGUT.

The Power of the Navy.—Early Years of Farragut.—Remarkable Instance of Boyish Bravery.—Forty-eight Years of Quiet Life.—Union Sentiments.—Extract from Private Letter.—Castilian Ancestry.—Naval Combats on the Mississippi.—Capture of New Orleans.—The Bay Fight at Mobile.—Lashed to the Mast in the "Hartford."—Official Tour of European Ports.—Personal Habits of Farragut.

DURING our last war, the United States Navy became a powerful instrumentality in upholding the glory and unity of the Republic. It maintained the most difficult and stupendous blockade known to history. Six hundred ships garrisoned the coast of the United States, and fifty-one thousand soldiers of the sea garrisoned the ships. This fleet on the sea, dazzled, with its splendor of action, nations afar off and compelled not only the admiration, but the respect of Old-World principalities and powers. In the midst of that invincible New-World armada we can see, even yet, the stalwart figure of Admiral Farragut, shining in bold prominence, as King of the Fleet, by the divine legacy of genius.

This remarkable soldier was born in 1801, at Campbell's Station, in East Tennessee. His first baptism of warfare was received when only nine years old, on board Commodore Porter's ship, the "Essex," in its combat with the English sloop-of-war "Alert," April thirteenth, 1812. It took just eight minutes for the

"Alert" to strike her colors, with seven feet of water in her hold. Porter was a friend of Farragut's father and had given the boy a midshipman's berth. The brave lad was wounded in this first, brief but bloody battle, and bore himself so nobly, that in Porter's report he was honorably mentioned, with the added regret that he was "too young for promotion."

After 1812, Farragut received a general education, added to some instructions in military tactics, and then, in obedience to a pronounced inclination, followed the sea. For forty-eight years his record ran from lieutenant in 1825, to commander in 1841, and captain in 1851. He had voyaged up and down the world, in quiet seas, hither and thither, unknown to fortune and to fame. But the last civil war gave him the key to both—golden opportunity.

On account of Farragut's southern nativity and southern family ties, it was supposed he would go with the seceding South. His residence was at Norfolk, and when he boldly avowed his Union sentiments, it was intimated that a further residence among the people there might not be pleasant. "Very well," he replied, "I will go where I *can* live, with such sentiments."

He moved to Tarrytown, on the Hudson River, and received his first appointment as commander of the naval expedition to New Orleans, January twentieth, 1862. On February third he set out from Hampton Roads, in the flag-ship "Hartford."

. . . In a private letter from Farragut, written in response to an inquiry as to his ancestry by one who had discovered that the French Charlemagne's physician bore the name Farraguth, the Admiral said:

"My own name is probably Castilian. My grandfather came from Ciudadela, in the island of Minorca. I know nothing of the history of my family before they came to this country and settled in Florida. You may remember that in the seventeenth century, a colony settled there, and among them, I believe, was my grandfather. My father served through the war of Independence, and was at the battle of the Cowpens. Judge Anderson, formerly Comptroller of the Treasury, has frequently told me that my father received his majority from George Washington on the same day with himself; and his children have always supposed that this promotion was for his good conduct in that fight. Notwithstanding this statement . . . I have never been able to find my father's name in any list of the officers of the Revolution.

"With two men, Ogden and McKee, he was afterwards one of the early settlers of Tennessee. Mr. McKee was a member of Congress from Alabama, and once stopped in Norfolk, where I was then residing, on purpose, as he said, to see me, as the son of his early friend. He said he had heard that I was 'a chip of the old block'—what sort of a block it was I know not. This was thirty years ago. My father settled twelve miles from Knoxville, at a place called Campbell's Station, on the river where Burnside had his fight. Thence we moved to the South, about the time of the Wilkinson and Blennerhassett trouble. My father was then appointed a master in the navy, and sent to New Orleans in command of one of the gunboats. Hence the impression that I am a native of New Orleans. But all my father's children were born in Tennessee, and as I have said in answer to inquiries on this subject, we only moved South to crush out a couple of rebellions.

"My mother died of yellow fever the first summer in New Orleans, and my father settled at Pascagoula, in Mississippi. He continued to serve throughout the 'last war,' and was at the battle of New Orleans, under Commodore Patterson, though very infirm at that time. He died the following year, and my brothers and sisters married in and about New Orleans, where their descendants still remain.

"As to the name, General Goicouria, a Spanish hidalgo from Cuba, tells me it is Castilian, and is spelled in the same way as the old physician's—Farraguth."

The wonderful series of movements and naval combats on the Mississippi, in which the gauntlet of miles of forts was run, resulting in the capture of New Orleans and the opening of the river, is a feat unparalleled in history. Genius, generalship, patience — a hundred rare qualifications were needed to bring such an attempt to successful fruition. Wise forecast, quickness of inventive faculty to meet sudden crises, untiring labor, and the highest kind of courage were required; but Farragut showed himself royal in the possession of all kingly qualities of resource and command.

"The 'Bay Fight' at Mobile, and the resulting capture of Forts Powell and Gaines, was another scene as terrible as New Orleans, and still more splendidly illuminated by the perfect personal courage of the Admiral, . . . as he stood lashed in the rigging of the old 'Hartford,' clear above the smoke of the battle, and, even when he saw the monitor 'Tecumseh' sunk —the ship he had been waiting for, for months—yet ordered his wooden fleet straight forward, despite forts,

FARRAGUT AT MOBILE.

gunboats, ram and torpedoes, and won a second victory of that most glorious sort only possible to the high, clear and intelligent courage of a leader who is both truly heroic and truly wise."

After the war, while in Europe as a representative of the United States navy, he received enthusiastic testimonials to his genius and his individual standing as a man of lofty character and aims, aside from the mere deference paid to his official position.

Farragut's personal habits were ever strictly temperate, and as a consequence, he enjoyed vigorous health. A story is told regarding him, of a bishop with whom he once dined, who, after the repast was concluded, offered him a cigar. "No, Bishop," said the Admiral, with a quizzical glance, "I don't smoke —*I swear a little, sometimes.*"

Not only has the muse of History baptized Farragut, and the breath of Art breathed upon him as he swung aloft in the "Hartford," lashed to the mast, but he has gone into poetry, in whose immortal music he will live forever.

Few heroes as grand have ever been illumined by the blaze of Fame—few types of manhood as noble, have thrilled to strains as lofty the harp of human life.

CHAPTER XXXIV.

FRANZ SIGEL.

Early Military Education and Career.—Espousal of the Cause of the Revolutionists.—Exiled.—Arrival in the United States.—Life Previous to the War.—A Volunteer in the Union Army.—His Military Ability.—At Wilson's Creek.—The Battle of Pea Ridge.—Fighting Against Enormous Odds.—Splendid Skill Exhibited by Sigel.—Difficulties with Halleck.—New York Indignation Meeting.—In Command at Harper's Ferry.—Battle of Newmarket.—Close of Military Career.

THE German general—Franz Sigel—was born at Zinsheim, Baden, November eighteenth, 1824. He was educated for the military profession and attained distinction in his native country. But during the German revolution of 1848, his sympathies were so thoroughly and strongly republican, that he resigned his adjutant-general's commission and became a leader in the liberal movement. After the defeat of the revolutionists he was exiled from his country on account of the dangerous influence he exerted as a liberalist. He came to the United States in 1850, and between that period and 1858 he taught school in New York and St. Louis.

On the outbreak of civil war he entered the volunteer service and was placed at the head of the Third Missouri Regiment, as its colonel. He went to Springfield, Missouri, in June, and from that point was sent to hold Price and Jackson in check. He came upon their united forces near Carthage, July sixth, where a severe battle ensued. When he discovered that the enemy, greatly outnumbering him, were trying to get between him and his trains, he ordered a retreat. The ability which he displayed in cutting his way through Carthage and back to his trains, lifted him at once into fame, and the name of Sigel became a war cry among his countrymen.

At Wilson's Creek he made a tremendous blunder by mistaking the enemy's troops for Lyon's men, and therefore failed to bring on a concerted attack in the Confederate rear while Lyon assaulted their front. Owing to the gloom of the morning and the absence of all uniform, this mistake is easily accounted for. When the soldiers of Sigel's command waved their flags in welcome to their supposed comrades in arms, a destructive fire burst upon them which covered the ground with the dead and the dying, and at the same moment a Confederate battery opened upon them from the hill. Utter confusion and rout resulted. Colonel Sigel, in his efforts to arrest the disorderly retreat, narrowly escaped capture. In this action he lost about one thousand men and five guns.

In August, he was made brigadier-general and placed over a division in Fremont's army, and in the following October was sent in search of Price.

At the battle of Pea Ridge, Sigel showed himself so conspicuously capable and exhibited such a high order of warlike skill, that his name at once blazed into national repute and gave promise of shining bright among the brightest.

This famous action occurred on the seventh and eighth of March, 1862, and was fought under the shadow of the Boston Mountains, in northwestern Arkansas. Price and McCulloch had been driven to this point from Sugar Creek, fifty miles away, and were there reinforced by Earl Van Dorn's troops, which included a large band of Indians.

The hostile array, confronting the Union generals, was made up of nine thousand Missouri troops, six Arkansas regiments, five Texan regiments and three thousand dusky Indians, making an aggregate of twenty-five thousand men. General Curtis awaited the onset of this force a short distance south of Pea Ridge, preparing himself for the coming battle.

Meantime, on March fifth, Sigel, then at Bentonville, ten miles away, received orders to join Curtis at Pea Ridge, and on the next day the command was promptly executed. But it was a hazardous and difficult achievement. Four Confederate regiments attacked his rear-guard, which consisted of the Thirty-sixth Illinois and Second Missouri. But the attack was useless, for these brave men cut their way through the solid living wall of rebel soldiery, and rejoined their comrades, though with a loss of twenty-eight killed and wounded, and a number of prisoners. For the entire distance of ten miles Sigel contested every step of his advance. Supported by the infantry, his guns were halted, and the advancing rebel ranks, unable to stand before the discharges of grape and shell from the effective aim of our artillerymen, broke and fled in confusion. Before the scattered ranks of the enemy could reform, the guns of Sigel were limbered and the troops fell back into position behind another battery planted at the next turn in the road. This programme was continuously enacted for the entire distance of ten miles between Bentonville and Pea

Ridge. At last Sigel arrived at the west end of Pea Ridge, where he formed a junction with the divisions of Generals Carr and Davis.

The Union position was on the main road leading from Springfield to Fayetteville. The first two divisions of the Union troops were commanded by Sigel, and when the intention of the enemy to attack his right and rear became apparent, General Curtis changed front and Sigel had the left wing. The line stretched across Pea Ridge.

The battle opened on the morning of the seventh, and soon raged with fury along the whole line. During the afternoon, McCulloch, on the left wing, endeavored to form a junction with the troops of Van Dorn and Price, thus surrounding the Union army on three sides, and cutting off their retreat. But the quick eyes of Sigel detecting the movement, he ordered forward three pieces of flying artillery and a force of cavalry to take a commanding position and delay the movements of the enemy until our infantry could be brought up in position for an attack. But these pieces had hardly been placed in position when an overwhelming force of the enemy's cavalry swept down upon them, capturing their artillery and driving the horsemen. A desperate fight at this point then took place, and just as the ranks of the Union cavalry were broken and victory seemed to hover on the enemy's banners, Osterhaus and his Indiana regiments came up on the double-quick, and sending a murderous fire into the enemy's ranks, charged immediately after with the bayonet. This bold charge put to rout the Indians and Texans, and the three captured field-pieces were recovered. The command was then reinforced by General Sigel, and the action re-commenced with greater fury than before.

The heavy guns of the enemy were brought into position, and an artillery battle took place which resulted in the retirement of the enemy in confusion, leaving the Union troops masters of this part of the bloody field. Night let fall her intervening curtain of darkness between the contending armies, with Union success on the left, defeat on the right, and the battle yet unfinished. At dark the firing ceased from all quarters, and the exhausted soldiers slept upon their arms. Carr's division now occupied the centre, with Davis on the right, and Sigel still holding the left. Near the position occupied by our forces a hill rose abruptly to the height of two hundred feet, very precipitous in our front, but sloping gradually to the northward. On this eminence the enemy during the night had planted batteries which commanded our forces, and also at the right base of this hill, batteries and large bodies of infantry were posted. At the edge of some timber to the left, supports of infantry were disposed, while beyond the road, to the extreme left, were posted their cavalry and infantry.

At sunrise our right and centre, with their batteries, opened fire upon the enemy, while Sigel, having learned the exact position of the enemy's batteries, advanced with the left wing to take the hill, forming his line of battle by changing front so as to face the right flank of the enemy.

Sigel then ordered the Twenty-fifth Illinois into position along a fence in open view of the Confederate batteries, which immediately opened fire upon them. One of our batteries, consisting of six or seven guns, several of which were rifled twelve-pounders, was at once thrown into line one hundred paces to the rear of our advanced infantry, on a rise of ground.

The Twelfth Missouri then wheeled into line with the Twenty-fifth Illinois on their left, and another battery of guns similarly arranged a short distance behind them. But the crushing array was not yet complete, for still another regiment and another battery wheeled into position, until thirty pieces of artillery, fifteen or twenty paces distant from each other, formed one unbroken line, with the infantry lying down in front. As each piece circled into position, its fire was discharged at the enemy, and the fire of the entire line was so effective as to silence every Confederate battery, one by one. For two hours and over this terrible rain of fire continued.

It would have required *more* than human bravery to withstand it. The ranks of the foe withered under it by the hundreds, yet they stood fast. Sigel and his awful guns drew nearer and nearer, until the shortness of range grew more deadly. "No charge of theirs could face that iron hail or dare to venture on that compact line of bayonets. They turned and fled. The centre and right were ordered forward, the right turning the left of the enemy, and cross-firing on his centre. This final position of the enemy was in the arc of a circle. A charge of infantry by the whole line completely routed them, and they retreated through the deep, impassable defiles of Cross Timber, towards the Boston Mountains, closely pursued by the cavalry."

Not long after the battle of Pea Ridge, Sigel resigned his commission on account of alleged ill-treatment from Halleck. An indignation meeting was called in New York, "to express dissatisfaction with the course pursued towards him," and when brought to the notice of the President, he promised to see that justice was accorded him. Sigel was, therefore, promoted to major-general in the following summer, and put in command of Harper's Ferry. He subsequently commanded the division of Fremont on Fremont's resignation.

At the battle of Manassas or the Second Bull Run, General Sigel figured boldly and well. During the first day of action until mid-afternoon, he fought the battle alone, and succeeded in driving the enemy. On the day following, also, he bore his part gallantly, retiring afterwards with the army to the vicinity of Washington.

On the fourteenth of September he was placed over the Eleventh Corps, and in November was stationed in the gaps of the Blue Ridge. Soon after, he again marched towards Washington, and established his head-quarters at Fairfax Court-House.

In the Richmond campaign Grant gave him a separate command in the Valley of the Shenandoah, "to protect his flank." But in a battle near Newmarket he was overwhelmingly defeated by Breckenridge, losing five guns and nearly seven hundred men. On account of the dissatisfaction which this defeat caused at government head-quarters, he was relieved of his command and superseded by Hunter.

His war career ended during the last invasion of Early. At this time he was in Harper's Ferry, which he evacuated. He subsequently resigned his commission, and became the editor of a German paper in Baltimore.

CHAPTER XXXV.
HUGH JUDSON KILPATRICK.

Born for the Cavalry.—Romance of Early Life.—Married on the Eve of Going to the Front.—Her Name on his Banner.—Big Bethel.—Wounded.—To the Front again.—Falmouth Heights.—Kilpatrick's First Famous Raid.—Brandy Station.—"Men of Maine, Follow Me!"—Aldie.—Gettysburg.—Night Battle at Monterey.—New Baltimore.—Attempt to Rescue Prisoners.—Atlanta Campaign.—Resaca.—Wounded.—Georgia Campaign.—Waynesboro'.—At Savannah.—Sherman's Letter.—Promotion. —In the Carolinas.—Close of the War.

LIKE the French Murat, Kilpatrick seems to have been born to become a very demi-god of cavalry. Daringly heroic on the field, he displayed a supreme genius for war, especially for that department of the service whose alarum cry is "To horse!" and whose sweeping squadrons, with wild clatter of hoofs, seem to the fervid imagination to be making a race for glory, even though it be through the gates of death.

It is quite in keeping with everything about Kilpatrick that he should choose the cavalry as a vehicle for his high ambition and noble patriotism. Such energies as his could scarcely be content with less dash or less brilliance of action. The beginning of his war career was one of romance, and his previous life indicated an unusual range of abilities. He first figures as the boy orator, speaking in favor of a congressional candidate, with all the fresh warmth and enthusiasm of his young nature. Then we see him as cadet at West Point, from which he graduates fifteenth in his class, and is given the honor of valedictorian. The day of graduation is hastened a few months by the startling guns of Sumter, which proclaim treason rampant and fire all loyal breasts with a desire to rush to the rescue of their country's beloved flag. The impatience and enthusiasm of Kilpatrick could not be restrained, and through his influence a petition was signed by thirty-seven of his class to be allowed to graduate at once and go to the front. The request was granted, and that day was one of especial significance at West Point. It was also one of equal significance in his life; for the little chapel where had rung out the words of his farewell address, also witnessed the sacred ceremony of his marriage with the lady of his love, and on that evening the young soldier and his bride took the train for Washington and the front. We know little of the bride except that she was enshrined in her husband's love, and that her name—"Alice"—was inscribed on the silken banner under which he fought and so gloriously led his troopers to victory and renown. No one can tell how much that name may have had to do with his future marvellous success. To natures like his, the magic of a name thus loved, fluttering aloft in the smoke of battle, becomes talismanic, and inspires almost supernatural heroism.

Kilpatrick's first battle was fought at Big Bethel on June eleventh, 1861, where, in command of a portion of Duryea's Zouaves, he led the advance, and in the first charge received a grape-shot wound in his thigh; but though covered with blood, he led his men in several subsequent charges, and was finally borne from the field fainting from exhaustion. After this engagement he returned to New York, and was not able to take the field again before September.

During that month he went to Washington, received the rank of lieutenant-colonel in the Harris Light Cavalry, and began preparations for the front. He had also received the promotion of first lieutenant in the First Artillery in the regular army. In addition to this he became inspector-general of McDowell's division, and was also on the board for examining cavalry officers of the volunteer service.

In the grand movement on Manassas, March eighth, 1862, Kilpatrick's cavalry had the advance, and drove the rear-guard of Lee's army from that place. He advanced to Catlett's Station on the next day, where he remained until April.

When McDowell marched to Falmouth, he was once more at the front, and in conjunction with Colonel Bayard and the First Pennsylvania Cavalry, made a brilliant night attack on Falmouth Heights, routing Lee's cavalry and capturing the place. For this dashing achievement Kilpatrick received the thanks of the commanding general. Afterwards, under Pope's command, he made his first famous raid in breaking up Stonewall Jackson's line of communication with Richmond from Gordonsville in the Shenandoah Valley, over the Virginia Central Railroad. At Beaver Dam, Frederick's Hall and Hanover Junction, he burned the stations, destroyed the tracks, and daringly attacked the enemy wherever he could find him. These events took place during July and August, 1862, and the boldness of the operations in the very heart of the enemy's country, filled the north with Kilpatrick's fame.

In Pope's disastrous campaigning, Kilpatrick's regiment was with Bayard's cavalry protecting the rear of the army on its march to Washington. When Hooker was placed at the head of the Army of the Potomac, the cavalry was reorganized under Stoneman as chief, and that general, in the following campaign, assigned to Kilpatrick the work of destroying the railroad and bridges over the Chickahominy. Four hundred and fifty men were given him for the work; but with this small force he brought to the difficult mission his usual skill, and, avoiding large forces of the enemy, raided to within two miles of Richmond, where he captured "Lieutenant Brown, aide-de-camp to General Winder, and eleven men within the fortifications." He says: "I then passed down to the left to the Meadow Bridge on the Chickahominy, which I burned, ran a train of cars into the river, retired to Hanovertown on the Peninsula, crossed just in time to check the advance of a pursuing cavalry force, burned a train of thirty wagons loaded with bacon, captured thirteen prisoners, and encamped for the night five miles from the river." This was the manner of his conquering quest, until on the seventh, he again struck the Union lines at Gloucester Point, having made a march of about "two hundred miles in less than five days, and captured and paroled over eight hundred prisoners." In the accomplishment of this splendid feat he lost only one officer and thirty-seven men.

After Chancellorsville, when Lee came into Maryland and massed his cavalry at Beverly Ford, Pleasanton was sent forward on a reconnoissance and met the enemy in battle at Brandy Station. This is renowned as the greatest cavalry battle of the war. General

Gregg arrived upon the field at half-past ten in the morning, and though his noble squadrons fought well and bravely, their columns were rolled back, and for a moment all seemed lost and overwhelmed by the superior numbers of the foe. But at this crisis, Kilpatrick, posted on a slight rise of ground, unrolled his battle-flag to the breeze, and his bugles sounded the charge. He had under his command the Harris Light, Tenth New York, and First Maine. The formation for an onset was quickly made, and the disciplined squadrons of these three regiments were hurled upon the enemy. But the Tenth New York recoiled before the murderous fire of the enemy's carbines. So did the Harris Light. Kilpatrick was maddened at the sight. He rushed to the head of the First Maine Regiment, shouting, "Men of Maine, you must save the day! Follow me!" Under the impulse of this enthusiasm, they became altogether resistless, and in conjunction with the reformed squadrons of the other two regiments, swept the enemy before them, and plucked victory with glorious valor from the very jaws of defeat.

On the next day Kilpatrick was made brigadier-general, and the battle of Aldie was fought soon after.

At Aldie he came upon the advance guard of Fitzhugh Lee. This place is in a gap of the Bull Run Mountains, and lay in the direct line of Kilpatrick's reconnoissance southward. The encounter here was unexpected, but Kilpatrick, equal to the moment, dashed to the front, made a rapid survey of the situation, and then sounded the charge. Fitzhugh Lee was at first taken by surprise, and did not oppose the headlong advance, but afterwards rallied and fought desperately for two hours. He occupied a strong position on the crest of a hill behind a barricade of rails and haystacks, and made a bold stand. Kilpatrick ordered forward a battalion of the Harris Light, pointed to the field of haystacks, and said to Major Irvin commanding, "Major, *there* is the opportunity you have asked for. Go, take that position."

This was an allusion to a request made by the regiment on the morning of that day to "retrieve their reputation," knowing that they had failed to meet Kilpatrick's expectations at Brandy Station. It is almost needless to say that the position was gallantly taken.

But the enemy rallied again for a last desperate attempt, and success for the Union arms now seemed wavering. Kilpatrick rushed to the rescue, and at the head of the First Maine swept down upon the advancing Confederate ranks with such fury that they reeled and broke in confusion. They were driven as far as Middleburg, and night alone saved the remnant of the command.

An incident occurred during this fight, which is worth mentioning: "Colonel Cesnola, of the Fourth New York Cavalry, had that morning, through mistake, been placed under arrest, and his sword being taken from him was without arms. But in one of these wild charges, made early in the contest, his regiment hesitated. Forgetting that he was under arrest, and without command, he flew to the head of his regiment, reassured his men, and, without a weapon to give or ward a blow, led them to the charge. This gallant act was seen by his general, who, meeting him on his return, said: 'Colonel, you are a brave man; you are released from arrest;' and, taking his own sword from his side, handed it to the colonel, saying: 'Here is my sword;

wear it in honor of this day!' In the next charge Colonel Cesnola fell, desperately wounded, and was taken prisoner."

On June twenty-first, Kilpatrick charged the town of Upperville—with sabres alone—and drove the enemy through Ashby's Gap.

Soon after this he was placed in charge of over five thousand cavalrymen—*vice* Major-General Stahel, relieved—the entire cavalry force now consisting of three grand divisions, commanded by Buford, Gregg, and Kilpatrick.

Just previous to the Gettysburg battle, Kilpatrick had a desperate engagement with Stuart's cavalry at the town of Hanover. For hours the fight raged furiously, but at four o'clock in the afternoon the Fifth and Seventh Michigan regiments came on the field fresh, and their weight in the scales gave victory to the Union arms.

While at the little town of Abbottsville, where the worn-out battalions were resting after their severe fighting, Kilpatrick heard, on the morning of July second, the thunder of guns at Gettysburg.

At once his bugles sounded "To horse!" and the splendid command dashed away towards the scene of conflict. Arrived on the field, he saw at once where he was most needed, and without waiting for orders, moved to the right and engaged the left of Lee's line—at Hunterstown. Late that evening, long after the clangor of contest had ceased between the infantry lines, the shout of Kilpatrick's galloping squadrons on the right, told that the battle there went well.

At daybreak, on the third, Kilpatrick having marched most of the night, occupied a position near

Little Round Top, on the extreme left. Skirmishing had begun at about ten o'clock in the morning, and by afternoon Kilpatrick was "far in upon the enemy's flank and rear." At four o'clock a heavy force of Confederate infantry endeavored to turn the position at Little Round Top, by a grand charge of Longstreet's entire corps. If they succeeded, the day was lost. But Kilpatrick comprehended the situation, and having under him the Regular Brigade and General Farnsworth with the First Virginia, Eighteenth Pennsylvania and Fifth New York regiments, a counter-charge on the enemy's flank and left was ordered which broke their lines, and, with the aid of the artillery fire that now rained upon them, produced terrible confusion. It was a grand but dearly bought victory when such generals as Farnsworth baptized the soil with their precious blood. But the country rung with well-deserved plaudits for the cavalry.

At daybreak, on the fourth, Kilpatrick's columns were in motion, marching for the nearest point on the Gettysburg and Hagerstown road, crossing the mountains at Monterey, with orders to intercept the enemy and harass his retreat in all possible ways.

When near the mountain top, in a long, narrow, winding road, with bluffs on one side and a ravine on the other, the enemy's artillery and musketry suddenly blazed out upon them in the midnight gloom. It was raining in torrents and the darkness was so great that friend and foe were alike indistinguishable. It did, indeed, require more than ordinary courage and generalship to prevent panic and compass victory. But as on many a previous occasion, Kilpatrick was equal to this. The recoil of his troops was only mo-

KILPATRICK AT BRANDY STATION.

mentary. Riding at their head, he led the attack with such skill and impetuous onset that the enemy fled, leaving in the victorious raider's hands "their guns, a battle flag and four hundred prisoners." He was now in advance of the retreating Confederate army, and on the following day "captured eighteen hundred and sixty prisoners, including many officers of rank, and destroyed Ewell's immense wagon train nine miles long." At four o'clock he met and defeated Stuart in an engagement at Smithburg, and then moved to Boonsboro'. The battle at that place followed on July eighth. It was a brilliant affair in which Kilpatrick and Buford shared equal glory. On the thirteenth, Kilpatrick came upon the enemy's infantry, under General Pettigrew, one mile from Falling Waters, and brought on an engagement in which that general was killed in a sabre charge by the Sixth Michigan Regiment.

From the battle at Hanover Farm until this period, Kilpatrick had conquered fifteen splendid victories in as many days, had driven the enemy from northern soil and was almost constantly in the saddle—riding hundreds of miles. "His division at the outset consisted of five thousand men, and at the end of the campaign he reported the capture of four thousand five hundred prisoners, nine guns and eleven battle-flags."

Unable longer to hold out against this terrible strain on his energies, he obtained leave of absence and went to his home on the Hudson, where he remained until September.

During that month he rejoined his command at Warrenton, and was received with unbounded joy. In the general advance of the army which followed, Kilpatrick crossed the Rappahannock at Kelly's Ford, and on the old battle-ground of Brandy Station, where Gregg and Buford were hard pressed, again decided the issues of conflict.

The last fight during October, on these famous plains, in which the great cavalry chiefs of the war distinguished themselves—the severe engagement at New Baltimore—the noble attempt made by Kilpatrick to rescue the Belle Isle and Libby prisoners in February of 1864—the death of his wife "Alice"—these events marked his record until he was needed in the great Atlanta campaign and summoned to join Sherman at Nashville, Tennessee.

When the grand armies moved, Kilpatrick led the advance, and in the wild and victorious charge at Resaca, reeled from the saddle and was borne from the field desperately wounded by a rifle ball. Through the long months of illness which followed, he was nursed into convalescence at his home on the Hudson, and when the news came that Atlanta must fall in a few days, nothing could restrain him from going at once to the front. He joined his command at Cartersville, and, not yet able to ride on horseback, went to the front in a carriage.

In the daring raid now performed by Kilpatrick on the enemy's flank, by means of which Sherman was enabled to get in rear of the Confederate army and take Atlanta, some of the most brilliant movements were executed, and no peril of any kind seemed too great to baffle his genius.

Then followed his ride through the heart of Georgia. On the fourteenth day of November, 1864, the long march from Marietta to Savannah began—Kilpatrick's command consisting of two brigades of twenty-five hundred men each. The plan of march was to sweep across the country in seven days by way of Atlanta to Milledgeville, thence to Millen and Waynesboro'—then to the sea. At Waynesboro' a hard battle was fought, and the enemy under Wheeler routed.

On December twenty-first, a triumphant entry into Savannah was made. Since November fourteenth they had "three times crossed from left to right, and right to left, in front of the army, and had marched over five hundred and forty-one miles." A letter from Sherman, December twenty-ninth, in the field before Savannah, shows the high value he placed upon Kilpatrick's services:

"But the fact that to you, in a great measure, we owe the march of four strong infantry columns, with heavy trains and wagons, over three hundred miles through an enemy's country, without the loss of a single wagon and without the annoyance of cavalry dashes on our flanks, is honor enough for any cavalry commander."

The valiant chief was promoted to the rank of major-general at Savannah, on January fourteenth, 1865.

In the great campaign in the Carolinas, rapid marches, feints and fighting were the order of the day, which at last resulted in the fall of Columbia, in the occupancy of Fayetteville, and the fight at Averysboro', where Kilpatrick made a stand on a battle-ground with a ravine in his rear to prevent the enemy from securing it. In this action, which occurred on March sixteenth, the cavalry and infantry fought side by side, mounted and dismounted, and behaved most gallantly. This action ended, the cavalry command went into camp at Mount Olive, on the Wilmington military road, and rested from its labors, after having endured marvellous hardships and rendered invaluable services. In a circular issued to his troops on March twenty-second, Kilpatrick said: .

"Soldiers, be proud! Of all the brave men of this great army, you have a right to be. You have won the admiration of our infantry, fighting on foot and mounted, and you will receive the outspoken words of praise from the great Sherman himself. . . . . With the old laurels of Georgia, entwine those won in the Carolinas, and proudly wear them!"

General Kilpatrick was born in New Jersey in 1838, and since the war has been appointed to high civic positions. Of him and the brave troopers with whom he nobly battled for country and the freedom of its institutions, let it be said:

"Honor the brave and bold!
Long shall the tale be told,—
Yea, when our babes are old,
How they rode onward!"

CHAPTER XXXVI.
PHILIP KEARNY.

Birthplace.—Where Educated.—In Europe.—Fighting Abroad.— Honors.—Participates in the Mexican War.—Loss of an Arm.— In Europe Again.—At Magenta and Solferino.—At the Front in our Last War.—Bravery at Williamsburg.—Promotion.—Kearny's Power over his Men.—The Battle of Chantilly.—Death's Sad Eclipse.—"Lay Him Low."

THIS gallant, impetuous, headlong fighter—a veritable son of Mars—was born in New York on June second, 1815. He received his education at Columbia College, and afterwards studied law. In 1837, he became a lieutenant in the First Dragoons, of which his uncle, Stephen Watts Kearny, was colonel. Soon after receiving this appointment, he was ordered by Government to visit Europe, to report upon the tactics of the French cavalry service. While there, he made himself proficient in the Polytechnic School at Saumur, and subsequently joined the Chasseurs d'Afrique in Algeria, in which his gallantry won him the decoration of the "Cross of the Legion of Honor."

In 1840, Kearny came back to his native shores, and when the Mexican war broke out, served on the staff of General Scott.

In 1846, he was made a captain of dragoons, and received the brevet of major for bravery at Contreras and Churubusco.

At the San Antonia Gate of the ancient city of Mexico, during the last assault, he lost an arm.

After the return of peace to that chaotic country, he was again on the war path in the far west, against the Indians on the Columbia River and in California.

In 1851, he went to Europe to continue his military studies, and during this sojourn in foreign parts he became volunteer aide to General Maurier, of the French army, who was engaged in the Italian war of 1859.

For bravery at Magenta and Solferino, Kearny received a second time the decoration of the "Cross of the Legion of Honor."

The outbreak of our last war brought him quickly home, and his patriot blade was soon unsheathed at the front. Government at once gave him the appointment of brigadier-general of volunteers. During the Peninsular campaign he commanded a division, and distinguished himself especially at Williamsburg and Fair Oaks.

At Williamsburg, when he came to the relief of Hooker, Kearny performed a feat of daring which made him the idol of his division. Wishing to disclose the enemy's concealed position to his command, he called the officers of his staff together, dashed out into the open field and rode leisurely along the entire line. Five thousand guns belched forth their death-dealing missiles, bullets fell around them like hail, two of his aids and three orderlies fell dead at his side, and before he reached the end of his perilous ride, he found himself almost alone. By this exploit he was enabled to accomplish his object of discovering the strength of the enemy; then riding back to his division, he shouted, "You see, my boys, where to fire!" Kearny now held his own until General Hancock came up and by a flank movement forced the enemy to retire to his fortifications.

At Harrison's Landing he was promoted to major-general of volunteers, dating from July fourth, 1862, and in the second battle of Bull Run he was again conspicuous for gallant conduct.

An eye-witness, who saw Kearny in the last action which preceded Malvern Hill, said that besides seeming to be omnipresent on the field, he gave "electric strength to his men wherever he appeared. Waving his brave one arm, more to be dreaded than two, and saying, with a smile into the eyes of every man, 'Gayly, my boys, go in gayly!' he drew them on into the thickest fight with an abandon which must have been seen to be realized.

"General Kearny possessed that rarest gift of intuitive anticipation of the enemy's plans—that sure instinct of the nearest danger which is almost a battle second sight and which would have made him, had he lived, one of our most famous generals."

On the first of September, 1862, at sunset, Stonewall Jackson made a sudden descent on the Union forces at Chantilly, under Reno. A furious thunder storm was raging in the sky above, while the battle raged on the plain below. The enemy was driven back at all points. But when General Stevens fell at the head of his command while leading a charge, confusion ensued and the first division of Reno, which it uncovered, also became demoralized. It was at this critical juncture of affairs that General Kearny, leading one of Heintzleman's divisions, advanced to the rescue and with a terrific charge drove the Confederates from the field. The victory was complete, but Kearny's life paid the forfeit. Amid the clash of battle and the crash of warring elements his life went out in a blaze of glory, leaving only the bleeding and inanimate clay behind.

"Flowers of red shot, red lightnings strewed his bier,
And night, black night, the mourner."

His soldierly impetuosity, never outdone in deeds of bravery, won him the admiration, the respect, the love of all; and that peculiar homage is his which we give to leaders who fall in the brunt of battle, while fighting in a glorious cause.

"Close his eyes, his work is done,
   What to him is friend òr foeman,
 Rise of morn or set of sun,
   Hand of man or kiss of woman?
     Lay him low, lay him low,
     In the clover or the snow,
     What carès he? he cannot know—
     Lay him low.

       .   .   .   .

"Fold him in his country's stars,
   Roll the drum and fire the volley,
 What to him are all our wars,
   What but death bemocking folly?
     Lay him low, lay him low,
     In the clover or the snow,
     What cares he? he cannot know—
     Lay him low."

CHAPTER XXXVII.
NATHANIEL LYON.

Of Soldier Ancestry.—Early Childhood.—Graduates at West Point.
—In the Mexican War.—On the Frontier.—Rescue of the St.
Louis Arsenal.—Given the Chief Command in Missouri.—At
Wilson's Creek.—Fighting Against Terrible Odds.—Twice
Wounded.—The Last Charge.—Lyon's Fall.—His Civilian's
Dress.—Funeral Honors.—The Sorrowful Multitudes.—Funeral
Oration at Eastford.—Resolutions of Respect.

BY the red torch of battle, lighted at Wilson's Creek, the warrior soul of Lyon was sent on its unreturning journey across the Stygian river, to the misty land of, the Hereafter.

He fell, deeply lamented by his country, sincerely mourned by thousands. No officer had been killed in battle previous to that date whose loss was felt to be so personal a sorrow. The shrouded form of the dead hero, touched by the strange magic of death, was borne from the field to his home in the east, amid a spontaneous outburst of sorrow from gathered multitudes all along the route. And in that last tearful incense of public bereavement his name still burns—"a name immortal, won by deeds immortal."

Lyon was born in 1821, at Eastford, Windham County, Connecticut, and from childhood listened with rapt interest to the recital of deeds of daring performed by brave ancestors in the Revolutionary war. It is not strange that his young and enthusiastic heart was fired by these oft-repeated tales, or that his choice of vocation was thereby the more strongly drawn towards a military life.

His paternal grandfather served in both the French and Revolutionary wars, and his mother's father rendered himself prominent and fought the fight of liberty at White Plains and Bunker Hill.

Young Lyon graduated from West Point in 1841, with the rank of second lieutenant of the Second Infantry, and performed his maiden service in Florida. Subsequently, he went on duty in the frontier territories.

In the Mexican war, he participated in every battle under Scott, from Vera Cruz to the City of the Montezumas, receiving promotions for gallant conduct. In June, 1851, he was given a captain's commission.

"After the conclusion of peace with Mexico, he was ordered to Jefferson Barracks, Missouri, preparatory to a contemplated march overland to California. By a change of orders from the War Department, his regiment was despatched by ship *via* Cape Horn, and reached California soon after its acquisition by the United States. His stay in California was prolonged beyond that of most of his fellow-officers, and his time unceasingly employed in operating among the Indians, subjected to long and tedious marches, constant alarms, and frequent skirmishes, living a large portion of the time in tents, and subject to the fatigues and privations incident to a campaign in that new and hitherto unknown country, so far removed from the comforts of civilization."

At the end of his California service, Lyon went again to the frontier, doing duty principally in Kansas and Nebraska. On the outbreak of the Kansas troubles, he was sent to the head-quarters of the Department of the West, at St. Louis. Here, by a bold and dashing stroke of genius, he rescued the St. Louis arsenal from the hands of his country's enemies.

When General Harney relinquished the chief command of this department, Captain Lyon, after having been chosen general by the Missouri volunteers, received the appointment of brigadier-general, and was given the chief command in Missouri. This he retained until Fremont was placed at the head of the Department of the Mississippi, on July ninth.

The sword, instead of the pen, has written at Wilson's Creek the remaining chapter of Lyon's life. The fatal engagement was the result of his choice between dishonorable retreat and an encounter with overwhelming numbers of the enemy. He did not for an instant hesitate in that choice, though fully realizing the dangers to be met. His plan of action was masterly, and if Sigel's forces had not mistaken the foe for Lyon's troops, it seems probable that the entire Confederate army under Price would have been routed.

Lyon, with intrepid leadership, fought in the thickest of the fray, inspiring his men by voice and example. A short time previous to his fall, he "had received two wounds, and had his fine dappled gray shot under him, which is sufficient evidence that he had sought no place of safety for himself while he placed his men in danger. Indeed, he had already unwisely exposed himself. Seeing blood upon his hat, one who was with him inquired, 'General, are you badly hurt?' to which he replied, 'I think not seriously.' He had mounted another horse and was as busily engaged as ever."

Lyon was filled with admiration at the bravery of

his men, and "praised their behavior in glowing terms with almost his last breath." He wanted a bayonet charge made, and three companies of Iowans at once offered to go. They asked for a leader. No time could be lost to select one, for the enemy was rushing to a fresh attack. At this juncture Lyon exclaimed: "I will lead you! Come on, brave men!" The charge was made, and the Confederates recoiled before their wild onset; but when the smoke lifted a little, the fearless Iowans were without their great leader. The noble heart had throbbed its last—Lyon was dead.

He had gone into battle in civilian's dress, with the exception of a military coat. "He wore a soft hat of an ashen hue, with long fur and a very broad brim, turned up on three sides. He had been wearing it for a month; there was only one like it in the command, and it would have individualized the wearer among fifty thousand men. His peculiar dress and personal appearance were well known through the enemy's camps. He received a new and elegant uniform just before the battle, but never wore it until his remains were arrayed in it, after his brave spirit had fled."

There is no doubt that Lyon made this attack fully comprehending that the "odds were fearfully against him, and that little short of a miracle could enable him to come off victorious. But he felt that the cause demanded it; that for him to abandon Springfield without a battle would demoralize and dishearten the Union men of southwest Missouri, and pain every loyal breast in the nation. . . . He had no alternative but to fall back to Rolla, or to attack the enemy. He obeyed the voice of patriotism and went out to danger and to death on that summer morning, as a man goes to his bridal.

Twice wounded, he was still undaunted, and refused to . . . seek a less exposed position. Even after he believed the day lost, he sprang eagerly from his dead horse into a fresh saddle, at the head of a forlorn hope, dashed into the thick of the fight, and died like a true soldier."

A guard of honor, chosen from among his brother officers and the St. Louis Home-Guards, escorted the loved remains to his home in Connecticut. After arriving at the village of Eastford, the body was consigned to its last resting-place, and the funeral oration pronounced by the Honorable Galusha A. Grow.

One of the resolutions adopted at a meeting of the citizens of Eastford, convened at that time, was as follows:

"*Resolved*, That as his fellow-townsmen, while we mourn our loss, we rejoice that we have his birth-spot among us to cheer us in steadfast devotion to our country; and we trust his grave among us will be the spot where future generations will gather, and be inspired with a noble emulation of his virtues, and the virtues of Sherman, Trumbull, Putnam, and others who have arisen in this State, defenders of their country's flag, and supporters of its government."

A great historian has said of Lyon: "His military services were beyond all praise; his character was beautifully earnest; and his sad death reflects infinite honor on his own memory, and I fear shame on those who let him fall a martyr to his duty, his patriotism, his zeal and the natural self-sacrificing element of his character."

"Roll, stirring drum, still roll,
  Not a sign, not a sound of woe,
That a grand and a glorious soul
  Hath gone where the brave must go."

CHAPTER XXXVIII.
ELMER EPHRAIM ELLSWORTH.

"How Knightly looked he as he rode to Hounds!"—Character.—An Enthusiast in Military Science.—The French Zouave Tactics.—A Noble Ambition.—Early Struggles.—The Chicago Zouaves.—Their Perfection of Drill and Character.—A Tour of Triumph.—In New York.—A Favorite of Lincoln.—The War Clarion.—New York Fire Zouaves.—Sword Presentations.—In the South.—Last Night at Alexandria.—Letter Home.—The Dread Tragedy.—Universal Grief.—Lincoln's Sorrow.—The Genius of Ellsworth.

WE love the memory of Ellsworth as that of our most chivalrous ideal of the young and glorious and knightly soldier. His pictured face wears a look prophetic of some high and unusual destiny. The eyes contain much of soul, and are of that kind which Emerson would designate as "full of fate." He is described as having been strikingly prepossessing in appearance, and his voice, which was "deep and musical, and instantly attracted attention," chorded well with so splendid a presence. "His form, though slight, was very compact and commanding: the head statuesquely poised and crowned with a luxuriance of curling black hair; a hazel eye, bright though serene, the eye of a gentleman as well as a soldier; a nose such as you see on Roman medals; a light moustache just shading the lips that were continually curving into the sunniest smiles." His tread was full of elastic grace, and gave to his figure its commanding ease of attitude. "No one ever possessed greater power of enforcing the respect and fastening the affections of men. Strangers soon recognized and acknowledged this power; while to his friends he always seemed like a Paladin or Cavalier of the dead days of romance and beauty." Every one with whom he came in contact was impressed with his intense vitality and the strength and warmth of his nature.

All this graciousness of physique did not belie the man. He was the soul of honor, the embodiment of high desires, and " amiable words and courtliness and love of truth, and all that makes a man." He might have belonged to Arthur's court, the stainless English king, and been numbered among those ancient and proud knights of the Round Table, " who reverenced their conscience as their king; whose glory was redressing human wrong; who spoke no slander, no, nor listened to it; who loved one only and who clave to her, and worshipped her by years of noble deeds," and worthily lived, " wearing the white flower of a blameless life."

By some prophetic forecast or singular chance, he had, for several years previous to the opening of our last war, been an enthusiast in military science, and was the first one who introduced into this country the French Zouave system of tactics. He amended both the French and Hardee, so that the movements in his manual of arms were each natural sequences of the others. "He studied the science of fence so that he could hold a rapier with De Villiers, the most dashing of the Algerine swordsmen. He always had a hand as true as steel and an eye like a ger-falcon. He used to amuse himself by shooting ventilation holes through his window panes. Standing ten paces from the window, he could fire the seven shots from his revolver and not shiver the glass beyond the circumference of a half dollar." "A photograph of his arm taken at this time shows a knotted coil of sinews like a magnificent exaggeration of antique sculpture."

His great aim was to reorganize the United States militia, which his keen eye saw to be full of defects. He went about this work in a clear and practical way, which won admiration from those in authority. There was to be an initial experiment—an operative demonstration of his theories; and consequently, on the fourth of May, 1859, he organized the United States Zouave Cadets of Chicago.

Previous to this date his life had been full of the tonic of untoward circumstance. Born at Mechanicsville, New York, April twenty-third, 1836, he acquired readily the common school education afforded by his native place, and thirsted for more. The limited means of his parents did not permit an outlay in that direction. The successive steps of his effort during this emerging period were from a printing office to New York city, from New York to Boston, from Boston a year after to Chicago, in 1857. Here he embarked in business only to be wrecked by the dishonesty of an agent. This rude blast of fortune he met uncomplainingly. The next year was occupied in reading law with determined application. He earned a meagre living, meantime, by copying outside of study hours.

With delicate sensitiveness he concealed from every one his struggle with poverty. "During all that time he never slept in a bed—never ate with friends at a social board. So acute was his sense of honor, and his ideas of propriety, that, although the most generous of men, he never would accept from acquaintances the slightest favors or courtesies which he might be unable to return."

On one occasion, he accompanied a friend to a restaurant for conversation, but refused to dine with him, though the aroma of the repast was well-nigh maddening to his half-famished stomach. "His hearty good humor never gave way. His sense of honor, which was sometimes even fantastic in its delicacy, freed him from the very temptation to wrong. He knew there was a better time coming for him. Conscious of great mental and bodily strength, with that bright lookout that industry and honor always give a man, he was perfectly secure of ultimate success."

One of his dreams was the intellectual and commercial conquest of Mexico, with a grand centre of operations at Guaymas, from whence the tonic influence of American progress was to arrest and rejuvenate the decay of Mexican nationality. He saw "annexation" as the end of this scheme, but not through warfare and bloodshed. It was rather the vision of one who should bear "the standard of the peoples, plunging through the thunder storms, till the war-drums throbbed no longer and the battle-flags were furled," and the seas should "fill with commerce—argosies of magic sails—pilots of the purple twilight, dropping down with costly bales."

And thus, under the warm rays of a genius like this, the Chicago Zouaves sprang into existence. Ellsworth threw aside together, old uniforms and old ideas. He taught his men a simpler manual of arms. The new uniform was his invention and left the wearer perfectly free in every movement.

"He drilled these young men for about a year, at short intervals. His discipline was very severe and rigid. . . . The slightest exhibition of intemperance or licentiousness was punished by instant degradation and expulsion. He struck from the rolls at one time twelve of his best men, for breaking the rule of total abstinence. His moral power over them was perfect and absolute. . . . Any one of them would have died for him!"

In several other towns in Illinois and Wisconsin he had companies under drill. In Springfield and Rockford he was especially appreciated. At Rockford he formed an acquaintance with a young lady, which resulted in betrothal and gave to the tragedy of subsequent events a touch of subdued romance.

"His company took the premium colors at the United States Agricultural Fair, and Ellsworth thought it was time to show the people some fruit of his drill. They issued their soldierly *défi* and started on their march of triumph. . . . Hardly had they left the suburbs of Chicago, when the murmur of applause began. New York, secure in the championship of half a century, listened with quiet, metropolitan scorn to the noise of the shouting provinces; but when the crimson phantasms marched out of the Park on the evening of the fifteenth of July, New York, with metropolitan magnanimity, confessed herself utterly vanquished. . . . There was no resisting the Zouaves."

At an exhibition given at the Academy of Music, that hall was filled to overflowing, by the *élite* of the city, and on their departure, they were "magnificently entertained at the St. Nicholas Hotel, by the Second Company, National Guard." "At Boston, Philadelphia, Washington and the other cities visited they were received with marked favor," and the Ellsworth Zouaves were rapidly acquiring an enviable repute.

After the completion of their journey, Ellsworth entered the law office of Lincoln, at Springfield, Illinois, and in the ensuing campaign became a popular partisan of that presidential candidate. In the heat of the canvass, his law studies could not receive undivided attention, and when the newly-elected President went to the capitol for inauguration, Ellsworth was one of the chosen few forming the presidential escort. "On that journey he was the life and spirit of the party."

Encouraged by Lincoln, he endeavored to perfect his schemes for military reform through the War Department; but just as he became disgusted with the office-hunting and abasement of principle rife at Washington, Sumter was attacked and at once he sprang to action. That action thrilled the nation.

The lieutenant's commission, which he had received from Lincoln in the hope of forwarding his plans, he now returned to the War Department, and was soon *en route* for New York to raise a regiment among the New York firemen. This was accomplished with marvellous celerity. In two days after he went to the chief of the fire department and issued his call for volunteers, twelve hundred recruits had enrolled their names. Selecting ten companies, he went to Fort Hamilton to drill. He labored there with enthusiasm, night and day, and in less than three weeks took his regiment to Washington. New York was enthusiastic over her Fire Zouaves, and three stands of colors were presented to them. The first was the gift of the city; the second was from Mrs. Augusta Astor, presented by Hon. John A. Dix, and the third was presented by Mr. Stetson in the name of the ladies of the Astor House.

Ellsworth "divided his regiment, according to his own original idea, into groups of four comrades each, for the campaign. He exercised a personal supervision over the most important and most trivial minutiæ of the regimental business. The quick sympathy of the public still followed him. He became the idol of the Bowery and the pet of the Avenue. Yet not one instant did he waste in recreation or lionizing. Indulgent to all others, he was merciless to himself. He worked day and night, like an incarnation of energy. When he arrived with his men in Washington, he was thin, hoarse, flushed, but entirely contented and happy, because busy and useful."

The succeeding weeks were filled with continued and unceasing industry. Everything went well in the hopeful, brave-spirited Zouave camp. On the fateful night of the twenty-third of May, Ellsworth called his men together and addressed them in a brief, stirring speech—announcing their orders to advance on Alexandria. When silence again hovered over the camp, he completed the business arrangements of the regiment, and at midnight, in his tent by the Potomac, wrote two letters; one to his parents, in which he communicated the impending advance and the possibilities of personal injury. "Whatever may happen," he concludes, "cherish the consolation that I was engaged in the performance of a sacred duty; and to-night, think ing over the probabilities of to-morrow, and the occurrences of the past, I am perfectly content to accept whatever my fortune may be, confident that He who noteth even the fall of a sparrow, will have some purpose, even in the fate of one like me.

"My darling and ever-loved parents, good-bye. God bless, protect and care for you. "ELMER."

The other letter was written to his beloved, and the tender message is forever veiled from all eyes save those for whom it was written.

The dread tragedy that followed was sad without relief. Ellsworth's regiment crossed the river in steamboats that night, and on learning that the place had surrendered without resistance to the terms proposed by the *Pawnee*, then anchored in the Potomac off Alexandria, Ellsworth proceeded, with a detachment of the first company, to take possession of the telegraph and stop railroad communication. While on this mission, the flag floating from the Marshall House arrested his attention. He entered with his party and asked what flag it was of a man whom he met in his shirt and pantaloons. This was James T. Jackson, the proprietor. The man professed to know nothing of it. Ellsworth ran up-stairs to the roof, cut down the flag, and was descending the narrow stairway again, when some one—it proved to be Jackson—sprang from a dark corner and discharged a double-barrelled fowling-piece full into his breast. The shot drove into his heart a gold circlet—one of his presentations—inscribed with the legend, "Non nobis, sed pro patria."

One who was with him at that fatal moment says: "The first thing to be done was to look to our dead leader. . . . The chaplain turned him gently over, and I stooped and called his name aloud, at which I thought that he murmured inarticulately. I presume I was mistaken, and I am not sure that he spoke a word after being struck. Winser and I lifted the body with all care, and laid it upon a bed in a room near by. The rebel flag, stained with his blood, we laid about his feet. . . . His expression in death was beautifully natural. . . . Excepting the pallor, there was nothing different in his countenance now from what all his friends had so lately been accustomed to gladly recognize."

His assassin met almost instant death at the hands of private Brownell, who was coming down the stairway in front of Ellsworth. When the remainder of the party came up, a litter of muskets was made, and the soldiers bore their beloved leader sorrowfully to the steamer. After reaching the Navy Yard, his body was taken to the engine-house, which was draped in mourning. But President Lincoln had him removed to the East Room of the White House, and there, on the twenty-fifth of May, the funeral obsequies were pronounced. The remains were borne to the depot, followed by the President and his cabinet, amid the tolling of bells and universal grief.

At New York he lay in state in the governor's room, and a funeral procession of immense length threaded its way through crowds that almost defied computation, to the steamer that was to bear him to his early home. At Albany, a similar testimonial of grief took expression, and while he lay within the shadow of the capitol, an organization called "The Ellsworth Avengers," rapidly formed itself. Arrived at Mechanicsville, at last, the martyred dead was given to his agonized parents, and, amid the fury of a raging storm which beat into his open grave—as if the very elements wept their wild sorrow—the body was committed to its long resting-place.

The excitement which followed the tragedy was very great throughout the country, and his name became a rallying cry for thousands. The grief of the President, who was tenderly attached to Ellsworth, was touching in the extreme. A gentleman, in company with Senator Wilson, who called to see Lincoln on the morning of the shooting, found him "standing before a window, looking out across the Potomac. He did not move till they approached very closely, when he turned round abruptly and advanced towards them, extending his hand. 'Excuse me,' he said, 'but I cannot talk.' He burst into tears and concealed his face in his handkerchief. Then, for some moments, he walked up and down the room, and they stepped aside in silence, not a little moved at such an unusual spectacle, in such a man, in such a place."

A New York city paper spoke of him as follows:— "It is about a month since a young man of soldierly bearing, of an unusually fine physique, of frank and attractive manners, and of great intelligence, called on us on the day of his arrival from Washington, to state his wishes and purposes in relation to raising a regiment among the New York firemen. A fortnight later we saw him on his way to embark for Washington at the head of his men, and escorted by the most imposing procession this city has ever witnessed. This man was Colonel Ellsworth, of the Firemen Zouaves. 'I want,' he said, 'the New York firemen; for there are no more effective men in the country, and none with whom I can do so much. They are sleeping on a volcano at Washington,' he added, 'and I want men who can go into a fight *now*.' The impression he made upon us was that of a fearless, gallant and energetic man, one of those possessed of . . . powers that especially fit them to be leaders among men. In him we think the country has lost a very valuable life."

Ellsworth was, in all respects, remarkable: not only in his genius as a soldier and reformer of military ethics, but in his beautiful symmetry of character. The light which he transmits is not merely the burning halo surrounding the brow of the hero, but that of a pure and complete manhood in which are clustered all the virtues, added to a sublime scorn of everything ignoble. We approach the unforgotten altar of his memory as would those who draw near a sacred shrine to lay upon it the mute worship of their odorous flowers; and we accord him the chivalrous love due a true knight of truth—a love akin to that which women lavish upon their bravest ideals. To us he can never grow old, nor change. The same radiant face will always be looking down on us from its white aura of clouds, and though gallant ones innumerable come to claim our admiration and affection, in all the long roll of honor given by the clarion of war, there will be but **one Ellsworth!**

CHAPTER XXXIX.
EDWARD DICKINSON BAKER.

The English Boy on American Shores.—Early Struggles.—Off for the West.—Efforts as a Young Lawyer in Springfield.—Congressional Honors.—Leadership on the Forum.—In the Mexican War.—Removal to the Pacific Coast.—Popularity as an Advocate.—Oration over Broderick.—Sent to the United States Senate from Oregon.—Union Square Speech.—Organization of the California Regiment.—To the Front.—Ball's Bluff.—Last Scenes.

COLONEL BAKER began life as an humble English boy, and was a marked illustration of that class of men who create their own destinies. His type radiates a full-orbed splendor. The obstacles which beset him in his early career only further demonstrated the force of a genius which pushed aside every difficulty in its upward path. Only five years old—a mere infant—when he first set foot on these American shores; his father—himself a Quaker—settled in the Quaker City of Philadelphia, and then, in a few years, died. Edward and a younger brother were thrown upon their own resources, penniless and alone, among strangers. The brave young lad managed to obtain work as a weaver's apprentice, in a small shop in South Street, and on the meagre earnings from this source, supported himself and his brother.

Passionately fond of reading, he delved into literature of all kinds, not passing by the alluring pages of romantic fiction. Through these slow years of formative growth, he worked faithfully, never tiring, ever patient. But no one dreamed that under that quiet exterior of modest endeavor, a volcano of genius burned in silence, throbbing with a wild longing to break through the crust of its monotonous existence into wider and more native fields of action.

The two young brothers became drawn in their desires towards the land of the wild west, and after some consultations and boyish but strong resolves, set out on foot over the Alleghanies. They took nothing with them but packs upon their shoulders and staffs in their hands; and thus equipped, perseveringly journeyed towards the setting sun.

At last they reached, what was then known as the Far West, the prairie State of Illinois. Springfield was the chosen spot for their residence, and it was not long before the boy-weaver, who had read law as well as romance in the Quaker City, was quite able to make a living under the shield of that profession. His ready gift of silvery eloquence aided him so well that he rose rapidly, and as rapidly became known as a popular advocate.

He entered the arena of politics, ardently espoused the Whig faction, and soon his star was seen glimmering and flashing in the halls of Congress. The honor which he reflected on his constituency in the legislative assemblies of the nation was of that lustre which might well make the wearer proud.

When the surges of war in Mexico touched our shores, Baker raised a regiment in Illinois and took it to the banks of the Rio Grande.

From Vera Cruz to the city of Mexico his glorious valor shone at the head of his command, and when

Shields fell at Cerro Gordo, Baker became the leader of the New York regiments through that bloody baptism

On his return from the wars, battle-scarred and glorious, he was once more sent to Congress, where he remained until 1850. His oration on the death of President Taylor was one of the finest given at that time of universal grief.

After a return from Panama, where he had tarried a while, the fascinations of the Californian coast drew him to the charmed land of the Pacific slope, where, in San Francisco, he at once took a high position as an advocate. Here, through years of successful pleading and an active life as a public man, especially a public speaker, he won the hearts of the populace. His name was on everybody's lips, and everybody hung with delight on the honied eloquence which dropped from his own. He was reckoned a latter-day Demosthenes, and acquired the cognomen of the "Gray Eagle."

But it was over the coffin of Broderick, who fell a victim to his anti-slavery sentiments, that Baker reached an almost unparalleled climax of eloquence, and thrilled the listening crowds as it is given to few men to do. The gathered multitude was swayed like the innumerable leaves of a mighty forest by a strong and mournful wind. It was the wail of a noble soul for a brother, dead. All business on the streets was suspended. Everywhere an ominous stillness prevailed, save for the slow tolling of the church bells which seemed to pulsate in space like the despairing throbs of a great heart. The people assembled in the main square, and with sad faces were silent or conversed in undertones. The shrouded coffin was there; at its foot a priest; at its head the tall form of the pale orator. For minutes after the audience became quite still, Baker did not speak. His look was not in the coffin of his friend, but his eyes were streaming with tears. At length when the silence was almost painful in its intensity his voice rose like a wail, and then an uninterrupted torrent of burning words of lofty pathos was poured forth with such all-powerful effect on the hearts of the sorrowing assembly, that every cheek was wet with responsive tears. "For an hour he held them as with a spell," and when with outstretched hands he leaned over the coffined body of the dead and pronounced the closing words: "Good friend! true hero! hail and farewell!" the vast audience sobbed aloud.

This event and the mockery of a trial which followed, fell with such sad effect on Baker that he resolved to leave the coast.

The progressive political element in Oregon at this crisis wanted a champion, and the choice of that faction at once fell on Baker. He went to Oregon, settled there, and with heart and soul worked against the Breckenridge Democracy. He was defeated in sending his man to Congress, but the legislature of Oregon was so strongly anti-administration that Baker was sent to the United States Senate to represent that State. His record here, though brief, was one of power and splendor.

When the struggle with Secession arose, "the Union at all hazards," became his motto. His reply to Benjamin of Louisiana, the delivery of which occupied two afternoon sessions, was memorable for its exhaustive arguments against Secession, and its forcible exposition of Union principles.

Great occasions always called out in him an immense reserve force that swept his audiences with resistless power. At such times he shone like a mighty star with fierce and burning strength. At the great meeting in New York, which filled Union Square with thousands of people, in April, 1861, Baker's passionate eloquence, which echoed a far deeper patriotism, held the audience with the touch of a master hand. The dense crowd shook visibly when the closing words of this great speech rang out upon the air:

"And if from the far Pacific a voice, feebler than the feeblest murmur upon its shore, may be heard to give you courage and hope in the contest, that voice is yours to-day; and if a man whose hair is gray, who is well-nigh worn out in the battle and toil of life, may pledge himself on such an occasion, and in such an audience, let me say—as my last word—that, as when, amidst sheeted fire and flame, I saw and led the hosts of New York, as they charged in contest upon a foreign soil, for the honor of your flag—so again, if Providence shall will it, this feeble hand shall draw a sword never yet dishonored, not to fight for distant honor in a foreign land, but to fight for country, for home, for law, for Government, for Constitution, for right, for freedom, for humanity, and in the hope that the banner of my country may advance, and wheresoever that banner waves, there glory may pursue and freedom be established!"

Baker immediately recruited the California Regiment, and was offered an appointment as brigadier-general. This and the rank of major-general, which was also offered him, he declined, preferring to go with his regiment as its Colonel.

His final effort in the Senate, previous to the last tragic scenes at the front, was made when he replied to Breckenridge in a Secession speech. Baker had entered the Senate chamber from his drill camp, two miles out, while the southern disunionist was in the midst of a partisan harangue. His reply was impromptu, but it finished his antagonist, and was accounted one of the most "thrilling speeches heard in the chamber for years."

The cloud of his overhanging fate seemed to make its shadow visibly felt to him before it came. This impression was so strong that it amounted to positive conviction. In August he said to a friend: "I am certain I shall not live through this war, and if my troops should show any want of resolution, I shall fall in the first battle. I cannot afford, after my career in Mexico and as a Senator of the United States, to turn my face from the enemy."

During his last visit to Washington, a few days previous to the battle of Ball's Bluff, a lady presented him with some flowers. "Very beautiful," he remarked, on taking them; "these flowers and my memory will wither together." He put his papers in order and gave special directions to his friend, Colonel Webb, concerning final arrangements in case he did not return.

Then came, on October twenty-first, 1861, the terrible tragedy of Ball's Bluff, when the Potomac became gory with heroic blood, and the overwhelming numbers of the enemy crowded the brave remnant of

Baker's and other regiments down upon the river's bank, there to make a last desperate stand or a more desperate and fruitless attempt to cross the river without means of transportation. Some one had blundered. But theirs was not to reason why. It was theirs only to meet death like dauntless patriots unquestioning to the end. A demonstration looking to the capture of Leesburg had been determined upon, a general reconnoissance was taking place, and the point of crossing for the California Regiment was at Conrad's Ferry. Once on the south bank of the river, Baker put his men in line awaiting attack, and the first onset was met with spirited determination.

The battle had been raging for an hour and over when Colonel Baker fell at the head of his command while cheering on his troops. A few minutes previous he had been surrounded by a body of Confederate cavalry and taken prisoner, only to be recaptured by his own men in a bayonet charge made by the right wing of the battalion. The fatal ball which sped him on his eternal exit was fired by a "tall, ferocious Virginian with red hair and whiskers," who rushed from behind a tree with a huge revolver in his hand, and "placing the weapon almost against the Colonel's head inflicted a mortal wound. Not satisfied with his deadly work he fired the second ball, while simultaneously the body was pierced with four bullets from the tops of trees, and the brave leader fell lifeless from his horse."

The assassin, like the murderer of Ellsworth, was instantly shot dead.

A flank movement had been made by the enemy to turn the Union line, just previous to the death scene, and Baker at once ordered the freshly arrived Tammany Regiment to meet it. It was while leading this charge that he fell—ten feet in advance of his column.

And thus went out in blood and battle, another noble life—a victim to the merciless Juggernaut of war. If one could arise to pronounce his eulogy as silvery-tongued as that voice whose music is forever mute, a fit apostrophe might be made to a hero whom we love to honor. His own passionate farewell over the body of Broderick, pallid in death, can be spoken with reverent affection here. If lives like his, altogether noble, or sacrifices like his, altogether glorious, are not lost on a world too grasping in its greed of gain, then surely the human soil which felt his influence must be fruitful indeed in all that is good!

CUSTER'S LAST BATTLE.

CHAPTER XL.
GEORGE ARMSTRONG CUSTER.

Early Life of General Custer.—School Experience.—First Love.—Sent to West Point.—Trials of a Plebe.—The Attack on Fort Sumter.—Graduates and Goes to Washington.—Ordered to Join his Regiment.—Incidents of the Battle of Bull Run.—Describes his First Emotions.—On Staff Duty.—The Peninsula Campaign.—Custer's First Charge.—Winning the Bars.—General McClellan Relieved.—Custer at Monroe.—The Course of True Love.—Battle of Aldie.—Made a General.—Battle of Gettysburg.—The Last Raid.—Appomattox Court House.—The Seventh Cavalry.—Life on the Plains.—Battle of the Washita.—Rain-in-the-face, Sitting Bull and Crazy Horse.—The Last Battle.

THE name of Custer will always be associated with everything that is brave, gallant and chivalrous. Coming upon the field of strife as a leader of cavalry during the war for the Union, his sword was not sheathed until treason received its death-blow at Appomattox Court House. The civil war over, he turned from the battlefields of the Rebellion to the protection of our Western Frontier, where he ably and heroically served his country, until his tragic death in the Valley of the Little Horn.

The brave troopers who followed Custer over the Plains of Manassas, down the Valley of the Shenandoah, in the trenches before Richmond, and through the dark recesses of the Black Hills, will ever connect him with the story of their glorious achievements, and allot him the highest niche in their memory of the heroic dead who fell at the post of duty.

George Armstrong Custer was a native of the State of Ohio, and was born in New Rumley, Harrison County, December fifth, 1839. New Rumley is a small hamlet on the border of Pennsylvania, from which State it was peopled in the early part of the last century. The family history gathered from the family Bible is that of an honest group of sturdy yeomen not ashamed of work, and satisfies us that the stock of which the future General came was good, and of that class which furnished the pioneers and frontiersmen of the last century.

Emmanuel Custer, father of the General, was born in Crysoptown, Allegheny County, Maryland, December tenth, 1806. His educational advantages were very meagre—in fact, all the education he possessed was acquired at home at such intervals as he could find away from the duties of the farm; but he gave his children the best opportunities that were afforded in those days in the early settlements of the border. He was married, in 1828, to Matilda Viers. His married life with Miss Viers lasted six years, during which time three children were born.

The maiden name of the second Mrs. Custer and mother of the General was Maria Ward. She was born at Burgettstown, Pennsylvania, May thirty-first, 1807, and was first married when a girl of sixteen to Israel Kirkpatrick. Mr. Kirkpatrick died in 1835, leaving his widow with three children. After two years of widowhood, Mrs. Kirkpatrick married Emmanuel Custer, and became the mother of the General two years later.

Armstrong Custer grew up a robust, frolicksome youth, with flaxen curls, and a nature the most gentle and amiable. He was fond of playing soldier, and executed the Scott manual of arms to the admiration of his schoolmates. An important era in his life was the marriage of his sister to a Mr. Reed, of Monroe, Michigan, where, at her earnest request, he came to reside, and entered Stebbins' Academy, in which he continued until his twelfth year. At a later period he obtained greater advantages with Rev. Mr. Boyd, an able man, who conducted the seminary. During his attendance at this institution, he was captivated by the charms of a pretty little girl—his first, last and only love—whom he married later, and left to mourn his loss. After four years at Monroe, he resolved to enter West Point, in case he could command influence enough to secure an appointment. After many difficulties due to politics, he attained his object through Hon. John A. Bingham, whose scruples vanished on a personal interview with the young aspirant. The desired commission duly arrived in 1856, and from that period to the end of his life he was a soldier. The germs of true heroism lay concealed in his nature waiting the season of germination.

The close application of Custer to his studies in the public schools and academies of Monroe had qualified him for the preliminary examination, and when he entered the famous Academy of West Point, he knew as much of mathematics as any of the one year cadets.

Tall, slender, frank, handsome, face rather girlish, seventeen years of age, is the picture of young Custer when he became a plebe in the summer of 1857. His physical strength and good nature enabled him to cope successfully with the peculiar trials of plebe life, which he bore lightly. Donning the uniform of a cadet, he marched out with his comrades to the encampment, where he was soon made acquainted with the various duties incident to life in camp. At the end of August, he commenced the monotonous routine of study and duties at the academy as a member of the fourth class.

He early became an excellent horseman, and made rapid progress in his studies; went home for a season after two years at West Point, and, returning, diligently pursued the same unvaried course until graduation.

But a mighty change had come over the nation, which was felt, perhaps, even more intensely among the cadets at West Point than elsewhere. Several States were preparing to secede from the Union, and the Ordinance of Secession was adopted by South Carolina, December twentieth, 1860, followed soon by Mississippi, Alabama, Florida, Georgia, Louisiana and Texas. In February, 1861, the Confederate Congress met at Montgomery, Alabama, and it was expected would authorize the appointment of a large number of army officers when applicants for position should be present to make their claims in person. Few of the Southern cadets waited for the diploma of the academy, and when they were gone the eyes of the nation turned anxiously to West Point, in which a spirit of close union and ardent love of country now prevailed.

When the national flag was insulted by the firing on Fort Sumter, every town and hamlet was in a blaze of patriotism, and the North, with one impulse, determined to put down rebellion. The influence was intensely felt at West Point, more especially, perhaps, as two of the officers now shut up in the fortress were

Lieutenants Hall and Snyder—comrades of the cadets but a few months before.

Omitting several minor occurrences, let us follow Custer to the seat of war and view him on the first field of battle. But before doing so, a few lines will suffice to tell the reader of his inner life without which sketch no life of him could be complete. In a word, a great change had come "o'er the spirit of his dream," due to the radiant charms of a little black-eyed girl seen some time back when but a child. She was the only daughter of Judge Bacon, of Monroe, now an accomplished and lovely young lady. The vision of a playful little girl haunted him as he recalled the event or incident of his childhood, when swinging on a gate she accosted him with, "Hello! you Custer boy!" and then, as if frightened at her own temerity, turned and fled into the house. She was enshrined in his manly heart of hearts, and, with the ardor of a gallant soldier, he pushed aside all obstacles, overcame the prejudices of her father, and after a constancy, a patience, a true sense of honor and integrity that do him credit, he at a later day carried off the prize of beauty and virtue, and found himself blessed with a dear wife and tender companion to his dying day.

Custer left West Point, and, after some preparation in New York, reached Washington about daylight on July nineteenth, 1861. At the Ebbitt House he met his room and tent-mate, Lieutenant Parker, now dismissed from the rolls of the army for resigning in the face of the enemy. They parted, each to pursue his own way; the one to serve against the government that had educated him, and which he had sworn to defend; the other to pursue the path of honor incumbent upon every patriot.

The Capitol of the nation was in a state of great commotion; immense numbers of despatches and orders were borne about by orderlies and messengers who were flitting from room to room in hot haste.

Reporting to the Adjutant-General, Lieutenant Custer was introduced by him to General Scott, who received him graciously, and made him the bearer of despatches to General McDowell. It was at that time not an easy matter to find a horse in Washington, and he sought one at all the livery stables in vain; meeting with a soldier whom he knew, a mount was secured, and he started for Centreville, near which the Federal forces lay. Arriving at his destination a little after dawn of the following day, he reported to General Wadsworth, of McDowell's staff, and was invited to breakfast. Though possessing a keen appetite, he thought upon such an occasion he should not indulge it, and declined. His horse was fed, however, and meanwhile discovering an old friend, Lieutenant Kingsbury, at headquarters, he was supplied with some hard-tack and coffee—the only food he tasted for thirty ensuing hours.

It is unnecessary to describe the battle of Bull Run, except so far as Custer was an actor in it; yet it is well to remember that the stream from which it derived its name lies between Centreville and Manassas, and along its right bank the Confederate forces were posted, their right wing near Union Mills, their centre at Blackburn's Ford, their left opposite the Stone Bridge and a small ford up stream. This army consisted of seven brigades with forty-two guns and twelve companies of cavalry. The commanders of these brigades were Generals Ewell, Jones, Longstreet and Bonham.

Their line extended from Union Mills on the right to Mitchel's Ford on the left. Holmes and Early formed a second line in support, while further to the left and guarding the fords was the last brigade under Colonel Cocke. To each of the four divisions of two brigades was assigned two companies of cavalry.

McDowell's forces, in four divisions, were commanded by Brigadier-General Tyler and Colonels Hunter, Heintzelman and Miles. Hunter and Heintzelman were to advance, cross the stream and turn the Confederate left.

Young Custer regarded all these preparations with a curious eye as he saw the field before him swarming with soldiers. As soon as his business at headquarters was despatched he remounted his horse and hastened in pursuit of his regiment. "Can you tell me where Company G, Second Cavalry, is?" he inquired. "At the head of the column," was the reply. And thither he went. Coming upon a body of cavalry he asked if the commander of his company was present. "Here he is!" was the response. "I am Lieutenant Custer, and in accordance with orders from the War Department, I report for duty with my company, sir." "Ah! glad to meet you, Mr. Custer. We have been expecting you, as we saw in the lists of the assignments of the graduating class from West Point that you have been marked down to us. I am Lieutenant Drummond. Allow me to introduce you to some of your brother officers."

This was his introduction to active service and first greeting from officers and comrades. He was now fairly launched upon the rugged life of a soldier, boisterous, tempestuous, variable, but the profession he delighted in from first to last.

The Federal cavalry, seven companies of regulars, under Major Palmer, rendered no further assistance in the battle than acting as supports to artillery. True there was a charge of a squadron at the opening of the contest, still Custer and his cavalry comrades were merely spectators at the battle of Bull Run.

The cavalry made a halt of half an hour at Sudley Springs, having attended Hunter's division in the march of the morning through the thick woods. The thunder of battle was heard not far distant and in their front, and a staff officer from McDowell came riding in hot haste desiring them to cross the stream, and to move up the ridge in support of a battery. Off they started, and in scaling the crest saw Griffin galloping into position with his battery, upon which the enemy had opened an ineffectual fire by aiming too high. Custer, following the battery, heard each shot, whose strange hissing sound inspired him with an interest different from that he felt during his artillery practice at West Point when the direction was *from*, instead of *towards* him. The cannon balls now told a different tale. Massed, near the foot of the crest, on which the battery stood, and sheltered from the enemy's fire, the cavalry waited, and once, the enemy threatening the battery, an order came for the cavalry to scale the crest, and drive him back. They were told that on reaching the crest it was probable they would receive the order to charge.

Custer had left West Point, a school-boy, three days before, and had never ridden at anything more formidable than a three-foot hurdle. His sabre had never encountered an antagonist more dreadful than a leather head figure stuffed with tan bark.

One may fancy his mind, as he ascended the hill, was in some degree filled with anxious thoughts. In front of his company of old soldiers they would watch to see how their new lieutenant would behave under fire. One comfort was that, while on duty with troops for the first time, and junior officer of all present with the cavalry, there was on duty temporarily with the company another officer, Lieutenant Walker, of the same rank, from civil life, totally inexperienced in military affairs, and his senior by only a few days.

Custer had found him deferential to his opinions as fresh from West Point, and thought he must know all that belonged to the art of war. And he felt no inclination to dispel his delusion. As they rode on, he asked: "Custer, what weapon are you going to use in the charge?" Now, the earliest notion of a perfect cavalryman formed by Custer was one whirling his curved sabre and cleaving the skull of every antagonist. Two weapons only they had to choose from; the belt of each carried a sabre and revolver. He replied, "The sabre," flashed out the glittering blade from its scabbard, and rode on as if he felt not the least concern. Walker, thinking "that was the way at the academy," did the same, and out came his sabre.

Custer was far from feeling as little concern as he aimed to make apparent. He tells us candidly: "I was far from enjoying that feeling."

Riding slowly up the hill he debated in his own mind the arguments in favor of the sabre, and of the revolver, as a weapon of attack: "Now, the sabre is a beautiful weapon; it produces an ugly wound; the term 'sabre charge' sounds well; and, above all, the sabre is sure—it never misses fire. It has this drawback, however; in order to make it effective, it is indispensable that you approach very close to your adversary—so close that, if you do not unhorse or disable him, he will most likely render that service to you. So much for the sabre. Now, as to the revolver, it has this advantage over the sabre; one is not compelled to range himself alongside his adversary before beginning his attack, but may select his own time and distance. To be sure, one may miss his aim, but there are six chambers to empty, and, if one, two or three miss, there are still three shots left to fire at close quarters. As this is my first battle, had I not better defer the use of the sabre until I have acquired a little more experience?"

The sabre returned to its sheath, and, silently drawing his revolver, he poised it, which his companion imitated. The mental calculation went on, as his hand grasped the revolver. The difficulty of taking fair aim in the hurry and confusion of the charge was the first consideration. Then it occurred that every shot might be fired and of no avail—that, by that time, the enemy would be around, and the combatants slashing one another, right and left, in which the sabre would be far preferable to an empty revolver. This last argument was a clincher; the holsters held the revolver, and the victorious sabre rose from the heroic shoulder, while his companion "went and did likewise." This mental logic was brought to an end as the cavalry reached the crest, and, after exposure to a hot artillery fire, as the enemy intended no direct attack, it sought a sheltered position. Everything promised a Union victory; the left flank of the enemy was turned, when, at a critical moment, Elsey's brigade of infantry and Peckham's battery under General E. Kirby Smith, fresh from the valley, hurled their force of three thousand men on the tired patriots. "We're flanked! we're flanked!" spread like wild fire through the ranks. A panic ensued, which ended in disordered flight.

We will not dwell upon a scene so sad and so well known, but follow Custer who, with his company and another of cavalry, with a section of artillery, moved under Colonel Heintzelman back to Centreville. They moved off the battle-field in perfect order, and were the last organized body to retire across Bull Run. They found the bridge at Cub Run blocked up by vehicles; there was no other crossing, and, as the enemy opened an artillery fire, the guns were lost. Finding a ford the cavalry crossed, halted a few hours in the old camp at Centreville, and pursued their march to Arlington.

The company was scarcely in camp when Custer stretched himself beneath a tree, hungry and exhausted. He slept in rain and mud without awakening for several hours. When he awoke, his thoughts were not enviable, nor were his present condition and future prospects at all flattering. But, in all the despondency of defeat, his faith was constant that the cause of the Union would ultimately triumph. This battle was fought July twenty-first, 1861, and soon after General McDowell was superseded in the command of the army by General George B. McClellan.

In a short time Custer was ordered to Alexandria, and became attached to the staff of General Philip Kearney, first as *aide-de-camp* and next as assistant adjutant-general. We shall note only a few events in his career at this period. One rather ludicrous incident was the attempted capture of a Confederate picket-post, which was approached in a calm, moonlight night. On nearing the post the party quivered like aspen leaves at the least noise. They were very much like boys going to rob an orchard. When the picket was reached, a musket-shot rang clearly out on the nocturnal air, followed by two others; but the last shots were a waste of powder, one would have sufficed. These valiant heroes took to their heels, and reached camp with the greatest alacrity. What would the same men have done a year hence?

On a brief leave of absence he visited at Monroe, and was not so careful at that time as afterwards of his deportment. His associates in the army, even his superiors, were wont to use profane language and participate in intoxicating beverages. It was common in the army, and he, young and inexperienced, fell into the way insensibly "of doing at Rome as Rome does." With some companions he indulged till on his return he described irregular lines, was seen in public—worse than this, *she* saw him whom of all he loved most, and began to look on him as beneath her notice. His sister, Mrs. Reed, sorrowed over him, closed the door, and reproved him in such terms as brought conviction, and rendered him at once ashamed of the course he was pursuing; and, what was better, he made a solemn vow never to taste a drop of intoxicating liquor as long as he lived. He kept his word, and became a true Christian gentleman.

When Custer returned to Washington he found it bristling with fortifications and the Army of the Potomac created. Transports were preparing to convey the troops to Fort Monroe. An advance on Manassas proved it to be evacuated. On the march to Manassas, Custer had his first experience of cavalry fighting. At the head of his company he first gave the order "Charge!" and gallantly he led. His men followed him with courage and the enemy was routed, burned the bridge over Cedar Run and fired from the other side. This introduced our hero into actual fighting.

During the siege of Yorktown young officers were in request for the engineers, and Custer reported to the chief engineer on General W. F. Smith's staff. Here he served, and gained valuable experience, till the unfortunate Union army was forced back from the Chickahominy. This stream aided his personal promotion. When on balloon reconnoissances he made many observations, and was nearly the first who gave information of the evacuation of Yorktown. The attack on Fort Magruder brought Kearney to the aid of Hooker, and meantime Hancock's brigade crossed a little run to the right, occupied two redoubts, and turned Longstreet's left. With this brigade Custer was joined at the time, and behaved on the occasion with great dash and bravery. He cut a queer figure at this period, wore an old slouch-hat and cavalry jacket, and muddy boots scarce worth a dollar.

May twenty-second McClellan made Coal Harbor his headquarters, when General Barnard, chief engineer of the army, began at once to explore the Chickahominy, near Bottom Bridge. He called Custer to his aid, not then knowing who he was, and both proceeded to the river. "Jump in," said the General. Custer did so at imminent peril from the enemy's sharpshooters, and on an unstable bottom. He reached the other bank, made his observations and gained satisfactory knowledge of the situation. Barnard became uneasy at his long stay, and when he returned, both went at once to headquarters. The subordinate was ignored, but it came out that Barnard had not made the exploration himself, and the General wished to see the young officer who had. He came dirty, muddy, pantaloons worn by the saddle, head unkempt, and in some confusion. After a few moments' conversation the General said, "You are just the kind of a young man I want. How would you like to come on my staff?" This was just the thing for Custer, who was glad of such good fortune, and was always attached to the General after this. Said he: "I could have died for him."

The first colors taken by the Army of the Potomac were captured by Custer from the Louisiana Tigers in the manner following: Custer begged General McClellan to allow him to capture the picket-post on the other side of the river, obtained his consent, and prepared for the attack at dawn, with two companies of cavalry and one of infantry. He explored the river, personally, and finding it favorable, rode down with the appointed detail. Anxious about the enterprise he did not closely scrutinize the troops with him, till the ford was reached. Then, being seen in clearer light, animated cries of recognition greeted him: "Why, it's Armstrong!" "How are you, Armstrong?" "Give us your fist, Armstrong!" Sure enough, it was his old school-friends from Monroe. He spoke to them kindly, said he was now busy, could not talk to them then except to say: "All Monroe boys—follow *me* ; stick to *me* and I'll stick to *you*—Come!"

The river was forded by the brave band; the enemy surprised, the Louisiana Tigers shot, stampeded, captured with arms and the colors, and our hero, Captain Custer, covered with glory, returned to his chief triumphant. It is not our province to tell of the disastrous campaign on the Peninsula, and Custer's new-won rank was not yet settled when a lowering cloud hung over the renown of McClellan. The "On to Richmond" cry sounded. Custer shared all the glory and ignominy of his chief in the "Seven Days' Fight," but he and Bowen once more shone conspicuous in a brilliant dash at Malvern Hill. On one occasion these cavaliers compelled the surrender of seven men, too near to the enemy to bring off, but they captured their arms and returned amid "inextinguishable laughter," each with an armful of sabres, carbines, revolvers and belts, while both armies were spectators.

Soon after, Custer made a brilliant dash into the enemy's lines. He had another series of heroic adventures in White Oak Swamp, during which he was separated from his regiment. The bugler-boy cried, "Captain! Captain! here *are two Secesh after me!*" He compelled the surrender of one, and sent him off with a guard. With another he had a wild, exciting race; he shot him, as he would not surrender, and captured a fine, beautiful bay horse, with splendid saddle and all the trappings. Captain Custer, during the Antietam campaign, attended as personal *aide* to McClellan, accompanied him everywhere, and, whenever the advance struck the enemy, was at the front.

General Hooker collected and organized the cavalry into three divisions under Pleasanton, Gregg and Averill. The battle of Chancellorsville had been fought, and an insolent enemy invaded the North. Hooker sent out the cavalry, and a brisk engagement took place at Beverly Ford, in which Custer distinguished himself. He was now on Pleasanton's staff, and displayed his peculiar dash and energy at Brandy Station, where the Federal cavalry on a fair field proved their superiority to the Southern chivalry.

June sixteenth, 1863, the Federal cavalry, under Kilpatrick, had a desperate encounter with Stuart's cavalry at Aldie. It was a trying time. Kilpatrick and Colonel Douty, with our hero, Custer, contended with a courage worthy the knights of chivalry. In the turmoil the orders of the leaders could not be heard. A young captain in a straw hat, his white curls flowing over his shoulder, and shabby uniform, attracted general attention. He waved his sabre, pointed at the enemy, and dashed upon them alone. Looking back, he waved his sword, and, with Kilpatrick and Douty, led his men to the charge. A dreadful fire met them, but the free use of the sabre, relied on in this battle, drove them in flight toward Ashby's Gap. The young captain shone out as a guiding star upon the field, and the men followed him. Kilpatrick's horse was shot under him. Douty was killed, but a charmed life seemed to belong to our young hero. He rode his favorite horse Harry, and bore the Toledo blade he had won in battle. A trooper turned round, fired and missed him; Custer almost severed his arm. Another opposed him in the same way, with the sabre this time. Then a wild race ensued. Suddenly Custer checked his horse, and met his enemy in front before he could stop. A few powerful blows with the weighty sword clove his enemy's skull, and he fell prostrate to the

GEORGE ARMSTRONG CUSTER. 433

ground. He had won his star, and was made a Brigadier-General for his bravery on this well-fought field —the battle of Aldie.

To follow him on the path of glory in an independent command would far exceed our limits. He became commander of the Michigan brigade, and selected his staff from his old Monroe friends. He rendered the greatest service to Kilpatrick at Hanover, when Wade Hampton pressed on his rear. At the battle of Gettysburg he led a company in person, and repulsed the enemy. On the third day of that bloody field he displayed great abilities as a leader, while the services of his men went far to gain the day. At Falling Waters he displayed all the coolness, courage and tact which so eminently distinguished him. In all the raids of Sheridan, and the historical fields on which renown was reaped by daring and effectual raids, he had no superior. He never failed. He gained great renown at Five Forks, and, when General Lee surrendered, he preferred to send in the first flag of truce to Custer, promoted to Brevet-Major-General.

There was a great parade before the army broke up; and Custer was sent to contend with the difficulties and discontents of the volunteers in Texas. In the changed circumstances of the army, in which regulars now filled the place of volunteers, and many anomalies were got rid of, a reduction of rank was inevitable. The Seventh cavalry was formed, and Major-General Custer became Lieutenant-Colonel of that regiment. While mustered out as General, he negotiated with the Mexican government to become chief of cavalry to Juarez against Maximilian, but the leave of absence for this purpose was not granted. While waiting for it, he returned to Monroe, where Judge Bacon was dying, and that good man expired in Custer's arms.

About this time he accompanied President Johnson, who was *swinging round the circle*. Mrs. Custer was with her husband, and the young couple found the jaunt a pleasure-trip without its expense. The movement was political, and Custer grew tired and departed. He was ordered, soon, to Fort Riley, Kansas, and became a "mighty hunter," possessing numerous dogs, guns, etc.

The Seventh cavalry was first mounted, armed and sent to the plains, in the spring of 1867. Here Custer began a new experience, and found himself often at fault. About this period the Hancock Expedition took place, organized and led by that general in person. The "Indian Ring" were bitter against Hancock for bringing on, as they said, an Indian war. Eight troops of cavalry, seven companies of infantry, and a battery of light artillery made up the force to about 1,400 men.

The Indians had robbed and murdered during the preceding summer, the Cheyennes and Sioux being the chief offenders. An expedition to check them was required. Appointments being made to come to a council, the Indians did not appear, and the chiefs made excuses, and, when the troops marched towards their village, they were found in imposing battle-array and mostly mounted. They were bedecked in their brightest colors, wore the brilliant war-bonnet, with the crimson pennant on their lances, strung bows and quivers full of barked arrows. They bore breech-loaders and revolvers, with the tomahawk and hunting-knife.

A conference ensued, and the Indians professed to be peaceful. This was a pretense, and, when the village was entered, they had decamped. Pursuit was made, but they were beyond reach. On this march Custer had his first buffalo adventure. The war was begun, and Custer left Fort Hayes on the first of June with 350 men of the Seventh cavalry and twenty wagons, proceeding toward Fort McPherson, on the Platte, two hundred and fifty miles away.

On this, his first Indian scout, Custer sent a train of wagons to Fort Wallace, to obtain supplies. Colonel West, with a cavalry squadron, was sent as escort halfway, while Lieutenant Robbins with one company was to proceed and return with the train, which was under the command of Colonel Cook. In the absence of the two detachments, the Indians made a sudden attack on the camp, near daylight. The report of a carbine roused Custer, and soon all were in arms to repel a whole swarm of Indians rushing on to stampede the horses and kill the men. The attempt was a failure. The Indians made an attack on the train, but were severely punished, with great loss, by the bravery of the men, led on by their officers in gallant style. Lieutenant Ridder and ten men, sent with despatches from Sherman to Custer, were massacred in the most barbarous manner by the Indians, and their bodies left nude, pierced often with fifty arrows. Strange fatality! that a man like Custer should have enemies; but few had more, or more malignant. He applied for and received authority to visit Fort Riley, about ninety miles east of Harker by rail, where his family then were; and then was court-martialled, and sentenced— suspended from pay for an entire year. Into these matters it is needless now to enter; certain parties regretted it, and Custer was magnanimous. Those who succeeded him failed; the summer campaign was abortive; he was invited back by Sheridan and the officers of the Seventh cavalry, and on his way was overtaken by a telegram from the War Department ordering him to report to Sheridan, now at Fort Leavenworth. After remaining a day, and receiving his instructions, he arrived at the main camp of the regiment, thirty miles southeast from Fort Dodge, and resumed command. The Indians had become so bold as to fire frequently at the pickets, which state of things he soon ended by sending out scouts. At this time he appointed California Joe chief of scouts. Shortly after ensued The Battle of the Washita. The plan of a winter campaign against the Indians, begun by Sheridan, met Custer's hearty co-operation. The regiment left Fort Dodge with some Osage Indians, November twelfth. A train of wagons and infantry guard were to accompany the regiment to the edge of the Indian country, make a depot of supplies, from which the men could march out for three days or more, and fall back on it as a base, from whence it got the name of Camp Supply. General Sully was in command, and Custer but partially so. However, he made such arrangements as were needed, and, on arrival of Sheridan at Camp Supply, was freed from Sully's control. The cold was intense, snow fell to the depth of one foot during the night, and at four o'clock the bugle sounded to horse amid a raging storm. "Prepare to mount!" "Mount!" then the signal to advance put the column in motion. The march began in a blinding storm; the guides, in a few miles, lost their way, and could not discover the place where it was intended to encamp. The undaunted Custer was not a man to be intimidated by obstacles and, taking out his pocket-compass, became his own guide to the destined place.

Crossing the Canadian River no Indians were found, and the storm, if an obstruction to the soldiers, was no less so to the savages.

When the last wagon had crossed, a courier reported to Custer the trail of a fresh war party, a hundred and fifty strong, apparently the last of the war party of the season, returning disgusted with the winter campaign, for they did not like the cold and absence of all forage for their beasts. Custer, in marching through the cold and blinding wintry storm, would have considerable trouble in finding the village. The forces were united, eight hundred strong; they had already reached the Washita Valley and were in close proximity to their enemies.

Mounting at ten o'clock, four abreast, they crept on silently as the panther upon his prey. No whisper was heard, no match for a pipe. Treading lightly they moved on till the sagacity of an Osage guide perceived the smell of fire, and breathless excitement was produced by the discovery of a few coals. They were found to be the remains of a fire made by Indian boys to warm them as they herded. Advancing, and peering over a hill, the guide remarked, as pointing to the place, " plenty of Indians there." The bark of a dog was heard and through the chilling air was borne the cry of an infant. At the midnight hour, Custer assembled his officers and laid the plan to ascertain the position and where the village lay. They put aside their sabres, sought the crest, and with their eyes scrutinized in the darkness the valley beyond. Crouching together in deep silence, broken only by the whispers of Custer explaining the situation, the motion was made to resume their sabres. On the frozen snow-crust the attack was explained, and each one's part assigned. The village was to be compassed ere day, and at dawning, when just enough light appeared, the attack was to be made in four detachments. In terrible cold Custer and his men passed the weary hours of the night discussing the probabilities of the coming fight, or muffled in their cloaks lying on the cold ground in deep slumber. It was silence all, and the sleepless thought on what the fate of to-morrow might be.

At dawn the sharp clear crack of a single rifle rang out from the far side of the village, and turning to the band leader, he ordered him to strike up, "Garry Owen." The inspiring notes resounded through the valley, cheer on cheer arose from the men of other detachments, ready for the attack. The bugle sounded the charge, and the whole command dashed rapidly in to the village.

The Indians fought with desperate courage, but a few moments made Custer master of the village, from which the inhabitants rushed and fought bravely under shelter of the trees, and wading the stream that divided it, some fought from the bank as a breastwork.

A large portion of the command were ordered to fight on foot; and one party encountered an old squaw who murdered a captive child when no hope of escape remained. In a moment a bullet avenged her victim.

Custer sent Romeo, the interpreter, to tell the women

and children in the lodges that they would be safe and cared for. California Joe brought in three hundred ponies, assisted by two old squaws whom he rendered useful.

Ten o'clock A. M. the battle was raging, and to Custer's surprise, about a mile from the village a small party of Indians were collected on a knoll, who soon numbered one hundred. These by accessions became numerous, and to solve the question Custer interrogated an old squaw, who informed him that a succession of winter villages contained all the hostiles of the southern plains, Arapahoes, Kiowas, Comanches, Cheyennes and Apaches, all within ten miles, the nearest within two. An attack in great force was to be expected, and Custer, when the firing had partially ceased, collected and reformed his men. An hospital was established in the centre of the village, the wounded cared for, and surgical assistance rendered. The loss was severe. Several brave officers were killed, and one missing.

The numerous body of Indians now surrounded the command, but the quarter-master brought up a seasonable supply of ammunition. The line had become a circle, with the village for a centre. The Indians fought with great prudence, but betrayed a lack of confidence. The attempt to draw the troops from the village failed. The lodges were pulled down and the captured property piled up and burned, and the village was but a heap of ashes. This brought on a general attack; but they were handsomely repulsed at all points. The Indians had now suffered a telling defeat, and to guard against the capture by them of the wagon train, Custer determined to kill the seven hundred ponies that were an impediment and could not well be retained. A suitable number were preserved to carry off the prisoners on the march. Thus a large force of the Cheyennes and other Indians under the great chief Black Kettle were defeated by Custer, involving a loss in killed of one hundred and three, including Black Kettle; the capture of fifty-three squaws and children, a large quantity of property, destruction of the village, and almost total annihilation of this Indian band. Sheridan's report is a fine eulogium on Custer; and this great battle was followed by an imposing review, which Sheridan regarded as a scene "one of the most beautiful and highly interesting he ever witnessed."

The closing operations consisted in the pacification and restoration of the Kiowas, Cheyennes, and Arapahoes to their reservations. The first of these was effected by Custer's capture of the two Kiowa chiefs, Satanta and Lone Wolf, and their detention as hostages, with the assurance that if their bands were not in camp next day at sunset, both chiefs would be hung at that hour, and troops sent after the Kiowas. To bring in the Arapahoes required either hard fighting and marching or great finesse, and Custer, who was allowed his own way in the matter, displayed great decision of character. Under the guidance of Little Robe and Yellow Bear, friendly chiefs, he marched with some forty picked men to their camp, and ended the dangerous enterprise by quietly locating the entire tribe under the guns of the fort.

The Cheyennes were pacificated by an expedition he made from near Fort Cobb to the North Fork of Red River, in which he rescued two female captives from the Dog Soldiers, the worst and most bloodthirsty savages of the plains. He had ended the work in the south-west, and proved himself one of the greatest Indian fighters of his time.

The Seventh regiment was soon broken into detachments, and Custer was sent to Louisville, Kentucky, with two companies. It was during his residence at Louisville in the winter of 1872 that he hunted the buffalo on the plains with the Grand Duke Alexis.

The Sioux were on the war-path at this time, and Custer was called to the Yellowstone, where he had a brisk encounter with the savages. He afterwards made a complete exploration of the Black Hills, starting from Fort Lincoln in July, 1874.

Rain-in-the-Face, one of the bravest of the Indian warriors, being convicted of the murder of two white men during the Yellowstone expedition and who was under sentence of death, escaped from prison and vowed the death of Custer. The most redoubtable chief of all was Sitting Bull, whose resources were great, and who had under him all the tribes within the semi-circle formed by the Little Missouri. Crazy Horse was another powerful chief, and against him an expedition was sent under Generals Terry and Crook. They last encountered him on the Powder River, but with little success, and the battle there was little less than a defeat. When Sheridan and Sherman planned Sitting Bull's destruction, it was ordered that the Dakota column should be commanded by Custer, for the simple reason, "Custer had never yet met with a single disaster while in command of an important expedition, and he had been blessed with more complete success in his Indian expeditions than any other officer in the regular army."

The plan was interrupted by Hon. Heister Clymer, chairman of a Congressional Committee, in the investigation of irregularities in the War Department, involving the Secretary, General Belknap, who soon after resigned. Belknap was a friend of President Grant, and Custer was summoned before the committee to testify what he knew. He went reluctantly, had little to say, but incurred the hot resentment of the President. Calling at the White House three different times to explain, the President refused to see him, and the result was, that the Dakota column would not be in command of Custer. He was finally permitted to proceed under General Terry, as a subordinate in charge of the Seventh cavalry. He won the friendship and confidence of Terry, and a total force of twenty-seven hundred armed men started west from Fort Lincoln against the Sioux. This was Terry's column, while that of Crook left Fort Fetterman on the twenty-ninth of May, and the latter's part in the great expedition brought neither glory nor advantage. Sitting Bull had the better of it, and Crook's battle on the seventeenth of June began with his being "unsaddled in camp," and the fact of a real defeat cannot be concealed.

Generals Terry and Gibbon, on June first, were in communication near where the Tongue joins the Yellowstone, and it was found that eighteen miles from the latter, and on the opposite bank, a heavy force of Indians had concentrated, and Indian pickets had stood in front of Gibbon's videttes for fourteen days. It was discovered that after scouring the Yellowstone as far as the mouth of the Big Horn no Indians had crossed it, and Terry at once began to seek them on the Powder,

Tongue, Rosebud, Little Horn and Big Horn rivers. Major Reno, of the Seventh cavalry, was sent with six companies a hundred and fifty miles, to look for Indians. Having reached the mouth of the Little Powder none were found. On his return he discovered a large Indian trail on the Rosebud, and it was now known that there were no Indians on Tongue or Powder rivers and the circle had contracted to Rosebud, Little Horn and Big Horn rivers.

Terry and Custer were waiting on the steamer "Far West," at the mouth of the Tongue, and on receiving Reno's report, Custer was sent up the south bank of the Yellowstone to a point opposite General Gibbon on the northern bank.

Terry pushed up the Yellowstone and kept abreast of Custer's column. After consultation with Gibbon and Custer, Terry adopted a definite plan of action. The Indians were thought to be at the head of the Rosebud or on the Little Great Horn, a divide of fifteen miles only separating these rivers; and Terry announced that Custer would strike the blow. "Custer," says he, in his despatch to Sheridan, "will go up the Rosebud to-morrow with his whole regiment and thence to the head-waters of the Little Horn, thence down the Little Horn."

In his orders to Custer, General Terry says:

"The column of Colonel Gibbon is now in motion for the mouth of the Big Horn. As soon as it reaches that point it will cross the Yellowstone and move up at least as far as the parks of the Big and Little Horn. . . . It is hoped that the Indians, if upon the Little Big Horn, may be so nearly inclosed by the two columns that their escape will be impossible."

We come now to Custer's *last battle,* fought on the right bank of the Little Big Horn, June twenty-fifth, 1876. The regiment left camp at the mouth of the Rosebud on the afternoon of June twenty-second, and marched up the Rosebud twelve miles and again encamped. On the twenty-third they continued the march for thirty-three miles, passing many old Indian villages and following a large but not fresh pole trail.

Next day on the march fresher signs appeared every mile till an encampment was made at the end of twenty-eight, that of the preceding day having been thirty-three miles.

Custer, at 9.25 P. M., informed the officers that without doubt the village was in the valley of the Little Big Horn, and that to reach it the divide must be crossed between the Rosebud and Little Big Horn rivers, which could not be done in the day-time without discovery. At 11 P. M. they took up a line of march, turning to the right from the Rosebud up one of its branches which led near the summit of the divide. The scouts told Custer about 2 A. M. that the divide could not be crossed before daylight. They then made coffee and rested for three hours, resumed their march, and crossed the divide at about 8 A. M. When they were in the valley of one of the branches of the Little Big Horn, Indians had been seen, and as they could not be surprised, it was resolved at once to attack. The command moved down the creek toward the Little Big Horn Valley, Custer on the right bank with five companies, and Major Reno on the left bank with three. Further on to the left and out of sight was Captain Benteen also with three companies.

As they came near a deserted village in which stood

one *tepee* at 11 A. M., Custer motioned Reno to cross to him, and he moved nearer to his column till half-past twelve, when the adjutant came and told him the village was only two miles off and running away. He ordered him to move forward rapidly, and then charge, when the whole column would support him.

He reached the ford of the river at a trot, crossed, halted ten minutes, and informed Custer he had everything in front of him, and they were strong. He drove the Indians over two miles down the river, grew uneasy in the absence of Custer, suspected a trap, dismounted and fought on foot near the edge of a point of woods.

With the loss of three officers and twenty-nine enlisted men killed, and seven men wounded, he reached the summit of a bluff and was joined by Captain Benteen, when their united forces were three hundred and eighty men. From the incompetency of this officer, and the disobedience of Benteen, Custer was left to contend with the swarms of Indians that assailed him without the help of his subordinates who heard his guns. The rest is soon told.

The trail showed that Custer came down to the river, and was driven back at the ford, from whence, in his line of retreat, he made several stands in succession, on the higher ground.

Captain Calhoun with his company lay as they fell, all at their posts where they had been placed to check the assaults of the savages. A mile beyond this, lay Keogh and his company in position, their right resting on the hill where Custer fell.

Custer, on the highest point of the ridge, made his last desperate stand, fighting heroically with Captain

Yates, Colonel Cook, Captain Custer, Lieutenant Riley and thirty-two others, till all were killed, himself the last, and by Rain-in-the-Face, in fulfilment of his vow. Here was another Thermopylæ. No Spartan bravery exceeded this, and Custer, with his noble band of heroes, will live in the remembrance of the latest posterity.

In the flash of his fame he died as he had lived— for his country. The offering was doubtless a glad one. He desired no better fate than such a death; he could leave no richer inheritance than such an example. While we feel as if destiny had robbed the future of the fame which such a nature must have won, we dare not regret that his career has been closed in its morning with this sunburst of glory. His memory will be gratefully cherished so long as honor has a victory, freedom a hero, or his country a name.

"The neighing troop, the flashing blade,
  The bugle's stirring blast,
The charge, the dreadful cannonade,
  The din and shout are past.
No war's wild notes nor glory's peal
  Shall thrill with fierce delight
The breast, that never more may feel
  The raptures of the fight."

TESTIMONIALS.

EXTRACTS FROM NOTICES OF THE PRESS.

Boston Traveller.

"Heroes of Three Wars," by the author of "Battles for the Union," and other works, is an intensely interesting volume, and will be welcomed by the reading public as a most valuable contribution to the military history of our country.

Philadelphia Times.

The soldier-author does his work in an artless, patriotic, beautiful style, and gives to his readers a real and not an imaginary idea of army life in all its lights and shades. Captain Glazier has laid his countrymen under lasting obligations to him, especially in his new book, "Heroes of Three Wars."

Washington Chronicle.

"Heroes of Three Wars" is written in a graphic style, and its thrilling delineations of many of the most important events of the Revolution, and our great struggle for the preservation of the Union, cannot fail to interest those who love their country, and glory in the achievements of its brave and victorious defenders.

Norristown Herald.

It is just the book for a winter evening. It inspires a spirit of patriotism, and gives a due appreciation of the labors and sufferings—and sometimes the more cheerful and fun-provoking experiences—of those who engaged in the great struggles for the nation's life and honor.

New York Herald.

Captain Glazier is one of the most pleasing writers who has added a contribution to our war literature. He takes you through the vividness of his descriptions into the very scenes which he portrays. "Heroes of Three Wars" cannot fail to interest every reader, and we predict for its sale a success unprecedented in the book trade.

Pittsburgh Gazette.

The nature of this book is very forcibly expressed in the title page. The writer wields a graphic pen. In the statement of facts he is painstaking and conscientious. Commencing with Washington, forty subjects are presented. The writer has the vivacity which is so essential in the composition of a work of this character. One is often thrilled as the panorama of war passes before his mind.

TESTIMONIALS.

Harrisburg Patriot.

In his new book the soldier-author introduces forty of the most illustrious names in the history of our country. The work is in fact a record of the privations, heroic deeds and glorious triumphs of the soldiers of the Union, and contains a fund of information not found in any other volume. Captain Glazier was a good soldier, and in the presentation of his subjects wields a graceful pen.

Syracuse Courier.

The book is perfectly reliable as history, with none of the dulness incident to most history. Dates and data are given, but they are not march d before you in slow and solemn procession, like the animals from Noah's ark, nor piled up in monumental array for you to laboriously master. On the contrary, the sketches are so spirited as to hold the attention of the reader from the opening to the closing chapter.

Toledo Blade.

This is a book which will never lose its interest so long as principle is considered worthy of human sacrifice, and men and women continue to admire deeds of heroism performed in their defense. It is a work of special interest at the present time to all who took part in the stirring scenes of the late war, and to the friends and relatives of those who suffered and endured for the cause of the Union, and so many of whom laid down their lives in its behalf.

Troy Times.

Captain Glazier writes with a full and accurate knowledge of the subjects introduced, and his thrilling sketches have all the vividness which none but a soldier and a participant in such scenes could give them. Simple in style, compact in matter, and vigorous in treatment, the book just meets the want of a large class of people who have no time for consulting the ponderous volumes which are too often imposed upon the indulgence of a generous public.

Buffalo Courier.

The author, himself a gallant soldier, writes of the exciting contests and the perils of the brave men who took part in them with the ardor of a genuine participant. The scenes of the bloody field are each so vividly described that we seem in reading of them to see the great conflicts of our three wars as in a panorama, and there is not a page which is not intensely interesting from the opening to the closing chapter.

Cincinnati Enquirer.

Captain Glazier rises above the conventional "war writer's" idioms, and gives his work a place in literature and history. Here is found the stern actuality of war's fearful tug; here the beautiful pathos of pure manly sentiment flowing from the heart of many a brave soul on the battle's eve; here the scenes of sad and solemn burial where warriors weep. The din of battle on one page, and the jest at peril past upon the next—the life test and the comedy of camp—these alternatingly checker the work over and give the reader a truer insight into the perils and privations of our brave defenders than any book we have read.

Baltimore Sun.

"Heroes of Three Wars" is written by the masterly hand of one who has evidently enjoyed a personal acquaintance with many of the subjects introduced, and is not only thoroughly imbued with the spirit of his work, but as thoroughly inspires his readers. Captain Glazier has familiarized himself with all of the details of interest in the lives of a grand galaxy of heroes, and has put on paper in a condensed and graphic form a clear picture of what he has treasured up in his own mind. We know of no book that contains so faithful a presentation of our brave defenders in so condensed and satisfactory a form.

Albany Argus.

The clearness and vigor of its style, together with its graphic and truthful sketches of the renowned soldiers presented, will render it famous from the Atlantic to the Pacific. The writer was one of the first to enlist and served to the close of the war of the great Rebellion, being promoted to a captaincy for gallant and heroic conduct on the battle-fields of Virginia, Maryland and Pennsylvania. The book should be in every household in the land, for the occasional perusal of its pages will serve to keep green in recollection those momentous and bloody struggles which are too soon buried in the oblivion of the past.

Boston Transcript.

The bivouac, the march, the hand-to-hand conflict with bristling steel, the headlong charge, the ignominious retreat, and the battle-field after the bloody assault, with its dead and wounded heroes, are all excellently portrayed, and with an ease and vigor of style that lend a peculiar charm to the book and rivet the attention of the reader from cover to cover. It is really refreshing to meet with such a work as this in these degenerate days of namby-pamby novels, so enervating to mind and morals. Captain Glazier's work elevates the ideas, and infuses a spirit of commendable patriotism into the young mind, by showing the youth of the country how nobly men could die for the principles they cherished and the land they loved.

Worcester Spy.

"Heroes of Three Wars" is a graphically written volume by no new candidate for public favor, but one who has already won the appreciative admiration of thousands of readers. An air of truth which is of romantic interest pervades the work, in the depiction of the terribly interesting events in the lives of his famous subjects. Captain Glazier was an active participant in the War for the Union, and followed the lead of Bayard, Stoneman, Pleasanton, Gregg, Custer and Kilpatrick. He portrays the daring deeds and glorious achievements of his heroes with an enthusiasm which fairly enchains the reader, and makes him feel for the time that he is either fighting his battles over again, or standing an awe-bound spectator of the clash of armor and fall of noble steeds and their brave riders.

Chicago Inter-Ocean.

It is correct in facts, graphic in its delineations, and in all its make-up is a most admirable volume. It will do the young men, and even those older, good to glance at these pages and read anew the perils and hardships and sacrifices which have been made by the loyal men who met and overthrew in battle the nation's enemies. The book is of absorbing interest as a record of brave deeds by as brave and heroic men as ever answered a bugle's call. The author writes no fancy sketch. He has the smoke and scars of battle in every sentence. He answered roll-call and mingled amid the exciting events he relates. No writer, even the most praised correspondents of the foreign journals, have given more vivid descriptions, soul-stirring in their simple truthfulness, than Captain Glazier in his "Heroes of Three Wars."

TESTIMONIALS.

Philadelphia Enquirer.

In Part Third of "Heroes of Three Wars," every man who participated in the Rebellion can live over again the days of his soldier life; can fight side by side with his old comrades; can charge again at the command of his old commander. And here it may be said that the way in which the old familiar names ring out throughout the book is truly inspiring. The work will doubtless be warmly greeted by one and all, but more especially will it be welcomed by the thousands of isolated farm-houses, scattered all over the land, from whom went out a son to fight for his country. It will make delightful reading for the long winter evenings so soon to be here. Moreover, it is a work that will not grow old. It will not change, like the majority of books, with the fashion. Its subject is one that cannot be encroached upon.

New York Tribune.

Captain Glazier's preceding works have gained him a wide fame, and in the present volume he has certainly lost none of the vigor, strength and power which characterizes his former writings. His style is easy and natural, and yet thrilling and graphic in the extreme. As he writes in Part Third of the new work, he witnesses again the scenes through which he passed with his famous subjects during the Rebellion, and his facile pen at once and with peculiar fidelity transfers the mental picture to the page before him. It is a wonderful power, and one which few men possess, to be able to carry with them through life the scenes of former years, and reproduce them at will for the pleasure of their readers. Captain Glazier demonstrates this fine gift with admirable force, and the fascinating pages before us are a moving, breathing panorama of the great struggles and heroic sacrifices for the preservation of the Union.

www.ingramcontent.com/pod-product-compliance
Lightning Source LLC
Chambersburg PA
CBHW032000300426
44117CB00008B/843